D0459421

THE COMPLETE DECORATOR

Kevin McCloud

THE COMPLETE DECORATOR

Special photography by
Michael Crockett

Ebury Press
London

For Z.

I would like to thank all those who have helped me produce this volume over its three year gestation. Denise Bates, my commissioning editor at Ebury, for her guidance and tolerance; Emma Callery for her enthusiasm for the subject, patience, unswerving editorial skill and powers of critical analysis; Paul Welti, who consistently applies an intellectual rigour to his design, for his commitment and for his conversation; Susan Berry for help with words; my agent Jane Turnbull for counselling and crisis management; Michael Crockett for his great skill and sense of humour; Nadine Bazar for wonderful picture research; and Elizabeth Baer of Pavilion Antiques for lending many of the objects photographed.

Also to Julian and his brush, Bruce and the Paint Shop Boys, and all the staff at McCloud & Co for putting up with my absences.

Finally, deep-felt gratitude to Susanna for feeding and watering me those countless evenings, supporting me, and not deciding to leave...

First published in 1996

3 5 7 9 10 8 6 4 2

First published in the United Kingdom in 1996 by Ebury Press
Random House, 20 Vauxhall Bridge Road, London SW1V 2SA

Random House Australia (Pty) Limited
20 Alfred Street, Milsons Point, Sydney, New South Wales 2061, Australia

Random House New Zealand Limited
18 Poland Road, Glenfield, Auckland 10, New Zealand

Random House South Africa (Pty) Limited
PO Box 337, Bergvlei, South Africa

Random House UK Limited Reg. No. 954009

A catalogue record for this book is available from the British Library.

ISBN 0 09 180762 X

Editor Emma Callery
Design Paul Welti
Special photography Michael Crockett
Picture research Nadine Bazar
Illustrations The R & B Partnership
Typeset by Peter Howard

Colour reproduction by Resolve Consultancy Limited
Printed in Italy by Officine Grafiche De Agostini - Novara 1996
Bound by Legatoria del Verbano S.p.a.

Contents

Introduction

I wrote this book because I wanted to make sense of its subject matter. Literally hundreds of books have been written about decoration and paint 'effects' in the last twenty years, and it's about time that these topics were put into their proper context. I hope this book does just that.

In writing it, two words loomed large, floating in the air above my word processor, CONTEXT and RESONANCE. My general feelings ran as follows: surely, to teach any decorative technique well, you should show, and talk about, how and where the technique must be used. For decades we have seen objects, rooms, even cars and toilet seats, painted with the most incredibly inappropriate finishes. They have not enriched our world; they haven't even made us laugh. A proper understanding of where something is appropriate, and what you can and cannot get away with, is highly important.

Of equal importance is to understand the power of what you are doing. Do not expect verdigris and rust, as finishes, to be somehow interchangeable; one suggests value, age and the presence of some nobler metal that has been worked at some time by a craftsman; the other reminds me of decay. This point illustrates how essential it is to discuss and explore the psychological impact and resonances of surfaces and finishes. Each use of paint or gilding as a surface treatment has some hidden powerful importance.

I have also been at pains to point out when a technique is easy and when it requires some practice. There are plenty of books that say it is all so easy. I have written those words many times myself, partly in a desire to see more people pick up a brush and have a go, to discover how easy it is to do something moderately well and find a way of expressing themselves. However, this book is for those of you who want something more; for those who are prepared to explore, experiment, study a little and, above all else, practise.

In working through this book I hope you will come to appreciate the biggest secret of all: the importance of knowing and understanding your materials. This is something that every good decorator understands immediately, even if he has never been told it.

The contents of a paint or medium, its list of ingredients, as it were, are absolutely key to our understanding of it and, more importantly, what we can do with it. If you understand a little of how acrylic paint performs and what makes it waterproof when dry, you are half-way to being able to develop and invent your own techniques. Of course, only one thing will take you the whole journey and that is the laborious process of practice, trial and error, experimentation and testing, as you put your materials through their paces. If you wish to advance your art, you should be prepared for this, rather than simply relying on every written paint recipe and technique as though they represent the end of the line.

I have invented some of the techniques in this book from scratch, others I have maybe refined or adapted, others follow the prescribed accepted canon (gesso, for example). In the studio, we have tested all of them and subjected them to criticism and scrutiny. As a result, for the moment I see many of them as about as refined as I can imagine them. For you, however, they may only be a starting point.

MAGIC AND SPONTANEITY: THE TWO MOST IMPORTANT IDEAS IN PAINTING

In my studio, I am rigorous about one principle: that paint effects must be like magic tricks, they must dupe you into believing that some force other than the human one has been at work. Sometimes, when the effect is a faux one, or particularly fine, this means that if you leave a careless brush mark, a run, or a thumb print in your work, you have broken the spell, because the viewer will then usually be able to work out how the trick was done. Equally, if your varnish coat betrays the poor undercoating by revealing the ridges of brush marks, or dries to a gritty finish, you have let the work down. A perfect, flat surface that is silky to the touch and resembles french polish, adds a sensual aspect to one's work and adds to the magic.

Of course, there are those rough and ready rustic techniques that absolutely require, rather than shun, the obvious hand of the painter in their execution. The Italian marbling and rustic graining techniques on pages 216-23 and 224-9 are examples. But in these, there is still something extra to be found, something which adds some magic to the finish despite their appearing obviously hand-painted; and that something is spontaneity.

Spontaneity is different. It has nothing to do with preparation or finish, requiring only grinding practice, research and experiment. Only after you have done it time and time again can a paint technique begin to assimilate spontaneity; you must be able to do it very fast and completely fluidly with total confidence in yourself and your materials. Again, we find the same touchstone ideas that permeate this book occurring; a knowledge of your materials and a readiness to practise.

Spontaneity, in its own way, is another kind of magic; it is the way in which the deepest part of yourself can suddenly find expression, and, as such, when it goes right, is intensely satisfying.

But to be spontaneous, you must, paradoxically, be entirely in control. To let your spontaneity run riot when you are not quite in command of your brushes or paints can be disastrous; the results are usually a mess. However, if you know what you are doing and how your tools and materials handle, and if you have practised a technique sufficiently for it to become an automatic procedure, then you can, by all means, give yourself over to the more expressive side of your nature. The results can be gratifying, and to the person who views your work, what you have produced will appear vigorous and strong. Interestingly, many such vigorous and strong examples of painting involve techniques which are extremely simple. Something which may otherwise have appeared crude can be transformed by the sheer energy of its creation.

Part One

COLOUR

A history of paint colour

If this text had been written ten or twenty years ago it would read very differently. Until the 1990s, ideas about what went into paint were conjectural and there were only a handful of respected academics around the world who concerned themselves with this somewhat anorak-ish subject. That has all changed. Painters and conservators used to cut back paint to see what the old colours were, by performing a 'scrape'. This technique has been responsible for the formulation of several 'historically researched' paint ranges that have now been proved rather inaccurate, thanks to the introduction of techniques and technologies that have been developed in the fine art world and transferred to the sphere of decoration. Nowadays, a paint analyst will use a polarizing microscope, chromatography and mass spectrometry to identify the constituent pigments and binders in a paint sample. The sample is a cross section of paint layers made by embedding a paint chip in a block of resin and then cutting it through. Because of such analysis, more old houses are now receiving appropriate colour treatments. If you are keen to find out exactly how your house was painted a hundred or two hundred years ago, enlist the help of a paint conservator or the conservation department of a local museum to help you make an analysis.

The contemporary world of building conservation is fraught with

personal agendas and the egos of those involved, and over the last decade or two, paint experts have wasted a great deal of time and public money debating the precise shade of colour with which old houses were painted – taking very imprecise names such as 'Wainscot' or 'Pearl'. In truth, it seems that since the decorator usually mixed the paint on site, colours varied enormously. The paint historian Patrick Baty quotes the following seventeenth-century account: 'Leaves to be brought to the architect whereof to make his choice

(ABOVE) *The Gothic revival of the nineteenth century led to the first serious study of historical colours in an attempt to recreate original medieval colour schemes, such as at the Sainte Chapelle in Paris.*

(LEFT) Regatta on the Grand Canal *by Canaletto (1697-1768). An insight into the historical use of paints on buildings can sometimes be gleaned from easel paintings, providing they are clean, not least because the artist may even have used the identical pigment to portray the building.*

as to the colour. The colours for rooms ought not to be taken at random but to be chosen according to the much or little light, or space of the place etc'.

The most interesting revelation in the past ten years has been just how many grand homes of the past were painted in bright colours. Indeed, if a fashionable home owner of any century between the fifteenth and nineteenth could obtain unusual and bright colours of paint, he would use them, not least because of their novelty value.

Ordinary vernacular houses were painted in somewhat dingy colours, mainly derived from local earths (although these earth colours found use in the grander buildings too) coloured with iron oxides or copper compounds to provide a palette that changed little for five hundred years from the beginning of the fifteenth century onwards. It is only in this century that we have obliterated the colours of the past and lost touch with our history.

LOOKING TO THE FUTURE

One thing, however, is sure. Thanks to old accounts and receipts (recipes) combined with the available technology for paint analysis today, it is possible to determine exactly which pigments were available to the decorators of the past. By employing the same colours and mixing them, we too can begin to approximate the colours they produced and make the types and colours of paint that they used.

But why should we bother? Surely modern paint ranges offer every conceivable colour in very consumer-friendly paints? And are we not getting hung-up on the past for its own sake, pursuing a nostalgia for 'dirtied' romantic historical interiors.

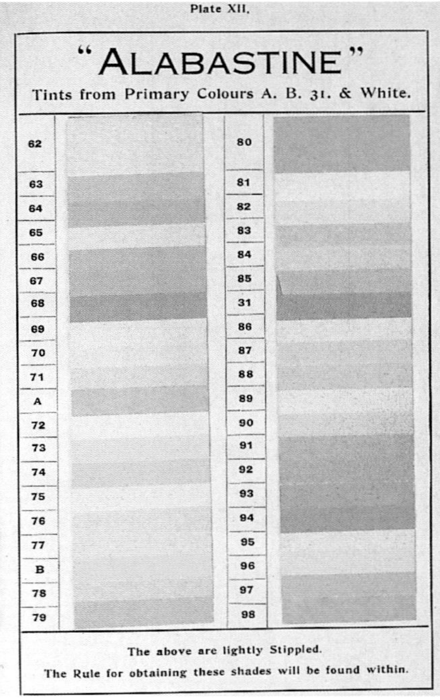

Plate XII.

"ALABASTINE"

Tints from Primary Colours A. B. 31. & White.

62	80
63	81
64	82
65	83
66	84
67	85
68	31
69	86
70	87
71	88
A	89
72	90
73	91
74	92
75	93
76	94
77	95
B	96
78	97
79	98

The above are lightly Stippled.

The Rule for obtaining these shades will be found within.

This manufacturer's swatch shows that as late as 1926 paint ranges were formulated to consist of a small number of familiar, tried and tested colours, using pigments that would have been known to decorators of the Middle Ages.

out of some atavistic navel-inspection? In a world of increasing complexity and threat, the domesticity of our homes inevitably offers us the easy option to escape the twenty-first century, and not create it. Shouldn't we really be forging and re-fashioning our new culture, not relying on one that was extinguished two or more centuries ago? To answer these questions, there are two points that are worth considering.

First, we should note that if we are to learn from the past (a necessary process to move forwards), we must ensure that what we see as history is as accurately represented as possible. When it comes to the subject of how colour has been managed historically and applied inside and outside our buildings, our ancestors have had an 8,000-year head start on us. There ought to be something we can learn from them.

Second, the colours they used were certainly limited by what was available; but they were also colours that were derived from the same sources as the buildings themselves; from rocks, clays and minerals. Thus the buildings they constructed 'grew' out of the soil and were dressed with pigments that came from the natural world. What is interesting is that despite modern technology, it is not possible to use synthetic dyes to reproduce all the particular qualities of a paint coloured with an earth pigment. The pigment granules are not dispersed in the same way and the result is a lifeless plastic coating. Traditional pigments, however, impart a subtle movement and life to a painted surface (see pages 250-6) and they also come with a proven track record of use and success. If, for example, you want to mix an excellent cream to paint your walls, use yellow ochre; it is just about the most ancient pigment there is. Like the family of earth colours to which it belongs, it is not simply an 'historical' colour, but one universally recognized as of immense value to the artist and decorator alike.

The colours on the following pages represent this core of ancient pigments that have proved their pedigree over thousands of years. If we want to decorate our private and public buildings well, surround ourselves with good colours and make the decoration of our homes sing, we should look to these colours as the way to do it.

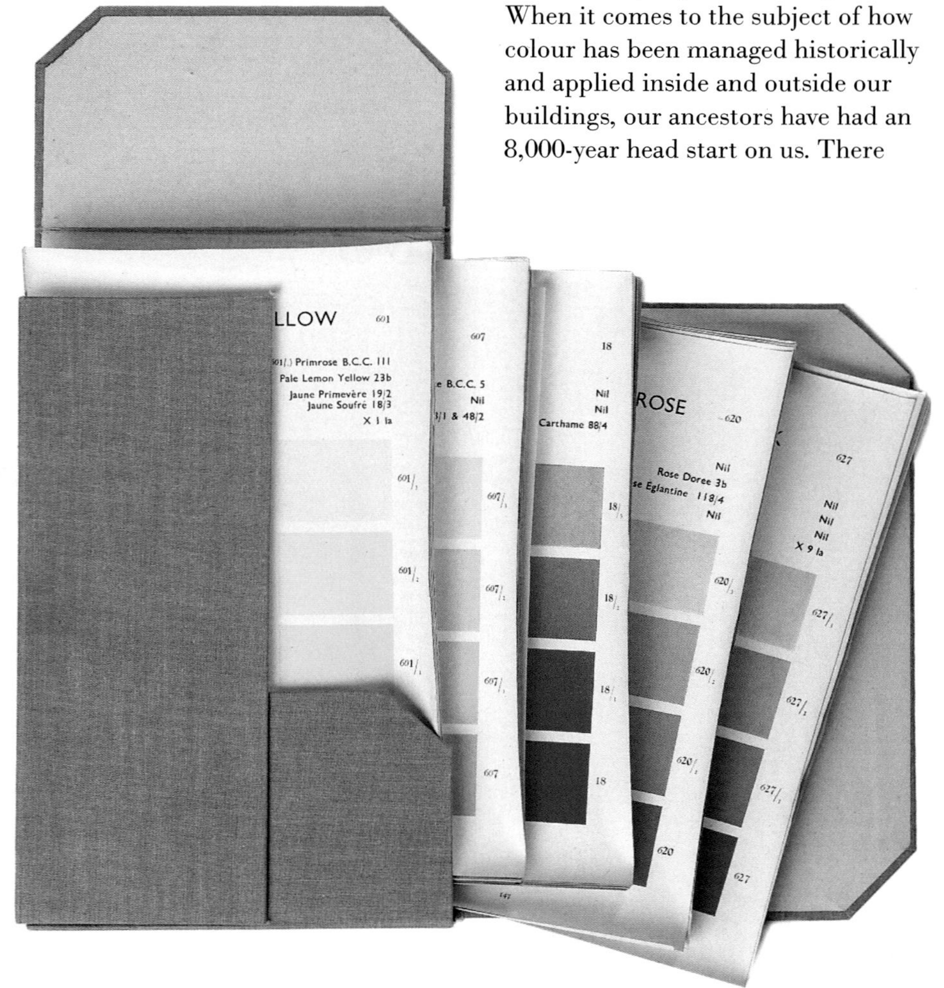

Paint colours were only formally standardized in the twentieth century. Until that time, the name of a colour such as 'salmon pink' was a matter for wide interpretation. Among the earliest attempts at classification was the Royal Horticultural Society's two volume manual of 1939, originally intended for matching flower colours.

Regional colours

'If you want to paint the outside of your house; get your neighbour to choose the colours.' Thus writes the eminent authority Jean Philippe Lenclos about the sensitivity surrounding the use of colour in our lives and the way in which we all bear a responsibility for properly integrating our homes into the built – and natural – environments.

The quote is underpinned by a truth about colour that I believe is much overlooked; that its psychological effect and significance is intimately bound to our culture. There is a connection between the colours we surround ourselves with and the way we live our lives. Historically, societies have even been visually stratified into their classes by the use of colour on architecture – cheap and expensive colours in correspondingly cheap and expensive houses. Yet the same societies have found themselves united under the colours of their national flags in times of stress. Colour means power because colour exercises such a powerfully emotional influence upon us in our homes and everyday lives.

Just as colours are historical, so they belong to different regions of the world. The essential core of colours that has been in use for several thousand years comprises about eight earth colours made from clay coloured with iron oxide and a few copper-based pigments for blue and green. They are to be found on virtually every continent on the globe, are the most stable common colouring matters, and because they are readily available and require little processing, have always been obtainable, cheap and therefore much used. The Pennsylvanian Dutch settlers did not have to change the vocabulary of colours of their native Swiss and German painted furniture when they moved across the Atlantic

(ABOVE AND BELOW) *Using paint swatches it is possible to build a theoretical palette for an area dependent on local building materials. The two examples illustrated show how stone colours can be complemented; on brown-grey stone (above), a wide variety of neutral colours will sit happily plus a number of soft grey-blue-green mixes. However, yellow stone (below) kills the pale blue-greys and can instead tolerate a wider range of brighter hues including red and yellow ochres, and deep blues.*

because similar pigments were readily available in the New World.

Yet from region to region within a continent, the colour palette subtly changes. This is particularly true within towns and cities where the use of pigments peculiar to an area has always helped to define a sense of place and has developed parallel to the architecture of that area. The Mexican town of Guanajuato, for example, is coloured with pigments of ochres and browns that tell the story of its native Indian and Spanish influences, while the towns above Passau in Germany have, over several centuries, developed a vocabulary of strong pastel colours on the outside of their buildings, delineated with white.

COLOUR CHAOS

This sense of place and belonging is all being speedily eroded by an attitude and advertising culture which favours brash plastic colours for signage, and uniform building materials and colours for modern developments. Housing estates in Miami, Scotland, and the suburbs of Paris are nowadays often built to look the same, not different, with no regard for traditional building methods, materials or colours for the particular area. An almost unlimited range of synthetic colours is available for the homeowner and architect and the resultant effect is of what has been termed 'colour chaos' or 'colour pollution' in our communities. As the architect and colourist Michael Lancaster puts it, 'Because we lack confidence in the use of colour, we tend to use it either timidly or brashly, and rarely with any understanding or control of the total effect. We need to develop greater ability to see how it can be used as a powerful and creative means of architectural and townscape expression to create a better, more satisfying environment. We should also remember that it is flexible, easy to change and cheap.'

(RIGHT) *When earth pigments are sourced locally and refined they may appear simply as a more consistent colour of the local mud. This is Owalato, the mud city of Mauritania.*

(BELOW) *These walls in Calcata, Lazio, Italy, are painted with colours that have been carefully modulated with white to produce tints of equivalent strength. The pigments used are a cool red ochre, ultramarine blue and yellow ochre.*

But luckily, the tide is turning thanks to the concerted efforts of a band of enthusiastic architects, planners and even paint manufacturers. The company Akzo, through their research arm, the Sikkens foundation, have for many years been sponsoring and developing colour programmes in several cities throughout Europe. These have taken place in Berlin, Norwich, Turin and, most famously, the Rambla area in the centre of Barcelona which was re-branded with a traditional colour palette on the outside of its buildings in time for the Olympic Games to be held there.

DEFINING COMMUNITIES

Predictably, many of the regional decorating colours that have been traditionally used by man are earth colours. Using the earth colours illustrated on the following pages (see pages 18-31), I can reproduce the paint colours of the Pueblo Indians of Santa Fe, or alternatively the red ochre and burnt sienna limewashes used to cover the houses of the Western Sahara.

But to say that all regional colours are the same earth colours is wrong. In the Souss plain of Morocco, it is the combination of rusty brown, delicate pink and deep brown ochre that dominates the townscapes and villages. Yellow is not used, nor umber colours – in fact, the soil is the colour of raw umber, but pigments to colour the buildings are brought from the mountains. Indeed, the use of pinks and red ochres (made from both purplish red ochre and warm red ochre) is absolutely unremitting, covering every surface of every building. From the perimeter walls and buildings of these mud cities and villages, the inhabitants have sent a strong and clear visual signal across the surrounding plains – that the people who live there, in choosing common colours, have more or less chosen a common identity, that they are a community.

It is not unreasonable to suggest that the sense of community and place so strongly created by these red ochre limewashes is something we can also reproduce in our own lives and communities by reviving the local colours that our forbears knew. As, in the western world, we witness the breaking up of our communities through all kinds of social upheaval, it is a cheering thought that around us lie hidden clues as to how our communities identified themselves in the past, and how they might do so again in the future.

Essential colours

There are about 900,000 paint colours in production, a figure that is barely comprehensible. And they are all produced synthetically, using carefully matched azo dyes and synthetic pigments that rely on modern petroleum and coal-tar chemistry, including at least forty which are considered totally permanent. Yet, despite this enormous choice, our ability to choose good colours and design decorative schemes is not improved. We still make mistakes over the most trivial matters and our queries remain unanswered; such as what constitutes a good cream paint colour and what exactly is that powerful blue I saw all over the buildings in Portugal on my holiday?

The answer must be not to increase the number of available colours even further, and not to try to explain or group the colours any more. That has been done by several manufacturers according to the Munsell system (see page 252) and we are still none the wiser. Nor is the answer to dream up ever-more evocative names for the colours (although I do like the nineteenth-century colour name, Gallstone). Instead, perhaps the answer lies in the way that pigments and colours have been used historically.

Mineral pigments are trapped in the earth, waiting for man to dig them up, mix them with a bit of glue and daub them on a wall. The cliffs at Hunstanton, Norfolk are of white chalk marl sitting on a band of red carstone. In between, lies a thin layer of red stained marl.

Until the middle of the twentieth century, on the whole, paints were manufactured using true pigments, powders that were mineral in origin and dug out of the ground (inorganic) or were processed from vegetable matter or animal bones (organic). Because the sources were limited, so the decorator's and artist's palettes were limited; greens were, and to some extent still are, difficult to produce. Pliny the Elder described in 50AD a decorator's palette that would have seemed perfectly adequate to the house painter of the 1890s: 'The bright colours that the client supplies to the artist are bright red, rich blue, vermilion, green, indigo and bright purple. The rest are dark. Of the whole palette some pigments are natural, some artificial. Natural colours are brown, red ochre, ruddle, white chalk, white marl, Melian white and bright yellow. The rest are artificial. Among the commoner kinds are yellow ochre, burnt white lead, realgar, vermilion, Syrian red and black.'

The enforced colour range of this traditional palette has also adopted a meaning over the last six thousand years. Because the pigments (of which there exist only a dozen or so) came from the ground and the vegetation around us, and because they also colour that same ground, and the rocks, marbles and stones we walk on, everything that was painted with them took on something of the quality of the natural world.

What is so appealing about this decorative palette today is that it can, in the instant of application, reinvest our buildings, rooms and objects with those same resonances, of the real, material world.

At the same time, what is interesting is that these colours have tremendous appeal to so many people. Yellow ochre, for example, produces superb creams and soft buttery yellows of a number of shades, all of which are highly pleasing to the eye, unlike the vast majority of synthetically produced yellow paints. The reason for this is not coincidental. We all carry with us in our mind's eye the colours of our natural world, the seas, rocks, plants and skies – our easy visual relationship with the natural environment depends on a retina and visual cortex that for thousands of years have been slowly adapting to respond to the particular ranges of light frequencies that are produced in the world around us. It is for this reason that we can perceive minute changes in shades of green but not in red; red occurs so infrequently in nature that we are not genetically trained or equipped to perceive its subtleties.

It is therefore not surprising that naturally derived mineral pigments mean more to us; they carry more messages and remind us of so many different contexts.

THE EARTH PIGMENTS

The first eight of the following colours (see pages 18-31) are arranged to form an open collection of swatches, each of which was hand-painted to show the pigment colour undiluted (across the centre of the swatch); how the pigment responds when washed out to reveal the undertones (towards the top of the page), and how the pigment responds when mixed into white paint, in this case titanium white artist's acrylic paint (towards the bottom of the page).

These earth pigments are coloured with iron oxides and form the essential historical core of pigments. Nearly all of them were in use in Minoan times, and they formed the decorative palette of the Romans, the medieval church painters, the vernacular house painters of the eighteenth century and even the

decorators of the early twentieth century. These pigments hold the key to successfully manipulating paint colour in interior design.

THE RARER PIGMENTS

On pages 33-7 you will find another five colours that have been added from Roman times, through the Middle Ages and on to the eighteenth century. They have been chosen as being representative of the rarer, brighter colours that can be obtained. Together with the earth colours they form an entire decorative palette that would satisfy even a fine artist for his uses, and yet all from 13 colours.

All the techniques executed in this book were executed in these colours, and by way of further illustration as to their potential, pages 38-41 illustrate a variety of mixes to produce an enormous range of secondary colours.

COLOUR AVAILABILITY

For each of the pigments described on pages 18-37, I list the names of the most readily available equivalent powders. They can be purchased from artist's and specialist paint suppliers (see pages 263-4), and these last also stock the universal stainers that are listed. I have not included any pigments with high toxicity levels.

PIGMENT TOXICITY

The most common pigments are given detailed toxicity ratings in the following section. Many references are made throughout the book to the health problems and dangers of handling pigments in powder form. Although many of them (the earth colours, for example) are considered relatively safe when handled as powders, you are strongly recommended never to handle any toxic pigments in powder form.

A number of specific medical terms are used in this section of the book to define the toxic effects of the pigments and materials discussed. These terms are:

Carcinogenic May cause cancer.

Mutagenic May cause hereditary mutation.

Teratogenic A substance that may cross the birth canal, causing birth defects.

Levels of exposure

There are no minimum exposure levels for substances known to have these effects. Instead, there are acute and chronic exposure levels. The definition of an acute exposure is a single-incident exposure where the substance usually takes immediate effect. Chronic exposure is where there are multiple exposures to a substance where the toxic effect is slowly built up.

Methods of exposure

The methods of exposure are:

Inhalation The breathing in of substances either in powder form or as fumes. They then enter the bloodstream via the lungs.

Ingestion Swallowing of substances which are passed into the blood from the digestive system.

Skin contact Usually the least harmful form of exposure, unless a substance collects under the nails to be later transferred onto food, or enters the bloodstream via a skin wound or cut.

For many artists, the pigment mines at Roussillon in southern France represented the most sought after source of fine earth pigments. The stone formations are stained with coloured clays in every conceivable iron oxide pigment from yellow to purple.

Yellow ochre

The reason yellow ochre is first among these Essential Colours is that it is probably the most universal traditional pigment and has the widest number of uses in decoration. Of all the pigments available to man, ochre, as it was historically known, must be one of the most pleasurable to handle. In its finest form it is a warm, bright and rich colour with no hint of greenness about it and when blended with a liquid medium becomes a little transparent, a feature which renders yellow ochre very useful for glazing.

Yellow Ochre pigment as powder (ABOVE), *and brushed out* (TO THE LEFT) *as a paint made by grinding the pigment in gum arabic.*

Yellow excites the retina and is often spurned as a decorative colour because of the way it can upset our sense of visual balance. In northern climes especially, yellows have a tendency to green because grey skies transmit a predominantly blue light, slightly warping true colour values. Consequently, yellow has virtually become the most difficult colour to handle successfully in decoration.

But yellow ochre is our saviour; its warmth ensures that whatever the climate, it will not tend to the green, an advantage that persists when mixed with white to form tints. In fact, it can safely be said that the best creams result from a mixture of yellow ochre and white; buildings all over the world bear witness to the universality of this truth. There simply is no better yellow for painting the outside of your house.

Interestingly, when mixed with white, yellow ochre loses some of the heat and mustard-like quality that it has in its pure powder form. It will consequently produce a rich golden yellow when mixed with a little white, and as more white is added, cooler, creamier tints. The swatch to the left, executed with pigment bound in a little gum arabic on watercolour paper, illustrates this point. The central bar of pure pigment is mixed into pure water towards the top of the page to form a graduated wash. You can see from this that even as it washes out, the yellow retains its strength and brilliance. Towards the bottom of the page, however, the ochre has been mixed with titanium white acrylic paint, an opaque and pure white that has the effect of dulling and warming the impact of the pigment. Thus it is possible to obtain a wide variety of yellows and creams from just one pigment.

ORIGINS

Any pigment that carries the description ochre must be prepared from natural earths, usually fine clays, that have been coloured by the presence of a large quantity of iron oxides (ferrous oxide and ferric oxide), better known as rust.

Earth is centred on a vast magnetic molten core with a very high iron content. Where iron appears on the surface it is usually in an oxidized form, since iron is in its most unnatural state when it is pure. The way in which it wants to rust so willingly, and return to its natural state is testament to that. In fact, the only known locations where man has been able to mine pure iron is from inside meteorites.

When iron rusts, it adopts a fantastic range of colours from deep reds through yellows and oranges to black and even dark purple, and all these colours have at some time or other been extracted and used in painting. The exact colour that the rust produces depends on the presence of heat and on the amount of water around; the more moisture, the yellower the colour.

Like many stones, marbles rely on iron oxides for their colours. So in the imitation of marble in faux work, it is best to use the appropriate pigments. Here we painted the Siena marble triangles in yellow ochre and white.

Little Hall at Lavenham in Suffolk, England, is painted in a dense coating of traditional limewash strongly coloured with a dull, regional ochre pigment.

Yellow ochre is one of a small family of earth colour pigments that rely on iron oxides to colour them, and the rest of these can be found on the following pages – red ochre, raw sienna, burnt sienna, burnt umber, terra verde and raw umber. The yellows are found in Italy, America, France and Britain, where the last remaining good supply, near Oxford (known as Oxford ochre), was mined and ground at a local windmill until the Second World War. France produces the best yellows, fine and pure and in their purest forms tending to a true golden cast; one of the best is known by its abbreviation JFLS, standing for *jaune fin, lavé, sur fin* (fine yellow, washed, extra fine).

MAKING YOUR OWN PIGMENT

The word *lavé*, meaning washed, not only suggests that impurities have been removed, but that the pigment has been refined by a simple process known as levigation. The technique was known to the Romans and is simply explained. Take a small lump of strongly coloured clay and leave it in a large coffee jar, with the lid on,soaking in water three times its volume for 30 minutes. Ensure you leave at least 2.5cm (1in) of air at the top. Once the clay is broken down, shake the jar vigorously and then hold it still for a couple of seconds before pouring the contents into another jar. What remains in the bottom of the first jar are heavy lumps and impurities that settled out after shaking. By repeating the soaking process and waiting for successively longer periods before pouring, you will be able to separate finer and finer grades of pigment from the water. The pigments can be dried and then ground in the desired medium when the time comes for you to use them.

You may have encountered a similar yellow, named Mars yellow, which belongs to the Mars family of pseudo-earth colours. These are man-made iron oxide pigments that are cheap and plentiful, being the by-product of many common chemical processes and which form a useful contribution to the colouring of manufactured coatings. Their brilliance of colour is often spurned by artists who prefer the quieter, more subtle qualities of the natural pigment.

THE ESSENTIALS OF YELLOW OCHRE

Commercially available as:
Yellow ochre, English ochre, French ochre, golden ochre, mineral yellow, yellow oxide, Mars yellow; yellow ochre universal stainer.

Contents
Iron oxide, clay.

Toxicity
No significant hazards.

Uses
* For tempera panel painting as flesh tones when mixed with white and red ochre.
* In fresco work, since the pigment will not be affected or changed by chemical attack, including the action of alkaline salts present in damp lime plaster. This feature also renders yellow ochre useful as a colorant for cement and concrete, in plaster casting and in limewash.
* On the exterior of buildings, in limewash or in silicate paints where not only is it resistant to acid and alkali, but will also not fade on exposure to ultraviolet light. (These powers of persistence are common to all earth colours.)
* Since the colour approximates gold, yellow ochre is often applied underneath gold leaf or paint to mask any cracks in the leaf. Under water gilding, a soft, coloured clay called bole is applied mixed with a little gelatine glue so that the leaf may be burnished once dry by polishing the bole through the leaf with a hard tool. The clay is really a cousin of the yellow ochre pigment, containing the same constituents but in differing proportions. Popular bole colours are red and yellow ochre, which are, and have often historically been, mixed to achieve a pleasing orange ochre.
* Yellow ochre may also be mixed with raw umber to produce interesting antiquing colours.

Red ochre

In terms of the colours of cities and buildings, red ochre must rank equal in importance with its sister, yellow ochre. Indeed, some would assert that the potency of red ochre places it as the most psychologically powerful colour from the traditional palette that an architect might use. The fact that an enormous number of buildings in ancient Rome were painted this colour supports this idea; even today, several districts of the Trastevere in Rome continue to feature buildings of a very uncompromising deep red-brown.

The brighter red is a true red ochre made artificially and sold as Mars red; it will produce salmon pinks when mixed with white. It is this colour which has been reproduced on the colour bar chart to the left. The darker pigment is native red oxide, a coarser, darker and more bluish colour. It has much greater staining power and produces quite mauve rose pinks when mixed with white.

Red ochre suffers from a confusion of identity, mainly due to there being several varieties with different names. Mars red is a synthetic, pure version, and light red is a scarlet-tinged ochre. The latter can replace traditional Venetian red, which is noted for its brightness and warmth and for the fact that it produces salmon pinks of a warm cast. Indian red (sometimes forms of this are sold simply as red oxide) has a bluish tone and therefore produces cooler, rosy pinks. Bluish red oxides have historically been more widely available due to their being impure native pigments with a high oxide content (85 per cent). In the paint trade they are often referred to as Spanish red, and in John Smith's *The Art of Painting*, a guide to 'vulgar painting' published in 1723, he refers to 'Spanish Brown well ground and mix'd very thin with Linseed Oyl as a priming coat for woodwork.' This practice reflects the time-honoured tradition of painters applying cheap paints as primers and undercoats.

CHANGING PIGMENT COLOURS

Today, red ochre can be sourced as a native earth pigment, manufactured easily (for example, by roasting ferrous sulphate), or made directly from yellow ochre. This last is an experiment that may easily be tried out at home by calcination (roasting).

Take an old metal teaspoon half filled with yellow ochre pigment and heat it over a gas flame, or place the powder on a flat tin tray over a cooker ring. Upon heating, the pigment will darken slowly, turning dark brown; once cooled it will lighten to a warm red, the equivalent of a good Venetian red. This process is irreversible and

When German and Swiss settlers began to move to Pennsylvania in 1683, they improvized with materials found in the New World, decorating furniture with native ochre-coloured paints, ground in oil or mixed with casein binders.

These two pictures illustrate the simultaneous use of native ochres in decoration and in fine art in Italy. The fresco is at Schloss Runkelstein at Bolzano, while the buildings, one of which is clearly washed with a salmon-pink tint of a Venetian red ochre, are at Ancona.

works by driving out water molecules from the pigment, converting hydrated oxides to anhydrous ones. Different temperatures will produce different colours, and the enterprising Mrs Merrifield, the venerated nineteenth-century translator of Cennino Cennini's *Il Libro Dell'Arte*, describes how earth from Roche in Cornwall produced a wide range of colours, including violet. Today, the Mars colours, such as Mars violet, are chemically produced in methods little advanced from this process.

The process of calcination was known in ancient Rome; Theophrastus wrote about it in the fourth century BC, describing it as a method for manufacturing false cinnabar (a naturally occurring dark vermilion). Yet painters have always seemed to prefer the naturally available pigment to the artificial (and purer) version, perhaps because a red ochre calcined from yellow ochre is never as powerful as its naturally occurring namesake. The low price and wide availability of native red and yellow ochres has meant that they have entered the visual vocabulary of almost every civilization and can be found in decoration around the world, from Aboriginal songline paintings to African houses.

THE ESSENTIALS OF RED OCHRE

Commercially available as:
Red ochre, Persian red, Persian earth, Prussian red, red oxide, Mars red, Indian red, Venetian red; red oxide universal stainer.

Contents
Iron oxide, clay. Mars colours are generally much purer.

Toxicity
No significant hazards.

Uses
* On tempera panels as flesh tones, mixed with white and yellow ochre.
* In fresco work and on the exterior of buildings, as for yellow ochre (see page 19).
* Red ochre is often applied beneath gold leaf or paint to warm the colour of the leaf when applied. This can be enhanced by rubbing the leaf to expose the ground. In water gilding, a soft coloured clay called bole is applied mixed with a little gelatine glue so that the leaf may be burnished once dry by polishing the bole through the leaf with a hard tool. The clay is really a cousin of the red ochre pigment, containing the same constituents but in differing proportions. Popular bole colours are red and yellow ochre, which are mixed to achieve an orange ochre.

Raw sienna

Raw sienna is often seen as a poor yellow in comparison to yellow ochre. But as a brown it possesses superb qualities; it is clean, light in colour and wonderfully transparent and rich when brushed out. This latter property can be fully exploited when antiquing or glazing a surface. Moreover, it has found a firm place in every artist's palette due to its permanence and readiness to mix with other pigments as a toning or neutralizing colour.

You can clearly see the difference in colour obtained by washing out the colour (from the middle to the top) and mixing it with white (from the middle to the bottom). The wash is vibrant and clear and the pigment loses none of its colour intensity when diluted. By contrast, when mixed with white, all the pigment's heat is lost; the results are a series of delicate buff colours that turn creamier as more white is added.

Like the ochres and umbers, the sienna colours are native earths, indicating that they are mined pigments that have undergone the minimum of processing or interference. However, whereas the ochres betray nothing of their origins, the names of the siennas and umbers indicate both their provenance and the processes behind them. The name sienna correctly suggests that raw and burnt sienna come, or at least came, from the area in Tuscany surrounding Siena. Not surprisingly, this region of Italy is veined with these colours; they are in the earth, the buildings, the riverbanks and the rocks. The same iron oxides in the pigment are found in the local clay that is used to make roof tiles and wall bricks in the city of Siena.

Raw sienna, like its brighter cousin yellow ochre, is simply dug out of the ground, washed and ground. When it is calcined (see page 20) it becomes burnt sienna. This process is identical to that which takes place when clay pots are fired; when cooked at a high temperature, terracotta clay changes colour from grey to a reddish burnt tone.

Other parts of the world also are coloured with this same pigment. In Britain, an area near Devizes in southern England has soil of exactly the colour of raw sienna, and there exist several local examples of houses painted with limewash tinted with local clay. Often a spring or stream will have accumulated strongly pigmented pockets of clay that can be washed and used in paints, in the manner of the traditional local decorator. Around the world it is almost impossible to dissociate the colours of the landscape, the rocks and soil from the traditional colours of buildings. Now that we prefer to use universally available colours in modern synthetic paints, we are in danger of losing the sense of geography that our buildings have traditionally had.

THE ESSENTIALS OF RAW SIENNA

Commercially available as:
Raw sienna, Italian ochre, Siena earth, Italian raw earth; raw sienna universal stainer.

Contents
Clay, iron oxides, aluminium oxides.

Toxicity
No specific hazards.

Uses
* In flesh tones, and in glazing over other colours; raw sienna is particularly useful in glazes and historically in oil and tempera work.
* In fresco work and on the exterior of buildings, as for yellow ochre (see page 19).
* In antiquing solutions or as colourwashes to tone underlying colours and neutralize them. Raw sienna is often mixed with raw umber for these uses.

The effect of freshly applied coloured limewash or plaster can often be shocking; we expect buildings in Mediterranean countries to have an uncared-for character and this is commonly reflected in their worn paints. On the right is a patched building in Spoleto painted in now half-removed raw sienna paint, a stock, cheap colour in the area. On the left is a freshly painted modest house in Burano. It is painted with the same colour, but is sharper and fresher.

Burnt sienna

Burnt sienna is deeper and richer than red ochre, but when washed out (see left) it shows some of the latter's brilliance and power. However, when mixed with white there is no mistaking this colour; whereas red ochre produces delicate brown-pinks, burnt sienna, when mixed into white paint, makes pinky browns. These pastels are invaluable to fine artists in rendering flesh tones. In decoration, burnt sienna has been used as a brown that carries no trace of dirtiness. For this use alone it ought to be prized.

THE ESSENTIALS OF BURNT SIENNA

Commercially available as:
Burnt sienna, burnt Italian earth, burnt Italian ochre; burnt sienna universal stainer.

Contents
Clay with iron oxides.

Toxicity
No significant hazards.

Uses
* In flesh tones, and in glazing over other colours; particularly useful in glazes and historically in oil and tempera work.
* In fresco work and on the exterior of buildings (see page 19).

The use of earth colours to decorate buildings is still widespread in less-developed countries. Algeria has many fine examples.

Black

When is black not black? When it is a pigment. The strongest, deepest black available is carbon black, produced by collecting the sooty deposits from the flames of burning oils. Its antecedent, lamp black, dating from prehistoric times, was collected in chambers positioned above the flame and graded according to how greasy the deposits were. Because of the oil content of any type of carbon black, it is not recommended for mixing in oil as it will retard the drying. Its oiliness also renders it difficult to mix with water, which it will instantly repel.

Other ancient pigments are ivory black or bone black, which are jet black with a useful brownish undertone. They both mix with oil or water, making them useful pigments to keep in powder form.

THE ESSENTIALS OF CARBON BLACK

Commercially available as:
Carbon black, lamp black, ivory black, bone black, drop black; black universal stainer.

Contents
Pure carbon with varying quantities of oily and tarry deposits.

Toxicity
Skin, inhalation, ingestion all moderate, but carbon is a known carcinogen and repeated contact may lead to skin cancer.

Uses
* Toning and darkening of other pigments, cement and plaster.
* Tinting white paints to delicate off-whites.
* Creating interesting pale blue tints when mixed into white paints such as casein wall paint, synthetic acrylic emulsions or distemper; bone black should produce brown-greys, useful for stonework.

Burnt umber

Burnt umber, a calcined version of raw umber (see pages 30-1), is perhaps the least used of the native earth pigments. This is partly because of its deep, unremitting brown and partly because the umber pigments are highly absorbent of any oil. This means that any oil paint for house painting that is manufactured to contain burnt umber will necessarily contain a great deal of oil medium relative to the liquidity of the paint. The result is a highly tough and leathery oil film on the paint when dry that is acceptable in a top coat but useless in an undercoat because such flexibility will lead further coats of paint to crack. For this reason, the pigment has never been used as a cheap undercoating colour in the way that red ochre has.

The deep velvety quality of burnt umber pigment does not always translate into a paint made with it!

However, burnt umber has found much historical use as a top coat. Earth colours that are truly native to any one country have always, until widespread manufacture of cheap synthetic pigments, provided the cheapest colorant. As a result, they are the colours most widely found in and on old vernacular buildings.

The swatch to the right of this page indicates the kind of tones produced when burnt umber is mixed into white paint (from the centre of the swatch towards the bottom of the page). However, when not mixed into white, burnt umber displays rich, warm undertones and these can be best viewed when the pigment is washed out, as on the right (from the centre of the swatch towards the top of the page). This appealing earthy quality, combined with the fair translucency of the pigment, is best appreciated when the colour is laid onto a warmer coloured ground such as a parchment or straw colour. These are common grounds for wood-graining, so it is not unusual to find burnt umber being employed by decorative artists to assist in faking some of the denser woodgrains such as mahogany and dark walnut. Indeed, in common with burnt sienna (another quite transparent pigment), burnt umber seems to have been used in graining for at least 300 years.

Fine artists have also appreciated the transparent richness of burnt umber for several centuries. Holbein preferred to sketch out his paintings in brown

The finest umber pigments come from Cyprus, but they are found worldwide. This wall is in Mauritania, West Africa.

monochrome, often apparently building up quite detailed modelling using black and umber. Likewise, this practice of using washes of brown for underpainting was employed by Italian artists of the same period.

THE ESSENTIALS OF BURNT UMBER

Commercially available as:
Burnt umber; burnt umber universal stainer.

Contents
Iron oxides, clay, manganese dioxide. Manganese salts have a catalytic drying effect upon oil paint and so any umber colour will shorten drying times.

Toxicity
Manganese, if ingested or inhaled at chronic levels, induces manganese poisoning. On a normal day-to-day level of contact, most decorators are unlikely to build up sufficient reserves of the metal in their bodies. However, observe the usual precautions when handling the pigment in powder and liquid form.

Uses
* For glazing and shading flesh tones in portraiture.
* In fresco work and on the exterior of buildings, as in yellow ochre (see page 19).
* Burnt umber may also be mixed with raw umber to produce plain neutral browns for antiquing, rubbing into craquelure and colouring in imitation of leather.
* In woodgraining, where it should be used in varnish or a glaze as either a tinting or graining coat.
* As an alternative to burnt umber use Vandyke brown (see raw umber, pages 30-1).

Terra verde

The basic palette of earth colours is conventionally seen as an arrangement of six colours, separated by name and characteristics into three pairs. Yellow ochre may be heated to red ochre, which is also naturally abundant, raw sienna may be heated to produce burnt sienna, both deeper and browner versions of the ochres. And raw umber, when roasted, will yield burnt umber.

Terra verde pigment is light and fluffy, indicating that in oil or water, it will prove ineffectual. Generally, the physical weight and density of a pigment relates to its intensity and covering power.

To this list I have also added black in this section, since it is the oldest pigment of all (see page 25), and finally a marginal outsider, but a valuable addition, terra verde, or green earth. (Roasting this pigment turns it brown.) Terra verde, as its name suggests, is an earth pigment native to Italy and it contains clay, iron oxides, like all earth colours, and some manganese (responsible, as in the case of raw umber, for some of the greening). Its peculiarity is that these are present in very small quantities, rendering the pigment extremely transparent and useless as a body colour, but therefore excellent as a glazing colour. The latter advantage is further enhanced by its slight bluish-grey tinge, redolent of verdigris. When mixed into wax, this makes terra verde a very useful glazing colour for bronze, whether real or fake.

The finest grades of terra verde come from Verona or Bohemia, but other sources include Cyprus and the Mendip hills in the west of England, where I live. I have found small quantities of local green clay and levigated them (see page 19) to produce an acceptable, if slightly dull, pigment. When I do this, I know I am repeating the same process that thousands of decorators and colourmen have used before me. Terra verde may not have the same Egyptian and Minoan pedigree of its sister earth colours, but it was certainly used extensively by the Romans, who valued its permanence in fresco wall paintings.

USING TERRA VERDE FOR ICONS

Around the end of the first millennium, the artists of the Greek church were perfecting the painting styles of religious icons, strictly formalized works that conformed to precise design and colour principles, and for which terra verde was an essential component. By the twelfth century, these artists were in employment abroad, teaching wall and easel painters in Italy the principles of their art and laying the seeds of the Italian Renaissance. Tempera panels, painted on gilded gesso grounds with figures of the seated Madonna and child, are typical of early Italian work and employ the technique of painting the flesh, first with a solid coat of terra verde, and then detailing it in verdaccio, a neutral green-grey of several shades and tints for painting in shadows and highlights. Thus a whole face was painted in green with all the features delineated and shaded. This served as the underpainting to give the later layers of flesh colours realism. Tempera paint consists of pigment suspended usually in egg yolk and so is somewhat glutinous and translucent when applied; this

This Byzantine icon of St Gregory from the Pushkin museum in Moscow displays the recognizable signs of age in a tempera panel painting. The gesso ground has cracked and the paint layers have been worn thin through centuries of handling. The result is that the pink flesh tones have worn away to reveal much of the terra verde ground and the verdaccio shading.

technique is difficult and relies on building successive layers of semi-opaque colours, resulting in an effect of great depth and life.

Cennini describes the final stage of painting flesh: 'You must prepare three gradations of flesh colour, each one lighter than the other, laying every tint in its right place, taking care not to cover over the whole of the verdaccio, but shading ... and softening off in the tenderest manner. On a panel more coats of colour are required than on a wall, and yet not so many but that the green tint under the flesh colour should be just visible through it.'

OTHER USES OF TERRA VERDE

The use of terra verde is by no means restricted to the artist's palette. It is a cheap green that house painters have tried wherever possible to employ, usually mixed with a little white to give it body and opacity. In 1692, at Burghley House in Northamptonshire, the decorative gilder assisting the painter Verrio bought 1lb of 'Italian Green Earth', sufficient, in fact, to paint the woodwork in a room or to serve as a colour under or against gilding. Today, terra verde is a little used pigment but it does deserve experimenting with, since once applied it is, unlike so many other green pigments, both lightfast and permanent.

THE ESSENTIALS OF TERRA VERDE

Commercially available as:
Terra verde, green earth, terre verte, verdetta, celadon green, Verona green (turning to Verona brown when roasted); green oxide universal stainer.

Contents
Iron oxides and small quantities of manganese.

Toxicity
No known hazards, although care should be taken when handling in powder form. Repeated and daily ingestion or inhalation could lead to manganese poisoning. For symptoms, see burnt umber on pages 26-7 and raw umber on pages 30-1).

Uses
* In fresco work, since the pigment will not be affected or changed by chemical attack, including the action of alkaline salts present in damp lime plaster.
* In oil glazes and varnishes as a decorative film over trompe l'oeil landscape painting.
* In tempera, oil and acrylic painting beneath flesh tones.
* In the artificial patination of bronze when mixed with wax and in faking verdigris.

Raw umber

Although raw umber can hardly be described as an exciting colour, its place in the decorator's palette is paramount because it is such a good and universal toning colour. Unlike its burnt equivalent (see pages 26-7), raw umber has no hint of hot brown; rather, it tends towards the green or yellow and so is distinctly cool in appearance.

Italy produces fine umbers derived, as the name suggests, originally from Umbria, the region south of Tuscany where Siena is situated. Chemically, umber is identical to all the ochres and siennas, differing only in that it contains much more manganese, rendering the pigment useful as a drying agent in oil. It is widely recognized that Cyprus produces the best grades, known as Turkey umber, and this name crops up repeatedly in historical references to paint colour.

Raw umber is obtainable in a variety of tones, each with a greater or lesser tendency towards green or yellow.

The uses of raw umber are legion. For the artist it proves a useful alternative to black in painting shadows, and for the decorator it is an excellent dirt colour, for use in varnish or wax as an antiquing colour. It can also serve as a neutral brown wash to suggest dried earthy plaster, and is perhaps best employed in the company of other washes laid above it, such as burnt sienna. A particularly fine parchment or skin colour is achieved by overlayering colourwashes of raw umber, burnt sienna and raw sienna (see colourwashing on pages 70-5 for a version of this employing raw sienna and raw umber).

Raw umber also serves a more subtle use as a greying toner when mixed with other colours. The effect of mixing it with a deep, solid colour such as yellow ochre or pea green is to antique it immediately and render the dried paint with a subtle complexity that synthetic paint colorants cannot match. To explore this, experiment by adding raw umber to a variety of colours.

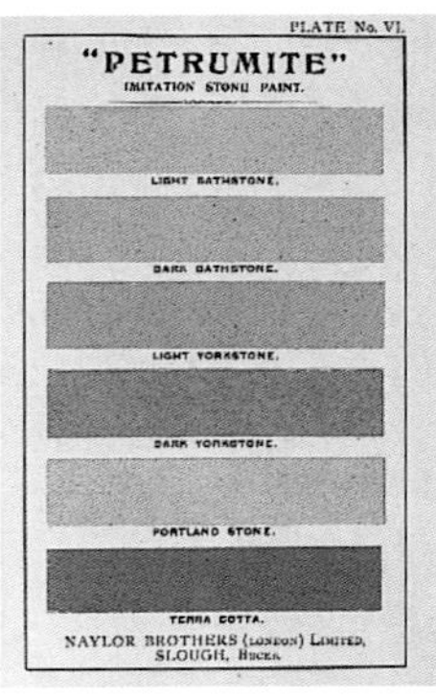

This manufacturer's colour chart of 1921 predates the widespread use of artificial colorants. Consequently, this textured stone paint is formulated with native earth pigments. It is likely that raw umber was added to at least the top five.

RAW UMBER AS TONER

A secondary, and almost more important, use of raw umber is as a toning pigment in pale colours and white paint. As the swatch to the right illustrates, when mixed with white paint (from the middle to the bottom of the page), raw umber loses all its greenness and independent identity, producing instead a warm grey that virtually no black can. This brown-grey colour is invaluable as a gentle toner, mainly as a way of eliminating searing white paints from interiors and pulling decorative schemes together. The problem with white paint is that, other than snow, there is nothing in the natural or built environment coloured pure white. Given this single connotation of pure white, it is hardly surprising that we perceive it as a symbol of purity but also as a sterile colour that sits uneasily against other colours. Even among modernist designers and architects, pure white has now been replaced with 'natural' whites, those of chalk and stone and skies.

Historically, too, the traditional colour of white-painted woodwork was, until the latter half of the twentieth century, much more subtle and quieter than that of brilliant white gloss, which is quite unsuitable for historic interiors. Appropriate and traditional oil paints formulated with lead carbonate or lead sulphate produced creamy-grey whites. These colours may be successfully imitated by using raw umber added to bought white paint, with the optional addition of a drop of raw sienna, burnt umber or black. Experiments with different combinations will yield slightly different off-whites to suit various decorative schemes. However, I have found that raw umber alone gives a very pleasing warm grey-white that seems perfectly at home in most colour schemes, especially those containing warm colours such as yellow ochre.

Raw umber may also be introduced to white

water-based paints, such as traditional distemper, for painting ceilings. In rooms where the decoration is strong or dark, you will be surprised at how dark a ceiling colour may be tinted and still appear as white to the eye when the room is finished. In this way, you will succeed in integrating a colour scheme in which there appears to be strong contrasts. The trick is not to then introduce anything that is pure white.

In both these roles, of toner for strongly-coloured paints and of greying toner for pale or white paints, raw umber is much superior to black, which tends to introduce a hard edge to the dried colour.

This landscape is on the Umbrian/Tuscan border where the soil is coloured by both raw sienna and raw umber colours.

VANDYKE BROWN AND VANDYKE CRYSTALS

Although not a pure earth colour, nor an ancient one, some mention should be made of this pigment as a useful replacement for the umbers, particularly burnt umber, the colour which it most closely resembles.

Vandyke is a native earth pigment that contains vegetable humus and bitumen as well as iron oxides. The poor grades are fugitive and when applied thickly as paint will eventually crack and wrinkle. However, when mixed thinly into varnish, glaze or shellac, this highly transparent pigment gives a warm luminous coating, especially effective on Dutch metal leaf or gold paint. Provided it is of a good quality, Vandyke brown will not fade. It is also very useful in graining and marbling,where its transparency adds to the effect of depth.

Vandyke crystals, soluble in hot water, are sold as a cheap woodstain. However, as it contains bitumen, the liquid can also be used as a graining solution since it requires no further binder to be added. According to the strength of the solution, a wide variety of colours can be procured from the crystals, from near-black to pale amber, making them versatile and essential for effective woodgraining. This is especially so over brighter grounds, emulating the richer woods such as rosewood, walnut and mahogany (see pages 230-5).

This primitive interior is finished in an interesting and ancient spattered finish on a ground of grey made by mixing raw umber and white.

THE ESSENTIALS OF RAW UMBER

Commercially available as:
Raw umber, Roman umber, Sicilian umber, Cyprian umber, Cyprus earth, Turkey umber; raw umber universal stainer.

Contents
Iron oxides, clay, manganese dioxide. Manganese salts have a drying effect upon oil paint and so any umber colour will shorten drying times.

Toxicity
Manganese, if ingested or inhaled at chronic levels, induces manganese poisoning, an illness resembling Parkinson's disease. On a normal day-to-day level of contact, most decorators are unlikely to build up sufficient reserves of the metal in their bodies. However, you should observe the usual precautions when handling the pigment in powder and liquid form.

Uses
* For toning white or pastel paints.
* For toning and muting coloured paints.
* In fresco work and on the exterior of buildings, as for yellow ochre (see page 19).
* In woodgraining, where it should be used in varnish or a glaze as a tinting or graining coat.
* For antiquing, when mixed with glazes or waxes.

White

It is impossible to write about colours and not talk about white. Although many see it as a non-colour, like black (see page 25), white is often only white by degrees, and each variety of it handles in a different way. So some of the various subtle forms of white deserve a mention.

CHALK

The most common and ancient of colouring materials, and also a cheap pigment, chalk has been powdered into simple wall paints such as casein and distemper for thousands of years. It also forms the basis of pastels and gouache paint. It is harmless and inert, dries quite opaque in water paints but becomes transparent in oil or wax. Chalk is particularly notable for its creamy umber off-white colour and the delicacy with which it renders the finish of all paints that contain it.

WHITE LEAD

Now banned from use on all but the most important historic houses because of health risks, lead carbonate is a quite pure white that was traditionally manufactured using lead sheets, spent tan and vinegar. It is not used in water paints owing to its toxicity and its tendency to blacken on exposure to hydrogen sulphide when mixed with poor water-based binders. However, white lead blends superbly with oil and the combination of the two is universally recognized as the most beautiful paint to handle under the brush. This is due to its ability to form a chemically intimate mixture with the fatty acids present in oil to make a tough, smooth and elastic paint. Lead paints will usually wear, not by cracking or peeling away like modern synthetic coatings, but by chalking and wearing thin.

A slightly less toxic, and less brilliant, form of lead paint has traditionally been formulated using lead sulphate.

LIME

A full description of this white is given under the limewash technique on pages 96-9. It is not commonly used as a pigment but as a coating and has a lightening effect on pigments mixed with it.

TITANIUM WHITE

In industry, titanium has become the most widely used white pigment, replacing many of its inferior antecedents such as lithopone. This is due to its inertness, exceptional covering power, stability, brilliant whiteness and non-toxicity. Despite a tendency to chalk in oil, it is the most reliable synthetic white.

LESS COMMONLY USED WHITES

Zinc white: bright white but translucent.
Lithopone: zinc sulphide and barium sulphate mixed together; used in cheap paints.
Blanc fixe and barytes: variations of barium and zinc whites.

The Neo-classical interior of Wardour Castle in Wiltshire is decorated with a variety of restrained schemes in wall paint. The shades of blue illustrated here may be reproduced with white paint tinted with vegetable black and some form of copper-based blue.

Ultramarine Blue

Ultramarine, which was once made by crushing the semi-precious stone lapis lazuli, originally came from a few mines in Afghanistan. Only certain grades of lapis are suitable and even they only yield a tiny proportion of the colour in relation to the amount of stone crushed. The name ultramarine literally signifies 'from across the sea', indicating that to reach Europe the material had to be shipped in. The cost of mining and of transportation together escalated the cost of ultramarine so that, historically, the finest grades cost more than their weight in gold.

Ultramarine blue pigment possesses a quite magical intensity and deep brilliance. Its purity is akin to that of a deeply pigmented flower petal and it is worth obtaining some of the powder to look at, even if you never intend using it.

Blue pigments have always been hard to find in nature, particularly those which are lightfast and resistant to alkalis and acids. Pliny does make reference to indigo, but not to ultramarine; there are no references to the colour before the twelfth century. It was then quickly adopted as a valuable component of the artist's and decorator's palette, and was kept in reserve for the most prestigious details in painted work, such as the Madonna's veil in tempera panel paintings. Partly because of this restricted use and partly because of the pigment's intensity, today we still recognize ultramarine blue as a colour with noble and opulent connotations.

This Moroccan courtyard is painted in an unusual combination of two blues; one a slightly greenish copper blue, and the other ultramarine blue mixed with white.

This Madonna's cloak was initially painted ultramarine blue but it has turned black, as this pigment so often does in the presence of sulphurous fumes from burning fires.

This is strange, given that in 1828, a Frenchman called Guimet won a national competition by discovering how to synthetically produce ultramarine reliably and cheaply. His method was a complex one involving a variety of materials including clay, soda, sulphur and coal. Since then, ultramarine blue has come into widespread architectural use for decorating the outside of houses, particularly in some Mediterranean regions such as southern Portugal.

THE ESSENTIALS OF ULTRAMARINE BLUE

Commercially available as:
Ultramarine blue; ultramarine blue universal stainer.

Contents
Originally ground lapis lazuli but now a complex silicate of sodium and aluminium with sulphur.

Toxicity
No specific hazards.

Uses
* To suggest skies and backgrounds in medieval/Gothic settings.
* To produce excellent lavender blue tints when mixed with white.
* To produce good violets when mixed with reds.
* As a background for gilded detail.

Copper blue and green

If you are going to keep ultramarine blue in your palette, then you are also going to need other blues to make green tones. Ultramarine is nearly always tinged with purple, and as such when mixed with yellow will not produce vivid greens; it is too far around the colour wheel (see pages 250-6). So, in order to produce good greens, you will need a greenish-blue pigment that will reflect a good deal of green light.

The paint swatch to the left has been executed in phthalocyanine blue acrylic paint, which in every respect is identical to Prussian blue. The pigment shown, however, is cerulean blue, a paler and brighter blue that produces very similar results when mixed with white.

Until the early nineteenth century, decorators had no choice. Like it or not, they were forced to employ bluish greens (even the natural earth alternative, terra verde, is on the blue side), and the only naturally occurring blues and greens available to them were based on copper.

Malachite was the brightest and most expensive naturally occurring green pigment known to the ancients; it was ground to a powder. Another naturally occurring copper compound, crysocolla, was also employed. By Roman times, though, artists had learnt to manufacture their own green verdigris (copper acetate) pigment by suspending copper sheets above basins of vinegar; in the fourteenth century, Alcherius called this 'Greek or Common Green'. A sharper, less blue green, composed of copper carbonate, was also common.

A simple method of turning the more common green into blue was recorded in Bologna in the fifteenth century. 'Take 1oz of sal ammoniac and 6oz of verdegris and grind these powders very fine with oil of tartar upon marble; then put them into a glazed vase and let them stand some days and you will find the verdigris converted into a very beautiful azure.'

This practice remained in use until the early 1600s, by which time another source of blues and greens was identified. The product was exactly the same as that which had historically been used, copper carbonate, but now it could be artificially manufactured as a by-product of silver refining. Throughout the seventeenth, eighteenth and nineteenth centuries, these pigments were known as blue and green refiner's verditer and found widespread use in decoration for the usual reason; they were cheap. However, they were also unstable, the blue often reverting to green.

Enter Prussian blue, a powerful deep blue pigment with greenish undertones, accidentally invented in 1704 and made from alum and animal bones. It was as expensive as ultramarine when first introduced and used only in the houses of the great and good until the middle of the eighteenth century, by which time mass production was in hand, and the price had fallen.

By the mid-nineteenth century, other more sophisticated blues and greens had entered the market, but all possessed the same family traits as their antecedents; the blues were greenish and the greens were bluish. Among them were viridian, a chrome-based green similar in colour

Copper blues and greens form an essential part of eighteenth-century middle class taste in decoration. This interior from Homewood House in Baltimore neatly juxtaposes schemes in both copper blue and green. Pea green can be produced from green verditer, yellow ochre and Prussian blue.

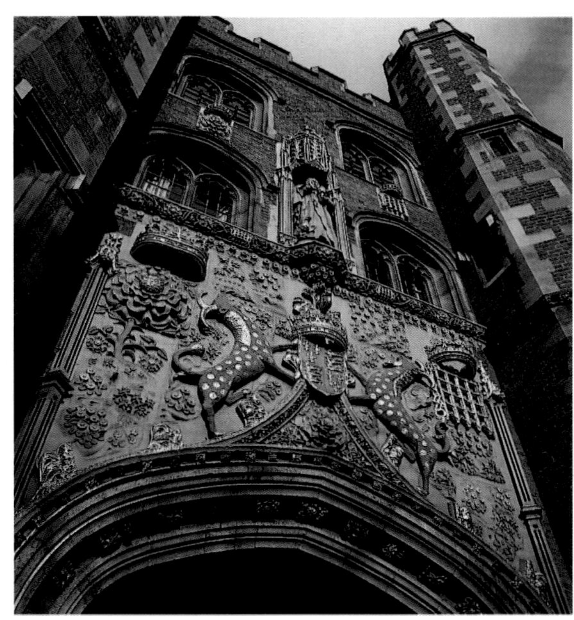

The rarer colours have always been incorporated into the vocabulary of heraldic colours such as at the entrance to St John's College, Cambridge.

to green verditer, and cerulean blue, a tin-based bright blue of a turquoise nature.

The reason for this potted history of colour is to show that, despite history throwing up dozens of blues and greens for artists and decorators to use, the majority have always been copper-based, hovering around the same area on the colour wheel. The marked exception is ultramarine blue, in use from the twelfth century on, which has a purplish tinge and was so expensive that it prohibited itself from everyday use.

Given that nature, and science, have historically given us such little choice, it seems inevitable that through the centuries, architecture has grown and developed with these colours in its vocabulary. If you need delicate blues and greens that convey the eighteenth century then you should use these colours in conjunction with yellow ochre and a little ultramarine blue (in imitation of indigo) to procure a palette of enormous range.

THE ESSENTIALS OF COPPER BLUE AND GREEN

Commercially available as:
Blues: cerulean blue, cobalt blue, Prussian blue; any standard blue universal stainer.
Greens: verdigris, cobalt green; any standard green universal stainer.

Contents
Originally, copper carbonate (azure, malachite, azurite or the verditers) or copper acetate (verdigris, which handles poorly and degrades). Modern synthetic equivalents handle better and are more reliable. They are phthalocyanine blue and green (again, copper compounds) invented in the 1930s and are permanent.

Toxicity
Copper carbonate has slight to moderate effects of irritation on the respiratory system, but with chronic exposure may lead to anaemia. Handle with care and avoid in powder form .

Copper acetate has similar effects but may be poisonous if swallowed. Exercise extreme care.

Viridian is hydrated chromium sesquioxide, to be avoided at all costs since chromium is a known carcinogen, teratogen and mutagen.

Phthalocyanine colours (phthalo, monastral or cyan colours, also present in some stainers) are extremely toxic, teratogenic, and are suspected carcinogens. Never handle in powder form and exercise extreme caution when in other media.

If you insist on handling blue and green pigments in powder form, choose a pigment known to be of relatively lower toxicity such as those listed in the *Commercially available as* section above. Do, however, exercise all caution and wear protective gloves, glasses and a mask.

Uses
* To fake verdigris and bronze colours.
* In the accurate rendition of period colour schemes, particularly those of the eighteenth century.
* To produce attractive wall colours when mixed with white paints such as soft distemper, emulsion or casein.
* To produce excellent exterior woodwork colours when mixed with white paint; suitable against brickwork, stone and concrete.

The pigment shown here is viridian (a false version made by precipitating phthalocyanine green dye onto an inert powder, and therefore as potentially dangerous as true viridian), which accurately emulates green verditer. The swatch has also been executed in viridian. Phthalocyanine green is darker, but produces very similar tones when washed out.

Vermilion

Although red oxides can provide us with a wide range of colours and tints, none is as intense a hue as vermilion. Originally invented by the Chinese, the colour was first manufactured in Europe in the thirteenth century by heating mercury and sulphur in clay pots to produce mercuric sulphide gas that condensed on the side of the pots as a brilliant red powder. The rarity of mercury and the extreme danger to which the manufacturer was exposed during the process, meant the pigment was expensive, but still cheaper than the naturally occurring variant of this colour, cinnabar. Despite its costliness, conservators continue to discover widespread use of vermilion throughout the Middle Ages; recently it was found that a large number of patterns and designs in Wells cathedral were executed in vermilion and not red ochre as had previously been believed. Indeed, vermilion is the bright medieval red seen on the painted tombs of knights, in heraldry and on what remains of painted medieval furniture. It was an important element in the language of Gothic and Tudor decoration.

This pigment is a synthetic, and much safer, form of vermilion, derived from azo pigments, and is known as vermilionette.

Cinnabar, as Theophrastus notes, occurred naturally in certain mountain cliffs in Spain, from which trained archers could dislodge lumps of it with their arrows. It was highly prized although inferior to vermilion. But it is not known whether cinnabar behaves as peculiarly as vermilion – which occasionally turns black in time due to atmospheric exposure.

For this reason, and for its poisonous nature, vermilion is not used in the printing or paint industry. In the fine artist's palette it has been replaced by cadmium red (arguably just as toxic, but more reliable) and in commercial work by the modern synthetic pigments that are produced in the petroleum and plastics industries such as toluidine red or quinacridone red, first synthesized in the 1930s.

THE ESSENTIALS OF VERMILION, CADMIUM RED AND SYNTHETIC REDS

Commercially available as:
Vermilionette, cadmium red, and synthetic red such as quinacridone; red universal stainer.

Contents
Vermilion – mercuric sulphide.
Cadmium red – cadmium sulphide with cadmium selenide.

Toxicity
Vermilion – Moderate by skin contact; high by ingestion and inhalation possibly resulting in mercury poisoning and damage to the liver and nervous system.
Cadmium red – Insignificant by skin contact but high by ingestion or inhalation. Cadmium in chronic exposure is carcinogenic and can cause other illnesses such as liver damage and anaemia.
Synthetic reds – Although pigments from similar groups (such as phthalo blues and greens) are known carcinogens, these pigments appear much safer. However, as a result of chronic ingestion or inhalation as powders, it is suspected that they may contribute to the likelihood of cancer.

Uses
* For bright detail work in period decoration covering Greek styles to the nineteenth century. Particularly evocative if used in conjunction with medieval dull greens and earth colours.

St George and the Dragon, a ninth-century Icon from Myria. Luckily the vermilion is still strikingly bright – this pigment was highly valued for adding such patches of colour.

King's yellow

Just as a bright red is useful in the decorator's palette for brightening other colours such as red ochre, so a bright yellow is indispensable for cheering up greens and yellow ochres. King's yellow, known as orpiment to the ancients, was mined by the earliest civilizations and prized for its brilliance, opacity and warmth. The name derived from auripigmentum, literally meaning golden pigment. However, it would not work when mixed with either copper- or lead-based pigments which precluded it from much use in the painting of houses inside and out. Also, Cennini mentions that even when used alone in wall paints, orpiment was likely to turn black once applied. Its rarity coupled with these strange handling properties means that there is little evidence for its early use in decoration.

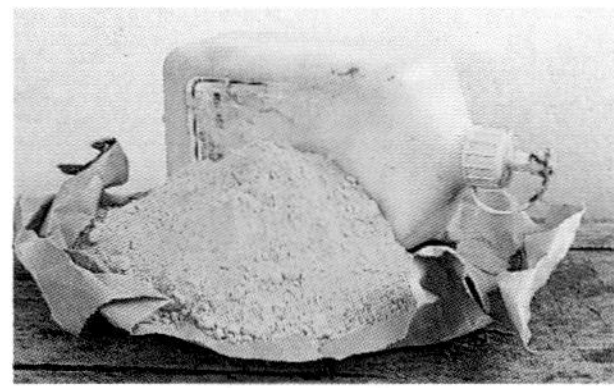

This pigment is a children's yellow powder paint, about the only yellow pigment which is safe to handle in powder form (children's powders are formed by dyeing chalk). This fact ought to be argument enough for the re-introduction of traditional yellow pigments such as Indian and saffron yellows, both made from vegetable sources. They are less stable in use but much less toxic.

As early as the fifteenth century this bright yellow was being artificially manufactured for use by artists, and by the early 1700s was in use as a decorative colour and known as king's yellow. However, since the pigment consists of highly poisonous arsenic trisulphide, its use must have been carefully considered. Nevertheless, it was used as a wall painting colour throughout the eighteenth century since any colour of such brilliancy was bound to attract the interest of fashionable aristocracy, forever in pursuit of the novel.

At that time the choice of pigment was between king's yellow, rather fugitive yellow lakes made from buckthorn berries, safflower or fustic, and the politely named Indian yellow, made from the urine of cows fed on mango leaves: some choice. Today, the warmth and opacity of king's yellow is best imitated by chrome and cadmium yellow pigments and

Claydon House, Buckinghamshire, exemplifies the elegance of the later eighteenth century. It is decorated throughout with fashionable distemper colours of the period, including blue verditer and king's yellow.

paints (both of which are also highly toxic and should be used only in the artist's palette). Synthetic yellows such as hansa yellow or a permanent yellow such as barium yellow, are not as opaque as either king's or cadmium yellows, but are considered safer to handle in paint form. Only cobalt yellow should ever be handled in powder form (unlike all the other yellows, cobalt is not a known carcinogen) and even then under strict conditions of safety and hygiene.

THE ESSENTIALS OF KING'S YELLOW

Commercially available as:
Cobalt yellow, chrome yellow, hansa yellow; yellow universal stainer.

Contents
Arsenic trisulphide (in King's yellow).

Toxicity
King's yellow is fatally poisonous. Modern equivalent yellows have their own problems. Zinc yellow, strontium yellow, barium yellow and cadmium yellow are known carcinogens and should never be handled in powder form or used outside the easel artist's palette. Chrome yellow is also a teratogen and mutagen, and hansa yellow is also a suspected carcinogen. Use the latter only in liquid form and exercise extreme caution.

Uses
* Tinting white paints to produce fresh bright yellow wall colours, as used in the eighteenth century for small rooms and print rooms.
* For brightening yellow ochre.
* In heraldic work and detail work in decoration from medieval times onwards.

Essential mixes

By looking at the essential 13 colours on the preceding pages, you can see that they belong to an obvious historical palette as well as forming the basic vocabulary of many regional colour schemes. Those of Mediterranean countries spring to mind particularly, because it is there that many of the listed pigments are employed full-strength and unmixed. However, the more subtle colours and delicate tints associated with northern climes were missing from these pages and it is these that are illustrated here and overleaf. As much as single pigment colours are used by themselves, they are also blended to form a variety of secondary and subtle primary colours. These 13 swatches each display a simple two-colour blend on the left-hand side. Each subsequent paint dab has then been made using the colour shown on the left mixed with increasing quantities of white paint to produce a series of tints.

The great advantage of this layout of swatches is that it shows just what a wide range of mixes are available by intermixing just a few pigments. Gratifyingly, most of these colours, such as putty, stone, pearl, pea green, grass green and drab, have come to be recognized as correct for buildings put up in the last two to three centuries. All are usually a mix of two colours from the traditional palette, plus white.

The series demonstrates, then, that it is easy to mix your own blends for authentic decoration, and that a fantastically wide range of decorative colours can be produced from the core of essential colours. Moreover, only a total of 8 of the 13 essential colours were used here, and so these swatches are by no means an exhaustive survey of the colours that can be mixed. To gain a true understanding of the potential of the basic palette it is a good idea to buy 13 tubes of acrylic or gouache paint, plus white and experiment yourself.

Most importantly, these blends are excellent decorating colours for a reason other than historical accuracy. The fact that they contain true pigments in simple, uncomplicated and unmuddied blends mean that when on the wall, or furniture, they appear much more lively and interesting than shop-bought blends containing synthetic pigments. In short, they look good, regardless of the exact quantity of white paint added, or of the exact blend of the two pigments.

The delightful colours mixed by our forefathers were nearly all compositions of more than one pigment, usually added to white. This simple rule-of-thumb for paint formulae is a decorating trick still practised by the expert interior decorators of today.

RAW UMBER ALONE
It is worth noting how this colour turns much greyer when mixed with white to produce an excellent antiquing colour, donkey browns, and superb off-whites.

RAW UMBER + RAW SIENNA
A hotter mix, also good for antiquing and colourwashing, and creating camel, oak and wainscot colours.

RAW SIENNA ALONE
Mixed with white, raw sienna makes fine stone colours of varying shades, and also biscuit.

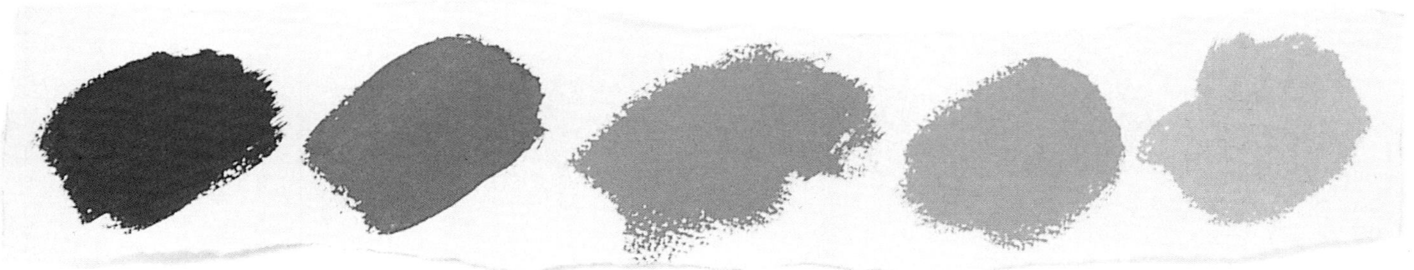

RAW UMBER + YELLOW OCHRE
Darker tones produce John Fowler's colour merde d'oie. *Mid-tones are the preferred blend for antiquing mixes over gold and metal leaf, and paler tints yield an excellent warm grey or putty colour.*

YELLOW OCHRE + RED OCHRE
Excellent terracotta plus good buff tints.

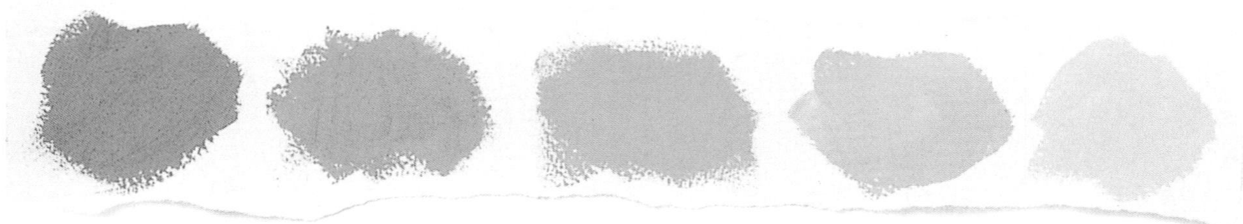

VERMILION + KING'S YELLOW
Much brighter orange, as to be expected. Beautiful peachy tints.

RED OCHRE + VERMILION
Superb oxblood yielding rosy tints made more intense by the vermilion. Good to try very pale.

VERMILION + ULTRAMARINE BLUE
Good rich purples with a warm rosy tinge. Fine mauve tints.

RED OCHRE + ULTRAMARINE BLUE
Duller blend but with more interesting, cooler tints resembling Mars violet. Excellent for use in schemes with earth colours.

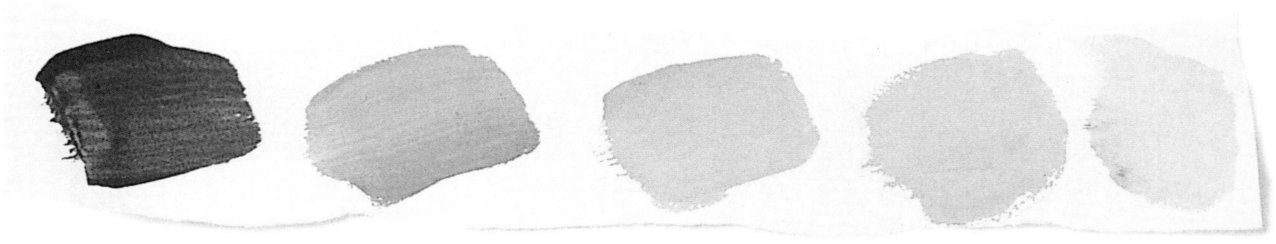

COPPER BLUE + COPPER GREEN
Bright aquamarine blues suggestive of Regency colour schemes.

YELLOW OCHRE + GREEN VERDITER
Fine deep green, pea green and eau de nil.

YELLOW OCHRE + ULTRAMARINE BLUE
Complex, oily greens excellent on furniture, fine neo-classical pale green.

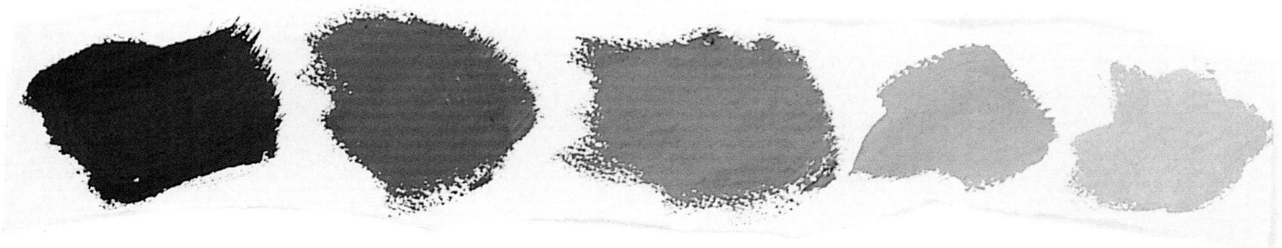

RAW UMBER + ULTRAMARINE BLUE
Good warm deep grey, excellent lead, granite and slate colours, and distinguished pale off-whites.

Part Two

PAINT

Essential materials and brushes

Before you begin painting, you must surround yourself with the necessary tools and materials; the right ones for the job in hand. It is commonly believed that the real sécret of skilled decorative painting lies in the choice of materials and tools. To an extent this is true, since, for example, the designs of many brushes have been perfected through centuries to suit particular tasks. Those used in this book are illustrated overleaf, but it is surprising to find how few these are.

Of course, there are also materials for which there are simply no substitutes and these are given opposite. Again, it is surprising how basic the list is. But it is better to understand a smaller range of materials in great depth than to have a passing acquaintance with many more. To carry the analogy further, you should not be afraid of the materials we use in this book, they should be your friends. By knowing them well, you will be able to control them better and exploit their strengths and weaknesses.

GOOD PRACTICE

* Avoid any extremes of temperature. Water-based paints will ruin if frozen, so do not keep them in unheated buildings. Keep any flammable liquids, including varnish, out of direct sunlight. All lids should be tightly secured to prevent evaporation, and necks of bottles should be wiped clean before screwing on the lid.

* Do not smoke, drink or eat in your place of work. Food can carry toxic material from your hands and fingernails deep into your system. Tobacco smoke also acts as a carrier of toxic powder and solvent particles, taking them much deeper into your respiratory system than if normally inhaled.

* Ensure your space is well lit. Point at least one lamp onto the ceiling to provide some overall ambient light to reduce harsh shadows from other lamps.

* Judge your work under normal working light, by tungsten light and by normal daylight if possible. Each may reveal a different colour!

* Clean up as you go to prevent paints and varnishes from drying on the sides of containers and paint kettles, and to prevent brushes from bending and sagging when left in pots.

* Decant spare mixes into appropriately sized containers with airtight lids to reduce air contact, and always label. Use (preferably) baby milk tins with easy-to-peel lids, or coffee jars with screw lids, for storing powders. A stiff lid may result in clouds of powder being released on opening.

* Do not leave brushes soaking overnight.

* Oil varnish brushes may be left between uses suspended in linseed oil (covering the metal ferrule) to preserve them. Clean in white spirit and dry before use.

* Store brushes in a ventilated cupboard to prevent dust from settling on them.

* Seal all draughts from the workplace and keep any work in progress warm at night; some materials such as oil-based varnish will spoil if kept cold during application or curing, or if the surface to which they are applied is cold. Others, such as gum arabic, are hygroscopic, becoming sticky in humid conditions.

* Cover floors and furniture with plastic sheeting for messy work. Do not constantly re-use plastic sheeting since dried paint may crack and dust off. Regularly wash cloth dust sheets.

* Sweep daily to keep down the dust. Spray the floor first with a plant mister to keep the dust down. Do not sweep if freshly varnished surfaces are drying since sweeping raises dust.

* Wash the floor, all shelves, tables, all paint pots and storage kettles/containers once a month to eliminate dirt and dust from all painting processes.

* Ideally, sand and abrade surfaces in another part of the workspace, to restrict the spread of dust.

* Remember three facts that could save your life:

1 Any solvent other than water is toxic and highly dangerous. Half-an eggcupful of white spirit or turpentine, if swallowed, is enough to kill a child within minutes. Always label solvent bottles and treat them with the respect they deserve.

2 Some powder pigments are carcinogenic and will have very damaging effects if inhaled or ingested. Steer clear of them and always use a paper or filter mask when handling powders.

3 Old rags soaked in linseed oil or varnish will quickly heat up if compressed, as in a bin. This is due to the oxidization of the varnish or oil on the rag. They can catch fire. Always lay them out flat.

ESSENTIAL MATERIALS

* High work surface to enable you to stand and work or sit on a stool.
* Clean newsprint paper for covering tables (cheap lining paper is an alternative).
* Paper tape for masking areas not to be painted.
* Plastic sheeting for covering areas of accessories and furniture not to be painted.
* Roll of industrial/domestic paper towels for mopping up and some decorative effects.
* Box of clean white, lint-free cloth (old hospital sheets) for use as a decorative tool in, for example, ragging, polishing, and making shellac rubbers.
* Box of mixed coloured rags, for cruder work and hand cleaning.
* Hand cleanser and barrier cream.
* Variety of masks, including solvent masks of rubber.
* Goggles.
* Medical, thin disposable rubber gloves for day-to-day wear. Heavy-duty elbow-length black rubber gloves for chemical patination and using limewash. All available from specialist paint suppliers.
* Aprons, overalls.
* Soap flakes and bars for washing brushes, brush pots and cupboard.
* Metal cabinet for storing flammable materials.
* Sundry scissors, pens, craft knives and scalpels.
* Hair dryer and extension lead for drying paints.
* Plenty of empty containers, such as yogurt pots and jars with lids, and clean paint canes. Labels for same.
* Collection of old wooden blocks on which to stand flat objects such as trays and table tops, when varnishing.
* Soft dusters and shoe-cleaning brushes for polishing waxes.
* Wet and dry paper (much superior to sand-paper for painted surfaces); 100 and 200 grit papers for basic work and 400 grit paper for final attack.
* Wire wool. One grade only is really necessary, and that is the finest: 0000 grade.

The equipment illustrated is:
ROW 1
RUBBER GLOVES *If you can, use the disposable, thin, hospital-type since they are more pleasant to wear and allow for a greater sense of touch. Use long ones for messier work and for limewashing.*
ROW 2 (FROM TOP TO BOTTOM)
RAGS *The best quality are from old sheets as, after countless washes, they have lost all their lint. Lint-free cloth is essential for the finest work such as when using rags to manipulate paint in certain paint effects.*
WIRE WOOL *Generally 000 grade is sufficiently fine for waxing and cutting back varnishes on mouldings and fine details, etc. 0000 is even finer.*
MASKING TAPE *24mm width.*
SANDPAPER *We use several grades, but prefer wet and dry paper (shown beneath), since by wetting, it keeps the dust down.*
SCISSORS, SPOONS, KNIFE AND TROWEL *Indispensable everyday equipment.*
ROW 3 (FROM TOP TO BOTTOM)
FULL FACE RESPIRATORY MASK *Over the top for the amateur, but essential for those with allergic problems and for professionals who come into contact with chemicals and the more toxic solvents such as aromatic hydro-carbons (toluene, xylene, etc).*
RUBBER FACE MASK *Good for everyday use, the replaceable filters can be bought containing charcoal to absorb light quantities of solvents and vapours.*
PAPER MASK *Not suitable for protection from solvents but useful in dusty environments.*

ESSENTIAL BRUSHES

Most of the techniques in this book are executed using a remarkably ordinary range of decorating brushes, the kind you can buy in any DIY store. However, some techniques call for specialist brushes, particularly the kind of techniques used to decorate smaller objects and accessories, where the scale of the finished effect is much finer. These are illustrated here.

Whenever I teach, I insist on demonstrating with, and making the students practise with, the cheapest possible brushes. I maintain that if they can soften with a 100mm (4in)-wide house painting brush, imagine how perfect their technique will be once they pick up a lily-bristle softener.

The first step in getting to know your brushes is learning how to hold them properly. A brush should be considered not as a tool held in the hand but as a physical extension of your hand. Anything over 100mm (4in) wide can be held in a four-finger grip, but below that size, a brush should be held as follows: place the handle of the brush in the cruck of your thumb and first finger and close the thumb gently onto it. Place the first few fingers on the metal ferrule to give you a firm but relaxed grip. This makes full use of the length of the brush's handle and provides a firm hold that will not tire the muscles.

Brushes should always be cleaned immediately after use and *not* stored in water as this may bend the bristles, rust the ferrule and rot and swell the cement into which the bristles are set. After cleaning in the appropriate solvent they should be washed with soft soap and warm water, dried, and then hung up in a dust-free environment. The exception are varnish brushes which may, instead, be left suspended in linseed oil between use to keep the bristles soft.

Varnish brushes should never be used for any other job since dried traces of paint left on the bristles will dissolve in varnish and be transmitted onto the varnished surface: something that no self-respecting decorator would wish to occur.

The brushes are (LEFT TO RIGHT):
LARGE ROUND FITCH *Useful for loading with large quantities of paint.*
DOMED FITCH *Also available with pointed end. Tough bristles for handling thick or sticky media such as shellac which it will brush out well. Also good for mixing.*
OVAL DECORATING BRUSH *Will hold more than its flat equivalent and is consequently useful for varnishing. Ensure that for this use, your brush is as soft as possible, preferably with split ends.*
FLOGGER *A specialist's brush for dragging or flogging a paint or glaze, as in woodgraining.*
OVERGRAINER *Another graining tool with which to have fun; it is really five pencil brushes braced together.*
PENCILS *Fine lining brushes for detail work. Available from artist's suppliers.*
(FROM TOP TO BOTTOM)
BADGER SOFTENER *Given that badger bristles are too delicate for use in oil glaze and paint, only use a small badger softener for the most small-scale, delicate work.*
LILY-BRISTLE SOFTENER *The pig bristles of this brush are springy and taper to fine points with split ends. This makes them ideal for softening both oil and water media. This softener is the most useful brush you can buy, and can be substituted by a fine- quality jamb duster (decorator's dusting brush).*
GOAT'S HAIR MOP *A mop is a brush with a broad, soft head of bristles. I find this one firmer and more springy than camel or sable mops (made primarily for watercolour artists) and, as such, more useful for the application of fine shellac coats and gesso.*

The secret life of media in this book

The message of this book is that once you know your materials, you can really begin to experiment and do exciting things with them. To that end, pages 48-57 act as an introduction to the media used in this book. However, before going any further, it is essential to know what is in paint.

The earliest paints, those used to decorate the walls of caves at Lascaux in France, for example, were simple concoctions. Men took coloured clays of red and yellow and charcoal from their fires, mixed them with water, and then daubed them on, probably with their hands, or with bunches of grasses. They soon learnt that these mixtures would powder off when dry and so experimented with sticky liquids to bind their paints and stick them to the wall. For example, they discovered that tree gums, like gum arabic from the acacia tree, or cherry gum (a crude form of gouache), would work well when blended with water. Likewise, egg yolks would also work, drying to a hard, waterproof finish (early tempera). Skimmed milk from their cattle worked (casein binder) as did the jellied stock left in the pot after the bones and skin of carcasses had been boiled up (gelatine). There is historical evidence that all these binders were in use by Egyptian times, whether as paint media or as glues, and in refined forms they still form an important part of the decorator's palette of materials.

Of course, modern paints are much more sophisticated formulations, at least on the face of it. Conventional household emulsion paint contains distilled water to stop it rotting in the can and a vinyl binder that forms a suspension in water (egg yolk is a suspension, as is an 'emulsion' of oil in water). It also has a pigment, which is nowadays the non-toxic and highly opaque pigment, titanium white. Thus far, emulsion paint is very similar to the caveman's homemade paint; it consists of a binder, a solvent and a pigment, the three essential components of paint.

But emulsion paint may also contain chalk, a jellifying agent, inert filler such as mica or talc, and maybe an extending additive to improve the flow of the paint under the brush. These constituents are there for only one reason, to save the manufacturer money. Generally, when you buy a paint you are buying a product that is formulated to do its job – but only just. Some manufacturers will, however, insist on only the best ingredients, and plenty of them at that, to provide you with a top-quality, high-performance product that will offer itself as a useful product for jobs you hadn't even thought of. By mixing your own paints, you will begin to appreciate the weaknesses and strengths of different binders and their combinations with different pigments.

Of course, some paints are not formulated to the exact equation of binder + solvent + pigment. Traditional gloss oil paint is formulated with just binder + pigment, using linseed oil. If its solvent, turpentine, is added, it is as a matting agent. Equally, some Scandinavian 'boiled paints' are of water and pigment bound with rye and wheat starches that are cooked with iron sulphate salts as a hardening and proofing agent. This equates as binder + solvent + pigment + agent. In a similar manner, distempers and casein paints may be hardened after application by spraying or lightly brushing on a coat of an agent such as acetone (see pages 56-7).

But perhaps the most interesting and unusual type of coating is limewash, which requires no binder. Its process of manufacture and drying are fully explained on pages 96-9, but its chemistry may be summed up as a series of changes that the material undergoes on exposure first to heat, then moisture, and finally carbon dioxide from the atmosphere. This results in a crystalline matrix being formed in the applied coat of limewash as it dries.

The list of media on the following pages is by no means exhaustive and contains virtually no reference to the wealth of products available on the industrial market. However, it does contain all those binders and paint media that are to be commonly encountered in any craftsman's paint studio and which are easily available for the homeowner to use.

Traditional water-based media

Each of these traditional media are used as binders when making paints and have been used for many hundreds of years. Lime cannot be properly considered as a binder that is added to paint, since it is a self-binding coating, which requires no additional medium if prepared correctly. See the limewashing recipe and technique on pages 96-9.

GUM ARABIC (Binder)

This medium is a natural vegetable binder from the acacia tree and so highly appealing for its 'green' and 'vegan' values. Paints made with it are hard and shiny (if much binder is added), and also entirely water soluble when dry. Its brittleness when dry may be tempered by the addition of up to 15 percent glycerine.

Uses Pharmaceutical and in confectionery. In television floor paint (where it can be washed off the next day). As a binder for watercolours, in gouache colours, for homemade washes and paints, in crackle varnish, and in cracked paint techniques.

Forms Liquid or, more usually, crystals (see recipe on page 60). The best grade to use is gum senegal.

Drying qualities Dries by evaporation in air; it turns from being colloidal (glue-like) to sticky and finally hard, as weak, incomplete proteins form a film. In damp weather it can be extremely slow to dry, taking up to several hours. Under dry conditions, it is touch dry in an hour or so.

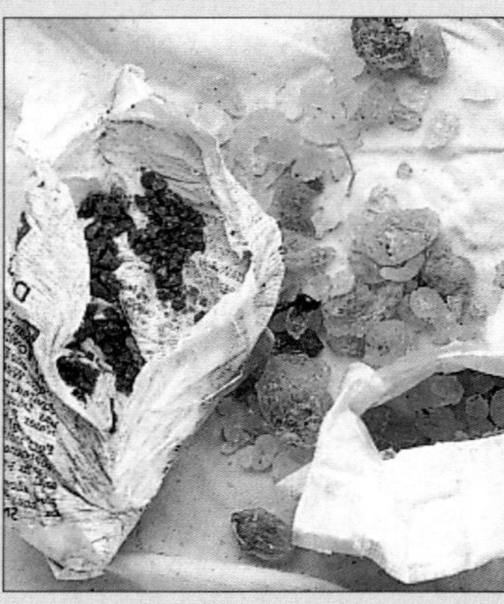

The large lumps featured here are gum arabic crystals.

Dissolving agent Paint bound by it can be dissolved when dry by water and alcohol, such as methylated spirits.

Shelf life Slowly decomposes as liquid unless preservative is added: use a little pine oil.

Failings Paints are brittle and break down if applied thickly. Some pigments swell in it.

ANIMAL GELATINES

(Binders, glues and sizes)

These ancient and traditional binders are familiar to us as the gelatine left over from cooking the Sunday roast. Common sources are the hoofs, bones and hides of cattle, and the crude opaque grades are simply known as glue. Gelatines are also soft binders; they remain water-soluble when dry. Their great advantages are their cheapness and ability to make paint that breathes.

A cup of rabbitskin glue – a typical animal gelatine glue – being added to water.

Uses As a binder in distemper and in gesso using finer grades. Traditionally, as a leather and wood glue. For sizing plaster prior to painting.

Forms Flakes, coarse granules or beads (pearl glue), sheets (parchment gelatine only), and as cooking grade powder or sheets. The darker the glue, the more impure it is. The glue is dissolved in hot water, which on cooling will jellify.

Drying qualities Dries in air by evaporation of water content. Turns from being glue-like to sticky and finally hard. If mixed warm into a paint or as gesso, the mixture will gel on cooling.

Dissolving agent Paint bound by it can be dissolved when dry by water and alcohol, such as methylated spirits. A spray coat of a hardening agent, such as acetone, applied to the dry paint coat, will harden the protein film, rendering it more water-resistant.

Shelf life As a dry powder, limitless. As a jelly, a few days. Once wet, the glue will rot extremely quickly, producing a foul odour with loss of adhesive power. Make glue and paints bound with animal gelatine in small, weekly batches.

Failings It cannot be used where it will come into contact with water. Brittle and fairly inelastic, these properties can be part-remedied by the addition of small quantities of glycerine (for elasticity) and dextrine (for strength).

CASEIN (Binder)

Casein is perhaps the most versatile of traditional binders. Just as gelatine is a meat product that contains incomplete proteins to form a film, casein is simply the protein content of milk, derived by powdering the washed curds from skimmed milk. Its proteins, however, are more complete and thus develop a harder film, so that the paint layer is more water-resistant when dry. Casein nevertheless makes breathing paints that have a dusty crystalline surface. It is available as washed and dried curds in various grades.

Uses As a wood glue and paint binder. To bind some distemper-type house paints and Plaka brand studio colours.

Form A yellowish-white powder. It must be mixed slowly into water into which an alkaline such as ammonium carbonate or lime is very slowly added to help it dissolve.

Casein paint made from casein powder (see page 60)

Drying qualities Dries on exposure to the air by evaporation. Most casein paints are dry in several hours but then cure over a period of several weeks to form a water-resistant surface.

Dissolving agents Paint bound by it can be dissolved when dry by water, if scrubbed into the surface, alcohol such as methylated spirits and other solvents. A spray coat of a hardening agent, such as acetone, applied to the dry paint coat renders the paint more water-resistant.

Shelf life Casein powder should be bought fresh and used within a few months otherwise its adhesion will be reduced. Once mixed into a paint, add a preservative to prevent the mixture from rotting. Pine oil is ideal; about 1 percent by volume is sufficient.

Failings Casein paints may crack and peel if built into moderately thick impastos. The breathability of casein paints is not as great as that of gelatine- bound paints.

USEFUL MATERIALS FOR USE WITH TRADITIONAL BINDERS

Formaldehyde

This preservative has a hardening effect on proteins and thus cannot be easily added to wet paint mixtures. It is, however, sometimes used to spray dry casein- or gelatine-type coatings to harden and waterproof them. A 40 percent solution can be diluted 1:10 with water and sprayed or brushed on.

Glycerine or honey

Used to help plasticize traditionally brittle binders such as gum arabic and gelatine and to keep washes made with them open and workable for longer.

Acetone

Although many solvents (especially alcohol) will break down proteins and therefore destroy paint made with these binders, acetone will not and can therefore safely be used to clean the surface of the dried paint. It also has the same hardening effect as formaldehyde on dry protein layers, such as those found in casein and gelatine binders.

NOTE: On no account should phenol (carbolic acid) be introduced to the workplace as a preservative in paints. Phenol can pass through the skin, with fatal results.

Modern water-based media

Modern water-based paints are all characterized by the fact that they are bound with a synthetic polymer medium that is nearly always a petro-chemical product. The two standard types of binder are based on the two plastics, vinyl and acrylic. Each plastic offers a number of complex compounds that find uses in paints and varnishes. Vinyl compounds are simpler and cheaper to formulate and so are found in water-based house paints. Acrylic co-polymers are more complex and can be borne in both solvents and water.
Because these plastics are essentially oily in basis, when suspended in water they conform to the true definition of an emulsion.

EMULSION PAINTS

These simple vinyl polymer paints bound with PVA or EVA are cheap and widely available. They are also remarkably tough. Emulsion can be enlivened if treated like a plain distemper and coloured up with powder pigments. It can also be strengthened by adding PVA, EVA or acrylic media to turn it into a 'super-emulsion'.

Uses On interior walls and ceilings, and selectively on furniture, if strengthened. Sits happily on oil-based flat undercoats, shellac and red/grey oxide primers, thus permitting its use on surfaces previously oil painted.

Emulsion paints are tough enough for any household applications.

Forms Standard grade for home use, trade grade, which is often thinner but with higher levels of useful pigment to permit one-coat coverage. Look for expensive own brands of white emulsion from small manufacturers; they are often formulated for performance not economy, and so are almost as good as acrylics, at a fraction of the price.

Drying qualities Dries by evaporation of water content on exposure to air, usually in a few hours. Remains water soluble when immediately touch dry, drying to a fairly tough and moderately elastic film that remains water-resistant.

Dissolving agents Paint bound by it can be dissolved when dry by petro-chemical solvents and especially alcohols such as methylated spirits.

Shelf life Years, if protected from frost and air contact. If water is added to the can to thin the paint, it adulterates the distilled water content with water laden with bacteria; the paint can therefore develop mould extremely quickly.

Failings Not the toughest or most flexible of paints. Non-breathing. Factory-coloured paints have a plastic quality when dry. Not for exteriors.

PVA/EVA (Binders)

Although these are the reliable vinyl binders found in pre-mixed shop emulsion paints, they can also be purchased separately for mixing your own paints and washes from which you require an emulsion-type performance. Available in tins from 250ml (1/2 pint) to 10 litres (5 1/2 pints).

Uses As a cement and concrete plasticizer in the building industry and in wall plasters and as white woodwork glue. May be thinned and used as paint or wash binder, as a sealant or weak varnish.

PVA and EVA are available in cans and have a paint-like consistency.

Forms Multi-purpose PVA or EVA or as wood glues (more expensive in this form); always a thick, paint-like white medium. Some paint suppliers sell emulsion glaze, in reality an expensive, thinned-down PVA.

Drying qualities As per emulsion, but turns transparent on drying. Paints, and particularly washes, bound with diluted PVA/EVA will therefore appear paler in the can than when dry.

Dissolving agents Paint bound by it can be dissolved when dry by most solvents and particularly alcohols such as methylated spirits.

Shelf life See emulsion.

Failings An extremely versatile medium, but not formulated for high-performance jobs or prolonged exposure to UV light. Will turn brittle in time.

ACRYLICS (Paint, binder and varnish)

Acrylic binders have revolutionized the coatings market because toxic, organic solvents have all but been eliminated from paints that serve high-performance uses. Acrylic paints are mostly water-borne and yet are waterproof.

Acrylics are like a very sophisticated emulsion paint; indeed, it is often difficult to differentiate between the highest-quality emulsions and the lowest-grade acrylics. Always buy the best possible quality product because it will serve the chosen use very well.

Uses When correctly pigmented, for artist's use. In masonry paint, exterior woodwork paints, floor varnishes, sealants for cork, wood and stone, metal and wood primers, furniture paints. Can be incorporated into acrylic scumble glazes for decorative effects and acrylic wax where silicone waxes are also combined.

Forms Varnishes and paints. The varnishes are the strongest, most concentrated forms of acrylic binders; you may dilute or use them as a binder.

Drying qualities Remains water-soluble when touch dry (takes a few hours), drying to an extremely tough and highly elastic film that remains water- and UV-resistant. The underlying softer coating will require longer to dry (taking up to 24 hours).

Dissolving agents Paint bound by it can be dissolved when dry by petro-chemical solvents and alcohols such as methylated spirits, although this may take some considerable time to work.

Shelf life See emulsion paints.

Failings Some early formulations have proved to have little resistance to UV light and have cracked and become brittle with age. Usually contains small amounts of organic solvent such as toluene as an emulsifier.

Acrylic paints are highly versatile, performing far better than emulsion.

Oil-based media

The slowest drying of all the decorator's materials are oil based. Many vegetable oils, such as olive oil, have little or no ability to dry at all. Others such as linseed (flax), walnut and poppy oil contain glycerides of linolenic and linoleic acids, key components in aiding the oil to absorb oxygen from the atmosphere and convert to a polymer film (see emulsion and acrylic paint formulations on previous page) that is highly flexible, resistant to solvents and tough, known as linoxyn.

Oil media should not be considered as a binding agent in paints in the same way as gelatines can be. Because the quantity of oil is so great in the paint, they are vehicles for the pigment.

Natural resins or saps from trees, are another traditional oil-type vehicle. They are present in varnishes and enamels, often mixed with oil. In fact, nearly all varnish products are a resin-oil mixture, be they traditional varnishes formed from rosin and linseed or tung oil, or modern synthetic products such as alkyd varnish. Some resins and gums are mentioned elsewhere in this section (gum arabic on page 48). Those mentioned here are exclusively soluble in turpentine or oil media.

DRYERS

Many oil and oil-resin formulations require a little assistance to help them oxygenate – at least to help speed up the process. Many pigments based on metals and other metallic formulations perform this role, and they are called dryers. Common dryers are those based on cobalt or manganese, and for this reason raw and burnt umber are useful drying colours because of their manganese content.

SOME OF THE STRONGEST DRYING PIGMENTS FOR OIL MEDIA	DRYING ABILITY
Raw umber and burnt sienna	***
burnt umber (for manganese content)	****
cobalt blue and green	**
cobalt yellow	****
lead pigments such as flake white	****
phthalo green and blue	***
Prussian blue	**
raw sienna	**

LINSEED OIL (Vehicle)

Linseed oil is a traditional vehicle for both artist's oil paints and proper house paints derived from the seed of the flax plant. Enough to say that no synthetic alkyd or polyurethane coating remains as flexible and elastic as linseed oil paint.

Uses In paints and varnishes, oil-type scumble glaze, glazing putty, linoleum and (mixed with hot gelatine glue) as a binder in eighteenth-century recipes for moulding materials such as composition. As an emollient and waterproofer in gesso and distemper, and as an emollient in French polishing. The principal ingredient of traditional goldsize, used for adhering gold or metal leaf to a surface.

Cold-pressed linseed oil is mixed here with pigments to make an artist's grade oil paint.

Forms Boiled, stand, cold-pressed, raw, blown, bodied, or sun-bleached oil.

Drying qualities Dries by absorption of oxygen from the atmosphere, forming linoxyn. Generally slow, the fastest oil still taking up to 12 hours to become surface dry. The drying rate is affected by the quality of oil, the amount of pre-oxygenation taken place (either in the can or at the factory), and the addition of catalytic driers, such as cobalt or manganese, which aid oxygenation.

Dissolving agents Paint bound by it can be dissolved when dry by alcohol, toluene and other rarer solvents if applied after drying. However, linoxyn becomes a remarkably durable and resistant coating which will repel most conventional solvents when fully cured (this process may take several decades).

Shelf life Dependent on type of oil used. If in airtight bottles, will improve with time.

Failings Long drying times. Tendency to yellow in darkness (reversible on exposure to light) and on absorption of dampness during drying. If thickly formed, linoxyn can crust.

ALKYD RESIN (Binder and varnish)

Designed to supplant traditional oils in the early years of the twentieth century, alkyds are a highly complex arrangement of alcohols and acids (hence al-cid) produced in chemical plants. When combined at a molecular level with the active constituents of a vegetable drying oil, alkyd resin is known as oil-modified alkyd resin, and as such, produced in vast quantities. It forms the binding vehicle for nearly every type of oil-based household gloss, enamel and eggshell paint. Alkyd varnishes, specially formulated for this job, are considered to be superior to polyurethanes as varnishes since they do not yellow so readily.

Uses Household oil-based eggshell and gloss paints. Enamel paints. Alkyd-type varnishes.

Forms Varnish and paints.

Drying qualities Dries by evaporation of the solvent content (usually white spirit) and then by oxidation as linseed oil. Drying times, however, are considerably faster, the coating reaching touch-dry conditions in less than six hours.

Dissolving agents Paint bound by it can be dissolved when dry by some of the rarer solvents, particularly coal-tar solvents such as toluene, xylene and benzene.

Shelf life Limited in paint and varnish forms. Will not improve with storage.

Failings A less elastic coating than linseed oil. Tendency to become brittle under exposure to UV light, and to crack and splinter off after several years' use in exterior conditions, where linseed-oil type paints would retain their elasticity and wear thin.

Alkyd resin is the binding vehicle for today's oil-based paints.

POLYURETHANES (Varnishes)

Whereas alkyd resins have found best use in paint formulation, polyurethanes have proved themselves as varnish resins. Early polyurethane varnishes were liable to crack, peel and blister under prolonged exposure to UV light, but latterly their formulation has improved, and the highest grades (generally those produced by the smaller manufacturers) rank on a par with alkyd resin varnishes. Steer away from two-pack polyurethane paints or varnishes that require the addition of a catalyst, since these can often be highly toxic.

Polyurethane varnish is best bought in small quantities as once the can is opened, the varnish will thicken.

Uses As a final varnish coat for paintwork and stained wood. As a bar and table top lacquer – it will cut back and polish very well.

Forms Varnish and lacquer.

Drying qualities Dries on contact with air by absorbing oxygen. Most available single-pack brands are specially formulated at the factory to enable them to dry within a few hours. This process affects the shelf life of the product.

Dissolving agents
Paint bound by it can be dissolved when dry by the rarer solvents, notably toluene. Ensure that any beeswax coating applied on top of a polyurethane lacquer finish is marked as being 'toluene free'.

Shelf life Months rather than years. It will thicken and deteriorate in the can once exposed to the air.

Failings As with most oil-type varnishes, it will penetrate wood easily and darken the grain. A sanding sealer should therefore be used beneath. Yellows rather badly, but newer formulations are better. Brittles with age. Scratches.

Shellac media

Of all the media mentioned in this section, shellac deserves its own corner because it is the only coating which uniquely dissolves in alcohol. Because alcohol evaporates so quickly, and is of relatively low toxicity, shellac has found a wide variety of uses in the decorator's armoury, including using refined grades for pale lacquers and for sanding sealers. Dense grades are used as knotting. Shellac is also an excellent quick-drying isolator for covering damp and mildew stains on painted surfaces, prior to redecorating. Arguably many of these uses could be fulfilled by oil-based varnishes were they not so slow drying.

SHELLAC (Varnish and binder)

Shellac is the refined version of a sticky substance that exudes from insects that swarm on trees in India, and is available in several grades and colours ranging from treacly brown to almost water-clear. For decorators, it is a highly versatile and essential medium.

Uses In French and other furniture polishing. In hand lacquering as a metal varnish, and a bright protective and colouring coat over metal leafing.

Forms Usually as flakes, but most prefer to purchase it in liquid form after it has been dissolved in alcohol by manufacturers. For most decorative purposes the standard orange shellac suffices and should be bought at the strongest liquid concentration. Several shellac products are pre-diluted to a required strength, something you can easily do yourself with methylated spirits.

Drying qualities Dries in a few minutes but requires several hours to harden fully. Shellac contains a certain quantity of natural waxes which render it cloudy in solution, but it dries transparent. Should be used in small quantities and regularly re-diluted with methylated spirits to maintain a workable consistency.

Dissolving agents Paint bound by it can be dissolved when dry by any alcohol, or methylated spirits will serve.

Shelf life Shellac flakes or sticks can perish if stored in a dry place, so buy fresh when needed. Within a few months, liquid shellac can lose its drying properties, so buy when needed and then store in glass or clear plastic bottles to prevent it from darkening.

When applying shellac for French polishing, use a rubber (see page 134).

Failings Orange shellac imparts a yellow tint to surfaces. Once applied, cannot be brought into contact with alcohol, damp or water, whereupon it will cloud and deteriorate.

OTHER TREE-GUM VARNISHES

There are several traditional, sometimes ancient, tree gums which have found reliable use as varnishes. Available as crystals or lumps (which often require crushing) from specialist suppliers and art shops, you may like to experiment with them. Ralph Mayer's *The Artist's Handbook of Materials and Techniques* offers recipes and formulations. The list below is not exhaustive.

Dragon's blood
Used as a red colorant and lacquer from ancient times. It is soluble in most solvents.

Elemi
An unreliable gum used for toughening other films, elemi is soluble in alcohol.

Gamboge
Excellent for use as yellow glazing pigment. Colour fades in bright sunlight. It is soluble in alcohol.

Mastic
Ancient varnish of a yellowish colour, soluble in both alcohol and turpentine. Glassy finish but can darken with age, but less so than oil-type varnishes such as copal.

Sandaric
Ancient in use, hard, highly brittle and yellowish. Soluble in alcohol and the more rare solvents. Often used in other oil-type preparations as a hardening agent. Inferior to mastic and dammar.

Xanthan gum or Botany Bay gum
Australian gum similar to shellac in behaviour.

Waxes

Although I have already mentioned acrylic wax under water-borne media, the product in question is an emulsion of silicone wax in an acrylic medium and so an entirely modern and synthetic product. To most people, wax suggests one product only, the best there is, beeswax polish. This is the product preferred by craftsmen painters and furniture restorers; it is the only wax we keep in the studio and the only one used in this book. However, in practice, most beeswax polishes contain other waxes to harden them; some cheaper polishes are adulterated and thinned out with paraffin wax.

Beeswax is made from hard beehive honeycomb gently heated to melting point, dissolved in solvent and allowed to cool to a paste. For good hard shines, the mixture is usually strengthened by small quantities of carnauba wax. For a perfectly blended solution, the best solvent is toluene. However, its powerful solvent action on varnish and paint layers means that waxes formulated with it should be avoided. Turpentine- or white spirit-based waxes are much better, although, strangely, wax is perhaps the only substance which behaves better when dissolved in white spirit rather than the more expensive turpentine; the latter causes the wax to swell into a crude granular mass.

BEESWAX POLISH

A ready-made preparation.

Uses Polishing furniture and painted surfaces. As a vehicle for patinating and antiquing powders for bronze and furniture. As a sealant for porous surfaces such as wood, stone and terracotta. As an antiquing solution when mixed with pigments/turpentine/artist's oil colours.

Forms Solid beeswax blocks, grains (both beeswax and carnauba are sold in this form), liquid preparations and paste in tins. Coloured antiquing waxes contain pigments, liming wax contains titanium white pigment. All can be introduced at home.

Drying qualities Does not dry or chemically alter by, for example, reacting with the air and polymerizing. The paste polish simply hardens by allowing the solvent content to evaporate. The wax returns to its natural condition; hence the need for the addition of hardening waxes such as carnauba.

Dissolving agents Paint bound by it can be dissolved when dry by the same solvents used to dilute it. Alcohol is also fairly effective at removing it.

Shelf life Indefinite.

Failings Absolutely nothing can be applied over a dried coat of wax other than another coat of wax; anything else will fail and rub or peel away (this reaction can be used to advantage – see Peeled and chipped technique on pages 170-3). If a previously waxed surface is to be re-painted, all traces of the wax must first be removed by scrubbing the surface down with white spirit and then with detergent and hot water. The surface should then be thoroughly re-keyed with sandpaper or wire wool. Commercial brands of de-waxing solution are available from specialist paint suppliers.

Beeswax polish is best applied using a small pad of very fine wire wool (see page 138).

Common solvents

Solvents are essential to the painter; they thin paint and varnish but also form part of the decorative process on occasion. The chemistry and functions of solvents are extremely complicated, so I have listed only those solvents with which you are likely to come into contact in your work.

Mercifully, as paint technology advances and the paint market changes direction in favour of more and more water-based products, our contact with solvents is becoming less frequent. As much as I have always tried to eliminate solvents from our work in the studio, we still use a few; those, in fact, that crop up in this book and are featured to the right, plus of course, water. In addition, you will also find opposite a list of the sources of many of the common solvents found in household products, and a list of their flash points, ie the temperature at which their vapours will ignite in air when exposed to a naked flame – useful to know!

TOXICITY

The toxicity of solvents varies enormously, but most are poisonous if swallowed, some with almost immediately fatal results. Moreover, some can be absorbed through the skin; toluene, xylene and benzene are three such, a sinister fact since they are all known or suspected carcinogens.

On inhalation, nearly every solvent can cause drowsiness, intoxication, irritation of the airways and eyes and, on high exposure, brain damage, narcosis and even death. It therefore pays dividends to study the contents of this page and to observe rigorous safety and hygiene procedures even when handling the more common solvents.

METHYLATED SPIRITS

Wood alcohol, distilled in large quantities for the decorating, chemical and pharmaceutical industries. Rendered undrinkable by the addition of colorants and petroleum agents. Pharmaceutical grades may contain up to 25 percent water and are therefore unsuitable for use as thinners.

Uses As thinner for shellac and shellac-based products. Useful for destroying and removing vinyl and acrylic-based water-borne paints.

Toxicity
By ingestion: high
By inhalation: medium
By skin contact: medium
Repeated and single incident exposure carry long-term effects, causing liver and kidney damage, narcosis, and damage to brain tissues and eyes. Ingestion causes blindness and death.

OIL OF TURPENTINE

A clear liquid distilled from particular pine resins, much favoured by artists; has a distinctive pine odour. Also known as gum-turpentine. A cheaper, more noxious-smelling turpentine is made by steam-extracting cruder resins from wood. Venice turpentine was considered for many centuries to be the finest, and artists have also historically employed oil of spike lavender, a sweet-smelling alternative.

Oil of turpentine is the best solvent to use for thinning oil paints.

Uses In artist's oil paints and as a superior paint thinner where odour is a consideration, such as on site and at home.

Toxicity
By ingestion: high
By inhalation: medium
By skin contact: medium
Irritating vapours with potential of skin allergies (more likely with cruder grades). Accidental swallowing can cause heart attack in the victim; often because they are forced to vomit, introducing the solvent into the lungs and thence the heart via the blood stream. In the case of children, a half eggcupful is sufficient to kill them if swallowed.

WHITE SPIRITS

A petroleum distillate, synthesized to replace turpentine, and indeed is also known as turpentine substitute.

Uses Throughout the paint industry, as a thinner and for cleaning up.

Toxicity
By ingestion: high
By inhalation: medium
By skin contact: medium
As per oil of turpentine.

TOLUENE

An aromatic hydrocarbon produced as a coal-tar distillation.

Uses As a solvent for some paints and thinners, often in association with xylene, when it may be called mixed isomers. As a thinner for waxes. As an emulsifier in water-borne plastic paints such as acrylics and emulsions.

Toxicity
By ingestion: high
By inhalation: high
By skin contact: medium
Can be absorbed through the skin to cause de-fatting. Once in the blood stream may cause organ damage. By inhalation will cause intoxication and eventually death. A popular solvent for glue sniffers.

XYLENE

As for toluene, above. There is some debate as to which of the two solvents is safer. Xylene has a higher flash point, but in its most refined form, toluene is purer. In the light of this poor knowledge, I recommend you use both of them as little as possible, and always with skin protection, goggles and a rubber face mask fitted with a solvent-type respiratory cartridge.

BENZENE

A note should be made about benzene, the sister distillate of toluene and xylene. It is a vicious poison and carcinogen. At no time should it or products containing it be used.

ACETONE

A note should also be made about acetone, for the opposite reason; it has a very low level of toxicity. Although it evaporates far too quickly for paint-thinning purposes, acetone is a good cleaning solvent.

SOLVENT FLASH POINTS

Most solvents listed here are formed by distillation: heating some form of crude liquid, for example crude petroleum oil or coal-tar. Solvents are listed in columns according to their source and are listed by decreasing level of toxicity, ie the most toxic solvent given is always at the top of the list. Solvents marked * should never be used.

DISTILLED ALCOHOLS	FLASH POINT
*Isoamyl/amyl alcohol**	*-46°C*
Methyl alcohol	*-16°C*
Butyl alcohol	*29°C*
Isopropyl alcohol	*16°C*
Ethyl alcohol	*16°C*
Benzyl alcohol	*100°C*

COAL-TAR DISTILLATIONS/ AROMATIC HYDROCARBONS

*Benzene**	*-15°C*
Toluene	*7°C*
Xylene	*24°C*

Coal-tar distillation also produces solvent naphthalene, a crude and impure solvent used to dilute asphalt and as a source for aniline dyes.

PETROLEUM DISTILLATES

Produced by heating crude petroleum oil. On reaching different temperatures, the various solvents are given off.

*Petroleum ether**	*-57°C*
Petrol (gasoline)	*-46°C*
Rubber solvent	*-46°C*
*VM&P naphtha (benzine)**	*-7°C*
Mineral spirits (white spirit)	*30°C*
Kerosene (domestic fuel oil)	*38°C*

Note to table: Usually, the lower the flash point of a solvent, the higher the toxicity.

If you don't recognize a solvent, don't use it until you know about it. Do not confuse Naphtha with Naphthalene, or Benzine with Benzene. Several publications contain essential information about the toxicity of materials; they are listed in the Bibliography.

Blending pigments and paints

MIXING PIGMENTS INTO A BINDER OR SOLVENT

To mix small quantities of pigments into a binder such as gum arabic or linseed oil, pour a little liquid binder onto a pile of pigment and combine the two with a knife. Do this preferably on a sheet of marble or thick glass. The mixture should then be ground under a muller to break down and refine the pigment particle size and thoroughly blend it.

On a larger scale, mix pigment and binder, say in equal quantities, in the bottom of a paint can with a brush or pestle. Take care to thoroughly combine them and remove lumps.

Because solvents are generally thinner than paint media, pigments will admix in them more easily. Wet the pigment with no more solvent than necessary and combine as above, adding more solvent than necessary. Once combined, you can store the mixture in an absolutely airtight jar, covering the mixture with a thin layer of additional solvent. This is a useful way of carrying pigments around from job to job. If dissolving in water, use distilled water and sterilize the storage jars beforehand in a moderately hot oven for 5 minutes.

ADDING PIGMENT TO PAINT

One method is to slowly add a minute quantity of paint to the pigment in a clean paint can, together with a little solvent. Once mixed, the rest of the paint can slowly be added, while stirring the mixture, as though you were making a roux sauce.

A better method is to blend pigment and solvent as above and then dilute it with further solvent until it is thinner than the paint to which you will add it. It can then be poured into the paint and whisked in. An essential tool for this is a plaster-mixing whisk attachment for a drill – but with the drill speed set very low! Be warned; if the pigment/solvent mix is thicker or as thick as the paint, you will achieve neither a satisfactory nor an even mix.

Synthetic colorants, or universal stainers, are convenient and available as concentrated liquid colours that are microfine pigments or dyes bound in castor oil. They should be added to paint and then thoroughly blended with the drill + whisk attachment.

Castor oil will mix readily with most paint types, but since it is a non-drying oil, the addition of too much will prevent the surface of the paint

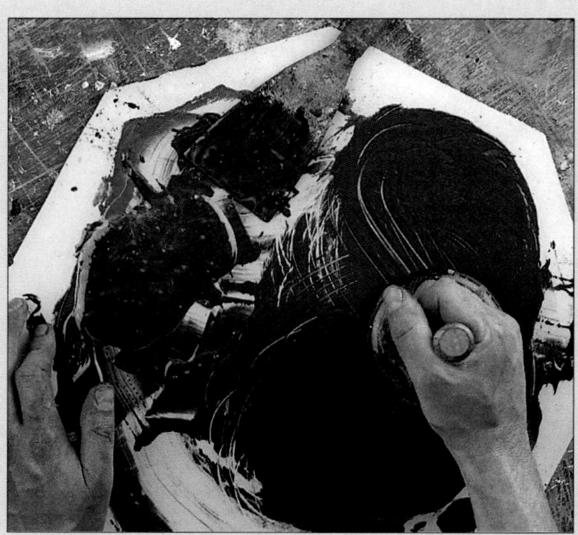

from drying altogether. For stronger colouring, use pigments ground or mixed in solvent.

THE IMPORTANCE OF GRINDING

Although many pigments can be adequately blended with paints, media or solvents simply by stirring with a brush, they ought really to be ground in whenever possible. When ground, the pigment particles are broken down to a very fine size. This has the double effect of ensuring a very intimate blend with the binder and of making the pigment go much further – when ground, a pigment has a much stronger colouring effect.

However, hand grinding is a laborious process and should be reserved for those paints that are for fine decorative use. You may, though, be lucky enough to lay your hands on a table-top paint mill for making your own house paints ...

BLENDING PIGMENTS AND PAINTS

Do not ever mix pigments as powders. The resultant colour may be nowhere near the colour of the eventual dried paint. This is because different pigments may each be of an entirely different particle size, with the result that one colour may eventually dominate. Moreover, some pigments are stronger and have more staining power, such as Prussian blue, which if mixed with a weak colour such as terra verde would entirely obliterate it.

Always mix pigments into a binder or solvent separately to make up individually coloured paints, and then mix these together judiciously.

When mixing different coloured house paints, start by mixing minute quantities measured in teaspoons, for example, to ensure that you know the precise ratio of paints to achieve your desired colour. The larger quantities can then be mixed in exactly the same ratios in a large bucket, without mistakes being made and the entire mix being wasted. The drill + whisk attachment is again very useful.

Once blended, any mixture of paints, pigments and solvents will benefit from straining to remove bits of dried paint, skin and lumps of pigment and impurities. An old pair of tights stretched over a paint can will serve admirably.

LIVERING AND FLUFFING

Some pigments will not mix with water. Lamp black, for example, contains a certain amount of grease, which prevents the pigment from mixing – it just floats on the top. Start by mixing the pigment with a little methylated spirits and then add the water. Alternatively, a tiny dot of washing-up detergent will break the surface tension of the water and allow mixing. The latter solution is hopeless, however, for making thin colour washes because the thinned paint will simply foam and bubble once brushed out.

DILUTING PAINTS AND PIGMENT/BINDER MIXES

Dilution should always be a slow process and the paint should be stirred continuously throughout. Once diluted, many paints then quickly settle out; the heavier masses of binder and pigment settling towards the bottom of the container. So stir continuously during use.

CHANGING COLOURS

Every pigment, solvent and medium has its own refractive index that determines how opaque or transparent it is in any of its states, wet or dry. For example, the traces of wax in shellac render it translucent when wet but brilliantly clear when dry. PVA is a white thick fluid but dries transparent, which means that emulsion paints do the same thing, and dry a little darker as the PVA binder loses its whiteness. Chalk in water becomes translucent, returning to an intensely opaque layer as a dry paint. Because of this, distempers and casein paints that are tinted will appear darker in the can than on the wall when dry. Calcium hydroxide, quick lime as it is before application to the wall, appears transparent as it is brushed on. On drying, it turns brilliant white. These processes can be précised as shown in the box below.

emulsions	*dry darker*
acrylics	*dry very slightly darker*
caseins, gouache, distempers	*dry paler and more opaque*
limewash	*dries much paler and opaque*
oil paints	*dry to the same colour and opacity*

Recipes

Here are a number of useful recipes. Further recipes are given in their appropriate techniques and these are:

Antiquing solution – page 180, 182
Distemper – page 76
Gesso – pages 90-5
Gold paint – page 236
Limewash – pages 96-7
Liming wax – page 118
Oil paint – page 86
Oil paint, artist's grade – page 88
Vandyke crystal solution – page 232

Basic binder recipes

LIQUID GUM ARABIC

YOU WILL NEED
Gum arabic crystals
Boiling water

Gum arabic crystals are available from artist's suppliers and specialist paint manufacturers in a variety of grades, the most impure being of a very dark colour. You may wish to sort a cheap mixed batch by discarding the darkest crystals.

In a container, pour the boiling water over the crystals (just sufficient to cover them) and leave. Any undissolved crystals will eventually dissolve if the mixture is reheated and stirred. Allow to cool and bottle.

If not preserved by the addition of 1-2 percent household disinfectant, this solution will deteriorate and mould.

SHELLAC VARNISH FROM FLAKES

YOU WILL NEED
1 part flake shellac
5 parts methylated spirits

Combine the shellac and methylated spirits in a container and seal with a lid. Leave for several days, whereupon the shellac will have completely dissolved. For a pale varnish, bleached shellac flakes may be bought, but these will dissolve less completely.

CASEIN BINDER

YOU WILL NEED
2 parts casein powder
1 part ammonium carbonate
16 parts water

Sift the casein powder and ammonium carbonate into half the water. Leave to stand for half a day and then add the remaining water.

This medium will serve extremely well as a size, prior to painting walls or furniture with casein paint, and as a vehicle for pigments, which can be ground into it to make casein paint. Thinned washes can then be made by adding water. It will also serve as a type of gesso when mixed 1:6 with whiting.

Casein powder should be bought fresh as its adhesive powers deteriorate within months. Do not be tempted to make your own from milk, since it requires great skill; all lactose and fat must be removed, leaving behind pure casein, the milk protein.

STANDARD GELATINE

YOU WILL NEED
1 leaf of gelatine
100ml (4 fl oz) water

Soak the gelatine in the water until it has swollen and jellified. Then heat the mixture in a double boiler and use warm. This is an alternative to the rabbitskin recipe on page 91 and may be similarly used as a paint binder, for thin paints, and as a size.

Gelatine in leaf form is extremely fine and pure and may be bought in packets.

STANDARD GLUE

YOU WILL NEED
1 part hide glue (or scotch, bone or pearl glue) in granule form
10 parts water

Soak the glue in the water overnight until it jellifies at the bottom of the container. Pour off the excess water and then heat the glue in a double boiler by suspending one metal bucket inside another with a spacer between, such as a block of wood. Fill the outer bucket with water, and pour the glue mixture into the inner bucket. Use warm.

OIL-BOUND DISTEMPER BINDER

YOU WILL NEED
20 parts gelatine/glue mixture (as above)
2-5 parts thick oil (sun-bleached linseed or stand oil)
1 part ammonium carbonate

Take any gelatine/glue mixture, such as the two above, or that on page 78, heat in a double boiler until at maximum heat (the water is bubbling) and then add the oil drop by drop, while stirring. The oil must be thick. Every ten drops, add one drop of ammonium carbonate to assist in the blending.

Use the eventual blend warm as a binder for distemper paints. Walls for such paints should be sized with a thinned glue or gelatine that does not contain oil.

This mixture will be a true emulsion, since the oil particles will be minutely suspended in the gelatine solution. This process helps the eventual paint film to be flexible and water-resistant. As such, this formula forms the basis of many so-called 'oil-bound' wipeable distemper paints.

Other recipes

STARCH GLAZE

YOU WILL NEED
1 handful washing starch
250ml (1/2 pint) cold water
500ml (1 pint) boiling water

Soak the starch in the cold water and stir until it is all dissolved. Add the boiling water until a jelly is formed. For use, the mixture may then be diluted to a thin liquid with cold water.

This mixture is invaluable as a size for plaster walls and as a protective coating on bare, unvarnished wood, paintwork and wallpapers, provided they are water-resistant. Once dirty, the starch solution can be washed off and recoated. Unlike gum, gelatine and glue solutions, this solution also has the advantage of being colourless. If lightly pigmented, it will also serve as a reversible antiquing solution.

TRANSPARENT OIL GLAZE

YOU WILL NEED
10 parts turpentine substitute
1 part whiting
6 parts boiled linseed oil

Blend together the turpentine and whiting and then add the oil, either in a food mixer (preferably a redundant one) or with a balloon whisk. Store in an airtight jar.

This mixture will dry in about 12-16 hours. For a faster drying time, add a small quantity of a terbene patent dryer. Follow the manufacturer's instructions for quantities.

HARD BEESWAX POLISH

YOU WILL NEED
1 part carnauba wax
2 parts beeswax
15 parts turpentine substitute

Gently heat all the ingredients in a double boiler until melted and blended. Allow to cool and store in an airtight jar or tin. Some recipes call for 1 part Carnauba to 5 or 10 parts beeswax, others for 2 parts Carnauba to 1 part beeswax.

Carnauba is a very hard wax ideal for fine polishing on furniture. However, it is brittle, and so needs the beeswax to impart flexibility. Its high price is probably the reason why many recipes call for the inclusion of small quantities!

RETARDING THE SETTING TIME OF A MIXTURE

A water-borne paint or wash mixture may be given a longer drying time by adding a maximum of 10 percent of glycerine or honey.

The setting time of plasters, including plaster of Paris, will be retarded by adding 15 percent glue (gelatine glue or PVA), liquid gum arabic or dextrine to the mix. Alternatively, add 5 percent by weight of powdered marshmallow root to the wet plaster. Each of these additives will improve the plaster's workability, allowing it to be used as a filler and improving the hardness when set.

Preparation and finishing

The preparation of surfaces and finishing are the two most important skills in painting. The craftsman decorator will always, but always, place more emphasis on the quality of preparation and finishing than, it seems, on the execution of the seen paint layer.

Under the old apprenticeships, young trainees would spend several years of their total of seven being inculcated in the mysteries of these essential aspects to the painter's work. The reason for this is that good preparation and finishing will serve an important function. A properly prepared surface will not subsequently fail for lack of proper de-greasing, rubbing down and priming; it will instead form a solid and reliable base for any subsequent paint layers. Most surfaces to be painted are slightly dirty and greasy from handmarks, soot and dust. Wooden surfaces are also liable to movement and to resin and moisture seeping out from the grain. Plaster may be actively alkaline and liable to salting on the surface, and old painted walls may require washing down to remove traces of old distemper.

The finish coat will also help to keep a painted or varnished surface clean; if a topcoat is wrinkled, sagging or a mass of nibs (the rough gritty bits formed by dirt and dust settling in or on the paint layer), it will catch the dirt and perforate more quickly.

PREPARING SURFACES TO AN IMMACULATE LEVEL

* There are paint finishes that specifically call for textured grounds, but most will perform best on a perfectly smooth ground. The first step must be to stabilize the substrate: remove and sand away any loose material and fill any holes with the necessary stopper; cellulose fillers are quick-drying and excellent for woodwork; plaster requires a water-based filler; metal is usually best filled with a two-part polyester (fibreglass) filler – the type used for car body repairs.

Cutting back a surface.

* Abrade fillers and the surface down to a fine smoothness. Start with 120 grit paper, perhaps proceeding to a 220 grit, or thereabouts for really fine work.
* In a paint studio or in a house, it is often much more preferable to rub down old paintwork and walls with wet and dry paper, using water in the process to keep the dust down. The use of water and wet and dry paper will prevent any (potentially lethal) dust from being raised off the surface. In any case, keep the rubbing down of old paintwork to a minimum; it conserves old paint colours and is often a waste of time. The function of rubbing down paintwork is to remove dirt and grease and provide a key for the next layer.
* Sugar soap can effectively be used to both clean old paintwork and to provide it with a key, by slightly cutting the surface.
* Before an undercoat is to be applied, most surfaces require some form of isolating layer, or primer. In the case of wood, plaster or metal, modern high-performance acrylic primers are now very adequate, although they may need to be thickly applied. Woods will benefit from an application of thinned shellac (mixed 50:50 with methylated spirits) as an isolator, which will penetrate the grain well.
* Oil-based traditional primers have in the main given way to water-borne acrylic primers – which also serve as undercoats.
* Plaster walls will require an isolating coat of either thinned glue, size made either from animal gelatine (warmed and diluted to a consistency so that on cooling it will only just set to a weak jelly), or with PVA binder, thinned 1:5 with water. The latter is not suitable for old walls that need to breathe. If casein paint is to be applied to walls or to furniture, it is best to prime the surface with a very dilute form of the paint which will penetrate the surface.

* Layers of paint should generally be worked from 'lean to fat', ie undercoats should have less binder in them than the topcoats. This prevents subsequent cracking and shrinking of the surface.
* Floors are best primed with acrylic paints that will flex with movement. If an all-over pattern is needed on floorboards, consider following the eighteenth-century habit of gluing down a linen cloth onto the boards prior to painting, something best done with a strong gelatine-type glue such as scotch, pearl or hide glue that is a reversible process with plenty of hot water. The linen bridges the gaps in the boards and offers a stabilized and even substrate for the paint, which will, in turn, cling better to the linen than to the boards. Again, paint and varnish with acrylic paint.

PUTTING MAGIC INTO YOUR FINISHING COATS

* Most decorative effects, especially those on table tops, doors and frequently handled objects, will require some form of protective coating. Water-borne acrylic varnishes are passably acceptable. Several thinned layers should be applied to avoid coarse brush marks, always with the softest brush, preferably one that is wide and flat such as a 50mm (2in)-wide synthetic sable brush. Once completely dry (allow 24 hours), the final surface may be rubbed back using a synthetic kitchen scourer pad that has been wetted either with water or water with a little methylated spirits added. The surface may subsequently be coated with a water-borne acrylic/silicone wax, or waxed and polished with beeswax polish.
* For the finest possible and most durable finish on a table top, consider using a minimum of three coats of alkyd or polyurethane varnish. Each coat should be rubbed down in the following way before the next application to avoid dust contaminating the subsequent varnish layer:
1 Apply varnish thinly; brush out swiftly from a well-loaded brush (some prefer to apply it with a hog varnish brush, and then use a wide flat brush to brush the varnish out).
2 Then, 24 hours later, preferably in the morning, rub down with 220 grit wet and dry paper with water.
3 Wash down the surface with clean water, dry thoroughly and leave all day to dry out.
4 In the evening, re-varnish, making sure there are no draughts to catch dust. Movable objects should be varnished *in situ* under some kind of protective plastic canopy rigged over the object to prevent dust settling on it overnight.

Waxing a surface for the perfect finish.

5 Repeat from step 2 until several varnish layers have been applied, and rubbed back to a perfectly flat smoothness.
6 A cut with 440 grit paper is optional, followed by the application of beeswax polish to the surface. Use 0000 grade wire wool to 'push' the polish into the surface. Use sparingly to avoid smearing, and allow to dry thoroughly before polishing hard with a soft dusting cloth and plenty of elbow grease!
* Never vacuum before varnishing; a vacuum cleaner will lift fine dust particles into the air.
* Many jobs simply require a coat of wax polish to finish them off; it is surprising how flexible and tough one coat of emulsion or acrylic paint can be on, say, an old piece of junk furniture, especially if subsequently wax polished with beeswax polish.
* Some elegantly finished objects are better suited to some kind of French polish finish, ie a shellac coating applied several times over with a cloth or cotton wad known as a rubber. This process is gone into at length on page 133. It is normal to finish the process with a coat of beeswax polish.
* Remember that nothing, but nothing, will adhere to a dried coat of beeswax or silicone polish. They must be thoroughly removed before any further work can be done to the surface. For this reason I do not recommend you wax plaster walls; they are better given a similar sheen by varnishing either with a semi-gloss oil-type varnish or with two coats of PVA thinned 1:3 with water.
* Floors can be finished with either the highly toxic two-pack acid-catalyst varnishes, which are extremely hard, or with modern, water-borne acrylic floor coatings. Brands vary in strength but most are surprisingly strong.

1 Traditional paints & techniques

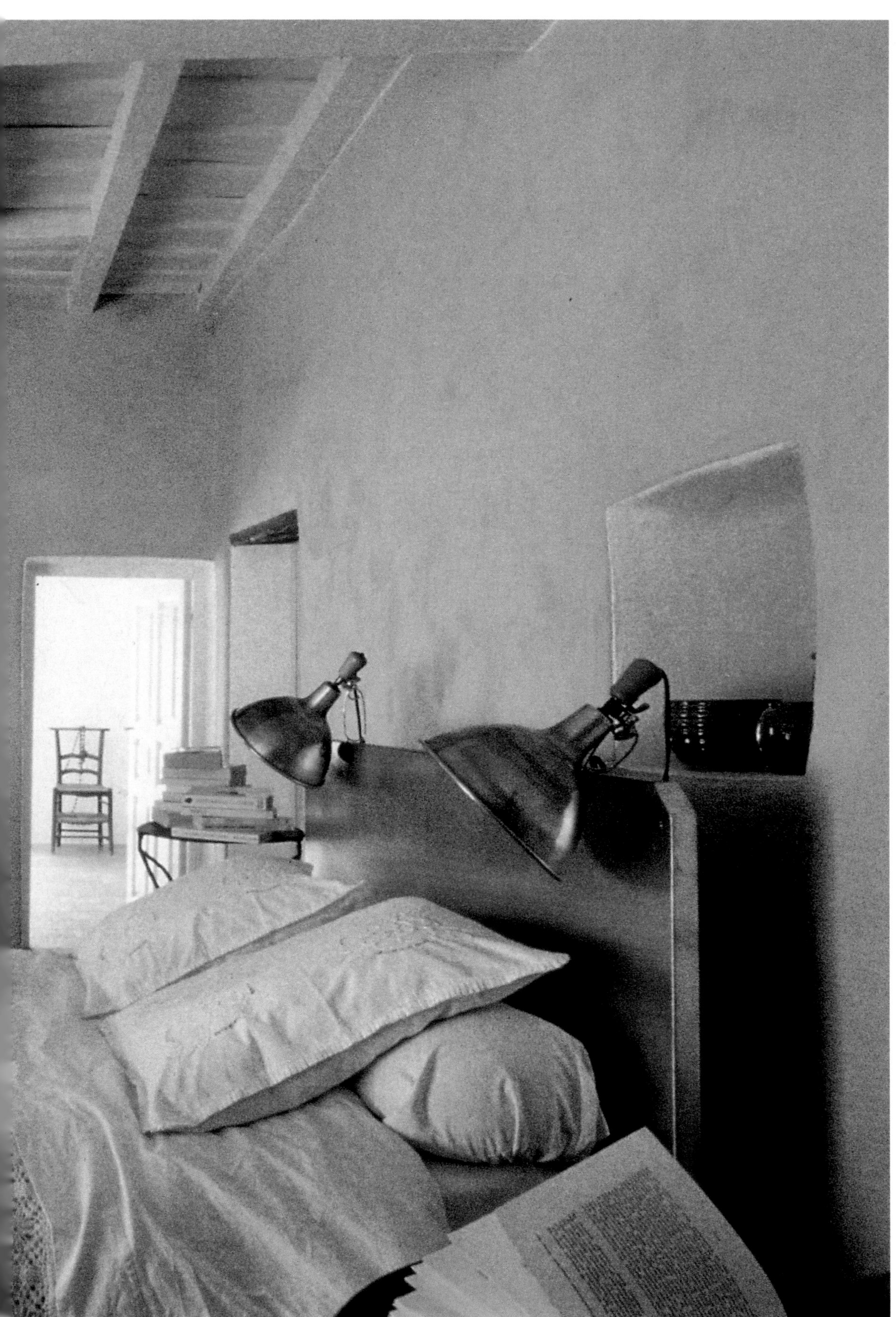

Traditional paints & techniques

This chapter may at first appear to be a motley collection of bona fide techniques and plain simple recipes for paint that produce no wild decorative effects at all. However, the latter each have a particular and rather craftsmanlike recipe for their formulation and they require a certain knack in application. I have kept them company with a selection of 'faking' techniques such as colourwashing (in the modern, emulsion-wash sense of the word) and veiling, both of which simply emulate the effects obtainable with traditional paints while employing modern materials that are tougher and more readily available. The reason for including these is that few of us are absolutely historically purist. We all need to know what the cheating methods are – even conservators and restorers have to rely on them occasionally.

But why choose a traditional paint as opposed to a high-performing modern product? There are three strong arguments.

First, on page 12, I touched on the historical value of traditional paints as coatings that are sympathetic to the fabric of old buildings because they breathe, allowing the damp in walls to transpire and then evaporate into the atmosphere. They can do this because these paints are composed of very similar materials to the walls themselves. In traditional buildings, the fabric of the structure may be timber, wattle and daub, brick, stone, even chalk blocks or mud and straw. They are often the readily available materials to hand, present in the landscape where the buildings were thrown up, and so create a strong intimacy between the buildings and their settings. Many old buildings sit very well in their immediate environment, appearing to have grown out of the ground on which they stand rather than having been plonked down upon it.

In many buildings, lime is the time-honoured material used to bind its structure together. It is the glue of many buildings, producing mortar when mixed with sand and aggregate, plaster when mixed with silver sand and chopped hair, and limewash when diluted. To give an old building a coat of limewash is to feed the building with more of what it is. It maintains the building's integrity, and seen in this way limewash can hardly be considered a coating of something alien to the building, rather it is a refined, finished version of what lies underneath. So there is a neat, intimate relationship between the paint and the building, just as there is between building and landscape.
In the same way, distemper offers a direct link to the rocks, earth and trees from which our buildings spring. It is not a modern plastic product but composed of chalk, simple glues from animal bones or cheese, and (usually) mineral pigments, also derived from the earth. It too is highly appropriate for old buildings, and whereas limewash has tended to be found on exteriors (there are exceptions, particularly in lowly dwellings), distemper is an interior finish. Both are considered in detail on the following pages, and both, justifiably, continue to be used as protective and breathable coatings. In the true sense of the word, they conserve the character and structure of old buildings by allowing them to breathe, move and sit happily in their historical and regional contexts. In

This effect of grey clouding can be produced in synthetic paint such as emulsion or acrylic, but may be best controlled by sponging/wiping on a paint of pigment bound with gum arabic – a soft, gouache-type paint that will repeatedly move under a damp cloth or sponge.

Emulsions and acrylic paints serve the technique of colourwashing very well. But when thinned, brushed on and allowed to half-dry, they may leave insoluble marks when re-worked. Rather than put up with it, the decorator has here used this to his advantage, applying the paint in a spiralling pattern to produce giant whirling blemishes in the paint layer. The finished effect, and colour, are redolent of polished plaster.

this role they are unique and of immense value to conservators and house owners alike.

TRADITIONAL PAINTS AS GREEN PRODUCTS

The second justification for such paints is that they are green products. Modern synthetic coatings, even water-borne emulsions and acrylics, are products derived from the plastics industry. They are made from petroleum, and even the most innocuous contain some small quantity of petroleum distillate such as toluene to assist as an emulsifier. These paints are not as safe as you think. Moreover, such products are manufactured in centralized facilities and then carried on often long journeys to their destinations; a great waste of resources given that the bulk of what is transported is water. On the other hand, as the paint technologist Peter Hood has pointed out, many traditional paints are simple enough to be produced by the decorator on site, employing materials that can be transported in dry powder form or even sourced locally (limewash for example). Transportation costs are low, the product price can therefore be kept low, and few resources are wasted.

TRADITIONAL PAINTS AND AESTHETICS

The third reason for considering the use of traditional paints, one that is perhaps even more compelling than their architectural or environmental value, is their aesthetic appearance. These paints simply look far better; and this fact applies to limewash, distemper, oil paint and gesso. All their surfaces seem to glitter or glow in a particular way, and when coloured pigments are added to them, subtle effects of movement and of differing intensity are produced. Above all, these paints seem to have a life of their own. The power that they can exercise over the decorative scheme of a room should not be underestimated.

This is not romantic tosh. In fact, the precise behaviour of the surfaces of these coatings is discussed on

Traditional linseed oil paint will not flake and fall away in the grubby fashion of modern synthetic gloss and eggshell. Instead, it wears back to reveal the grain of the underlying timber in a quite charming and delicate way. Limewash and distemper wear thin in a similar process that assists in blending these paint layers with the surface on which they sit. A reasonable imitation can be produced by part painting/part colourwashing wood.

pages 250-6. Essentially, their uniqueness stems from their coarse, simple structures and crystalline compositions when dry. Put another way, paint manufacturers have become too good at their job; in response to customer demands for a totally reliable product that provides an identical colour every time, they have plasticized and purified paints and pigments until the product is of perfectly even colouring, 100 percent reliable but also 100 percent bland. It is a story that parallels that of synthetic foods.

Now that we have accustomed ourselves to 30 years of rag rolling and colourwashing, it is worth reminding ourselves that in our search for broken colour effects and interesting painted surfaces we must not forget the delicate effects that are obtainable from limewash, distemper, home-made oil paint and gesso. Each has its own surface qualities (that I describe under the relevant technique) and each has a contribution to make to contemporary decoration, because their effects cannot really be matched using modern materials. This is an important point, because given the huge current emphasis on the historical value of traditional paints, their simple aesthetic value can be overlooked. They will work and look good in modern and minimal settings too. To help prove this point, some of the illustrations on these pages are of minimal interiors that demonstrate the use of broken colour and natural finishes.

The same applies to the exteriors of today's buildings. Our contemporary concrete buildings should be no lesser candidates for a coat of limewash than our historic manors, for the simple reason that a coat of limewash is a lot more interesting and lively to look at than a coat of plastic. It is a shame that instead we cover our progressive architecture with dull, flat paint. If, instead, we managed to synthesize modern design with traditional materials and paints, think how good our buildings would look and how well they would sit in their environment.

Colourwashing

A lot has been written in the last ten years about painting under the generic description of colourwashing; the technique has replaced oil glaze rag-rolling as the stock universal finish of most jobbing decorators. In fact, today's technique only vaguely resembles what people would have recognized as colourwashing in the seventeenth century (see over). These pages demonstrate a purely decorative technique involving the layering of broken colour that is merely redolent of old paint. According to the medium used, the effect can be quite different.

In its most sophisticated form, this technique is built up in several layers, each cancelling out the imperfections of the others, and constructing an effect that is greater than the sum of its parts. However, to perfect it, great practice over large areas is required.

Don't consider this an impediment; develop your skills by practising on large areas of blank, primed walls. The technique is quick and your trials can be soon repainted.

YOU WILL NEED
Emulsion, gouache or acrylic paint
Mixing container
Paintbrush dedicated to mixing
Water
Paintbrushes

1 *Brush a watery wash of colour (1 part paint to 5-8 parts water) onto a non-porous surface. Note that the brush should be moved quickly in every direction. As the paint begins to dry, re-brush it without loading any more paint, to soften the crude initial marks. You may find that the paint drags and lifts, creating interesting 'negative' marks, as in a solarized photograph.*

2 *When thoroughly dry (and this may take longer than you think), apply a second coat, usually another colour. For these pages I began with raw umber, then put on yellow ochre here. Again, the paint must be brushed out as it dries, superimposing more patches and marks.*

3 *Regardless of the number of coats, I find it usually necessary to knock them together with a final, pale wash. Apply this extremely thinly (1 part paint to 8-10 parts water) and quickly so that the brush marks simply blur together. Apply the wash with one paintbrush and, working simultaneously, soften it with another. The technique of Veiling (see pages 82-5) is a slight variation of this step.*

Oil glaze colourwash coloured with red and yellow ochres. Note how the effect is softer than the background below.

Colourwashing on stained wood. The timber drinks up the paint so that the eventual colour is closer to that of the wood.

This large area was colourwashed using only a single colour acrylic paint, raw umber. The marks it makes are consequently quite obvious.

CHOOSING THE MEDIUM

Like most techniques, colourwashing will produce different results according to the type of paint used. On the previous pages I used a diluted emulsion paint to establish quite strong but complex marks (acrylic paint, being a sophisticated form of emulsion, will yield identical results). This occurred because the paint dries quickly under the brush, and then will not easily budge.

However, oil paints – whether diluted artist's colours or diluted household oil-based paint – will remain workable on the surface much longer, allowing you to make very regular patterns (see above left). Within 20 minutes of being on the wall, oil paints have usually given off any solvent content and so begin to drag on the brush (at this stage making marks very similar to those reproduced on the previous page), but be warned that the paint soon ceases to be workable, developing an unpleasant sticky and dirty quality. By working quickly, though, initial marks can be softened with a lily-bristle hog softener to produce subtler brush marks (see opposite left) or even a faultless cloudy effect. Oil paints therefore offer the widest range of possible effects.

A paint made from pigment, water and a soft binder, such as gum arabic, beer or a dilute gelatine glue (for recipes see pages 60-1) will allow a very delicate finish simply because it remains water soluble, even when dry. Thus it is possible to paint a wall entirely 'in the rough' and then pass over it with a large moistened brush, reawakening the paint as you go and removing and softening unwanted blemishes. This sounds a little like a make-up advertisement, but it does

(RIGHT) *A much cruder example of colourwashing, produced by following step 1 of this technique. Although acceptable (indeed most decorators stop here) the effect is bland and two-dimensional.*

THE ESSENTIALS OF COLOURWASHING

DERIVATION

A late twentieth-century technique fashionably used to imitate old paint and plaster. The term derives from the sixteenth- and seventeenth-century habit of adding colour to ordinary distemper or whitewash, hence colourwash. These were applied fairly opaquely.

SURFACES

Interior walls and occasionally (if delicately performed) large items of plain furniture. Surfaces are best painted with pale colours, as any texture in the application of the base surface, such as roller or brush marks, will be highly evident in the finished effect (this can be used to advantage). Colourwashing is not suitable for exterior walls since there is little or no precedent for it. Limewash would be the correct exterior equivalent (see pages 96-9).

PREPARATION

Any non-absorbent, non-flaking surface such as oil-based or acrylic primer, a good-quality emulsion paint, or a totally cured casein wall paint. Cheap emulsion paints may be too absorbent to allow you to move the paint freely.

FINISHING

Under normal wear, no varnish or sealant is necessary. However, if not protected, the final coat may be worn off in areas of high traffic, such as stairwells. Consider using an oil-based veiling coat over water-based coats in these circumstances (see pages 82-5), or varnishing the work after with matt acrylic or synthetic oil-based varnish.

work. Gouache is a ready-made, if expensive, gum arabic paint.

Almost the most appropriate paint is that based on casein (widely available in small pots from artist's suppliers), which performs as well as softer paints like gouache because it remains water soluble for long after it has dried – up to several days. Casein paint, however, then undergoes a curing process whereby it gives up all its water content and forms a protein matrix (a natural version of what acrylic paint does) that becomes very hard and water resistant. If you apply casein paints too thinly, this curing process will fail.

HINTS AND TIPS

* From experience of teaching this technique, I have found that the most difficult problem is getting the right dilution of paint in the first place. Aim to produce paint of milk thinness, or even thinner, and experiment on a non-absorbent surface.

* The choice of colours is critical since the technique relies on the translucency of the paint over a pale ground to allow light to pass through and reflect through the layers. A combination of complementary colours may interfere with this process and produce a very muddy finish. I have found that the most successful combinations are those between colours occupying the same part of the spectrum, often including an earth colour, for example:

(LEFT) *Colourwashing's origins as a limewash and distemper technique are no better shown than in a lowly vernacular setting. In this farmhouse, a traditional paint has been employed, and the resultant patterns are not so much contrived by the brush, but rather occur as a feature of what happens when the paint is put on thinly.*

(ABOVE) *It is surprising how crude a finish you can get away with when your walls are then hung with pictures, mirrors and accessories. Their sharp edges, quality of detail and cast shadows contrive to 'push' the wall back and render it slightly out of focus. This is a useful trick for establishing a large visual depth of field on your walls.*

yellow ochre + king's yellow + cream

red ochre + crimson + pink made with red ochre

ultramarine blue + azurite blue + pale blue-green.

* Over large areas, brush control is highly important if you wish to obtain fluid patterns and not exhaust yourself. Most people work in too tight a fashion without using enough of their bodies; to paint a wall you must swivel at your hips as well as your shoulders. Using your whole body prevents groups of muscles from becoming tired. Grip the brush lightly, placing the shaft between thumb and forefinger; meanwhile the fingers, laid fairly flat, and thumb should rest on the metal ferrule.

* When using ready prepared paints, dilute them slowly, adding a little water/other appropriate solvent at a time to avoid lumps.

* When using powders, mix or grind them into the medium, such as linseed oil or gum arabic, before dilution (see page 58). Further colour can be added later provided it is always in liquid form. It also helps to add liquid colours in a slightly runnier state than the paint you are adding it to as this assists better mixing.

* When applying the paint, never use a brush that you have used for mixing; it will already be loaded with far too much pigment, resulting in an eventual diluting of the paint effect as it travels across the wall.

* Regularly stir very dilute paint mixtures as they tend to settle out. Powder pigments, and especially raw sienna, display this very markedly.

* Although not an historical technique, colourwashing happily imitates worn and ancient paint. Since walls in older buildings may need to breathe, it is best if the entire process is undertaken in casein-bound paints as they are microporous.

(BELOW) *Building three colourwashes together can produce effects of superb delicacy. This is a flower showroom which we painted in washes of cool, bluish red ochre with a thin white over the top.*

Distemper

Of all the paints used throughout history and throughout the world, none is as simple as distemper. Its dusty looking finish and delicacy essentially relies upon it being a cheap mixture of chalk and water with a binder added; usually a form of animal gelatine such as bone glue. Pigments can be added, and more sophisticated versions contain small quantities of linseed oil as a waterproofing agent. The recipe below sets out a method for making soft distemper in its most basic form.

Before painting any porous surface with distemper, the ground must be given a coat of clairecolle (a weak version of the gelatine glue used in the distemper) to size the wall and 'give it an appetite', as Cennino Cennini puts it. Make a separate, half-strength batch for this. Once dry, you may tackle the distempering with a happy heart.

To improvise a double boiler to heat the gelatine glue (see step 3), use two saucepans and a block of wood to space them apart.

YOU WILL NEED

Gelatine glue
Whiting
Bucket
Double boiler
Pigment (optional)
Whisk
Muslin cloth
150mm (6in)-wide, long-bristled paintbrush

1 *For about one room's worth, dissolve 340g (12oz) gelatine glue in 1 litre (2 pints) of cold water, stir and leave overnight to swell.*

2 *At the same time, sprinkle approximately 5.4kg (12lb) whiting into a bucket of cold water until it peaks just above the surface. Do not stir at any time. Also leave overnight.*

3 *The next day, pour off any discoloured excess water on top of the whiting and heat the glue in a double boiler. IT MUST NOT BOIL. Add the hot glue to the whiting, stirring constantly.*

4 *For a perfect mixture, I prefer to stir the ingredients with my hand. You can sense the temperature differences between whiting and glue, and in this way ensure that they are thoroughly combined.*

5 *At this stage, pigment may be added ready-mixed in water (see page 58), and again thoroughly combined, but this time with a whisk. Finally, sieve the paint through muslin and allow to cool to room temperature to form a weak jelly.*

6 *For a consistent finish, apply the paint very methodically, covering about 1m (1yd) square at a time. Then immediately begin brushing out the same area without loading the brush any more (if the paint drags, wet the brush with a little more distemper). Don't worry too much about evident brush marks because although the ground may grin through when wet, as the paint dries, the chalk content turns matt and much less transparent. Thus the paint becomes both paler and much more opaque.*

For the most part, wood and wall paints have always retained their separate identities. On wood, the traditional formula is a mixture of linseed oil and lead-based pigments (lead carbonate being the white pigment commonly used). However, where casein paints were used, the versatility of the paint sometimes led to its use on many materials.

CASEIN PAINT

For a finish that is similar to distemper but is more durable, there exists a paint made from cheese curds, with a pedigree as ancient as that of gelatine-based paints – casein paint. Writing in the twelfth century, Theophilus in *The Various Arts* lists a detailed procedure for extracting the casein, drying it and mixing it with an alkali (such as lime) to render it water-soluble. In northern Europe, casein seems to have been the standard binder for a large number of coarse wall paints, and this tradition spread to America with the settlers, where it is known as milk paint. However, research shows that casein paint had very limited use in Britain.

Casein's other principal use has always been that of a glue, of which the Cascamite brand is one example. As a paint, however, casein's chief advantages over soft distemper are that, once fully dry, it is resistant to water and abrasion. Indeed, I have used fine quality casein paints such as Plaka instead of gesso, since casein can be polished and waxed to create a beautiful finish.

It also breathes moderately well, and so can be used in ancient buildings (the power and hardness of a binder are generally in inverse proportion to its ability to breathe; hence emulsion forms an impervious layer and traditional coatings like soft distemper and limewash remain moisture permeable). Casein wall paints may handle less effortlessly than synthetic emulsions, but they do contain a high proportion of pigments other than whiting, such as lithopone and titanium white, which have extremely excellent covering properties. All in all, casein paint is not too dissimilar in handling or opacity to emulsion paint, while retaining some of the breathability and surface bloom of soft distemper. A happy compromise! (See also page 93 in Gesso for further uses of casein paint.)

THE ESSENTIALS OF DISTEMPER

DERIVATION

A term derived from the Italian 'tempera'; in English, it has now come to mean two distinct types of paint. Distemper is a water-based product bound with gelatine glue or casein for use on walls, while tempera in its more restricted sense designates a fine artist's paint whose vehicle is egg yolk. To the eighteenth-century English decorator, distemper contained glue, Spanish white (whiting) and perhaps some 'common colours'. In America, the term distemper is unknown, size paint being preferred. In France, the term 'detrempe' means both artist's tempera and distemper wall paint.

SURFACES

Walls (casein or washable distempers are desirable in areas of high traffic), ceilings (usually soft distemper only) and plasterwork, where synthetic paints should NEVER be used. Soft distemper has long been considered the essential coating for the insides of old houses throughout Europe. This is principally because it breathes so well, allowing moisture from a damp wall to pass through it without damage to the paint structure. Soft distemper can be removed with a sponge and water to ensure that subsequent coats of paint keep plasterwork crisp and defined.

PREPARATION

Size walls with clairecolle, as mentioned on page 76, or at worst a very dilute distemper mix. Substrates can be lining paper or just bare plaster. Distemper can be applied to clean, old emulsion, but this will not help an old wall breathe. Emulsion cannot be applied over soft distemper, which was always scrubbed off before re-decoration.

FINISHING

Soft distemper cannot be varnished or waxed. Solvents and waxes would render the chalk transparent, and so darken and patch the paint. This may read in rather a Draconian fashion, but this is simply because of the severe limitations of distemper's very simple ingredients: chalk is only happy as a pigment when it doesn't come into contact with oil or waxes, and gelatine glue will remain forever re-soluble in water.

The seven swatches on the following two pages were all painted with a distemper-type paint coloured with the limited essential colours range illustrated in Part I of the book. Although the paint could have been formulated using traditional gelatine glue as the binder, I instead chose a ready-made casein paint that chalks in the same way and has a delicate bloom on the surface. Note also how the pigments are not entirely blended with the paint, resulting in slight variations of colour intensity across each board.
The general advantage of casein paint is that despite being microporous, and hence useful in old buildings, it is tough and will accept the occasional clean with a damp sponge (and not dissolve off the surface). However, from experience these advantages seem to be present only in the superior brands.

Ultramarine blue produces a good lavender when mixed with white, a recognizably Mediterranean colour. Unlike the other blue, which tends to green, ultramarine has a reddish cast.

Good-quality burnt sienna pigment will yield acceptable soft pinks with a brownish cast, similar to the colour of polished brown plaster.

The most delightful pinks, clear and strong without being garish, strawberry or sugary, come from the type of red ochre that has a bluish cast. The resultant pink is cool.

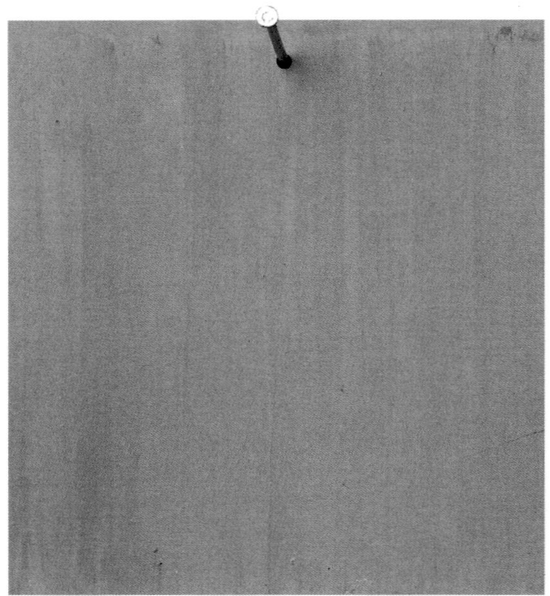

An orange salmon pink can be procured with a variety of colours; the usual source is an orange-tinged red ochre which I used here with a touch of vermilionette. Historically, it was common practice to adulterate vermilion with ochre, to lessen the cost, and vice versa to spark up the ochre.

Blue verditer, a green-tinged pale blue, traditionally provided a much used colour on the interior walls and exterior woodwork (in oil) of many buildings. I used Prussian blue pigment, but cerulean blue would provide a very similar colour.

You could attempt this sludgy green (which surprisingly has quite a high blue content) using terra verde pigment. Another method is to mix yellow ochre with a little ultramarine blue.

Yellow ochre used by itself in white will yield a surprising variety of bright pale yellows and creams. The brightness is a function of the type of ochre used and so will vary according to the pigment's source. Mars yellow, the synthetic variant, produces clean bright colours.

BINDING WITH OIL

One advertised feature of some distempers, whether casein- or gelatine-based, is that they are oil-bound: a peculiar thing, since they are, in fact, bound with casein or gelatine. What the manufacturer means is that during the manufacture, soap, fat or oil has been added to the glue in order to make the paint a little more durable – wipeable, as they say – on the wall. To make your own wipeable, soft distemper, mix in linseed oil (an eggcup or two) to the HOT glue at step 3 on page 76. It must be added drop by drop and constantly and vigorously stirred to emulsify it (just like making mayonnaise). To help it along, first mix a couple of teaspoons of water containing a little ammonium carbonate into the oil. The ammonium is alkaline and when mixed with oil will make a soap, thus rendering the oil so much easier to emulsify.

GUM ARABIC DISTEMPER

Making your own casein paint can be difficult and tiresome, but there is another simple alternative to soft distemper that you can make yourself, using liquid gum arabic. Gum arabic (see page 48) is the resin of the acacia tree, grown in profusion in Australia, Asia and Africa. Thick and almost tasteless, it is used as a binder in foodstuffs, and artist's water colours and gouache (the latter containing a little whiting) are bound with it. Gum arabic is shipped as lumpy crystals of differing colours, like amber, but can be easily transformed to a liquid by soaking overnight in just enough water to cover it (see page 60). Alternatively, you can buy it as a liquid.

To make the distemper, simply mix the gum arabic with whiting, as before, and add any pigments you may need to colour it. Although not advisable for making up wall paint, on the grounds of cost, it is extremely useful for small decorative projects where constant heating of glue proves irksome. In performance, its qualities of brittleness, and solubility in water even when dry, almost match those of soft distemper.

HINTS AND TIPS

* Clean the surface thoroughly before applying distemper. Soft distemper will crack and peel off if there is any grease or oil on the surface, and sometimes if it has been applied too thickly.
* Unlike modern vinyl emulsions, soft distemper is not necessarily a user-friendly paint. It can stick on the brush or it can decide to conveniently run down the handle and continue down your sleeve. The best advice for its application is to employ a 150mm (6in)-wide, long-bristled brush. This must be generously, and repeatedly, loaded since each time the brush is applied to the wall, the paint withstands very little brushing out.
* Soft distemper absorbs water and will also dissolve in water when dry, so always try to cover the walls with one coat only; otherwise you might find that the second coat may drag on the first, or remove it.

Because soft distemper cannot be gone over, by the eighteenth century, decorators had developed methods of manipulating it in other ways to create decorative effects, such as combing, stippling or dragging it to reveal the ground colour. This historic Finnish interior was spattered with several colours over pale blue.

Veiling

Veiling is an unashamed faking technique that perhaps sits a little uneasily in this chapter. It can be employed as a decorative effect in its own right, like colourwashing. But veiling is also useful in a setting where traditional finishes such as limewash, distemper or home-made oil paint have been applied to some surfaces and where you wish to copy the same effect elsewhere; or if, say, you want to hide heavy- duty heating pipes or ventilation ducts against a wall. It is also tougher than the more traditional finishes, so is extremely useful for such areas as hallways that might be liable to abrasion from children and pets.

YOU WILL NEED

Suitable paint (see Surfaces, overleaf)
Solvent
Container for mixing wash
Sponge
100mm (4in)- wide paintbrush
Absorbent cloth

1 *Working onto a synthetic paint ground that is either emulsion, eggshell, gloss or acrylic, use a pale tint of the same kind of paint. Make the tint into a very thin wash, using a great deal of solvent (8 parts solvent to 1 of paint) and lightly and quickly brush out the wash – the brush marks will blur away as the damp wash disperses on the surface.*

2 *You may need to dab the wash from time to time to eliminate runs. Or, as here, use an absorbent cloth to dab at the wash and make a light clouding pattern. This should not be obvious or forced, it simply serves to lightly patch the paint in a delicate and random way. This step is optional, particularly if your brush technique in step 1 is very good.*

PARE

PREGUNTAS?
Por favor comuníquese con nosotros antes de devolver el producto!
1 Visítenos a través del Internet para obtener la información mas reciente:
http://www.lenoxx.com
2 Envíenos un mensaje por correo electrónico para obtener una respuesta rápida:
evergo@att.net
3 Escriba a:
Lenoxx Electronics Corp., 35 Brunswick Avenue, Edison, NJ 08817, USA
4 Llámenos para obtener servicio rápido y amigable:
1-800-315-5885
Tiempo del Este:
Lunes - Jueves 08:00am-05:00pm
Viernes 08:00am-01:30pm
QUESTIONS?
Please check with us before returning!
1 Visit our website for the latest information:
http://www.lenoxx.com
2 Email us for a prompt reply:
evergo@att.net
3 Write to:
Lenoxx Electronics Corp., 35 Brunswick Avenue, Edison, NJ 08817, USA
4 Call us for fast and friendly service:
1-800-315-5885
Eastern standard time:
Monday - Thursday 08:00am-05:00pm
Friday 08:00am-01:30pm
STOP

NEVER TOUCH THE LENS!

A dirty lens may cause skipping or poor CD play. To clean the lens, use a special cleaning disk (not included) available in most music stores. Or you may use a cotton swab slightly moistened with alcohol. Wipe gently and dry.

NUNCA TOQUE EL LENTE!

Un lente sucio puede causar saltos o una reproducción mala del CD. Para limpiar el lente utilice un disco especial de limpieza (no incluido) el cual puede comprarse en la mayoría de tiendas de música. O puede utilizar en cotonete ligeramente humedecido con alcohol. Limpie suavemente y seque.

A50393R1

NE TOUCHEZ JAMAIS À LA LENTILLE!

Une lentille sale peut être responsable du mauvais fonctionnement du lecteur de CD ou amener ce dernier à sauter. Pour nettoyer la lentille, utilisez un disque de nettoyage spécial (non inclus) que vous pouvez vous procurer dans la plupart des magasins de musique. Vous pouvez également utiliser une tige de coton ouaté légèrement trempée dans l'alcool. Essuyez doucement, puis séchez.

3 On woodwork, adopt the same technique, but on mouldings apply the wash and soften it out (as in step 1), but then remove it from the highlight of the moulding with a sponge or rag. This leaves a dusty coat in the recesses, accentuating the form of the moulding.

A REFINEMENT

If you are reading this book in page order, then there are no prizes for realizing that this technique is really the third step of three-colour washing, used by itself. However, it is a little more refined in the variations obtainable by manipulating the wet wash with a cloth or sponge.

HINTS AND TIPS

* The delicacy of veiling depends on a subtle and confident execution, so practise this technique on large panels before committing yourself to a wall.
* If the wash forms nasty patches, it is more than likely too thick; thin it beyond belief and then re-try. Alternatively, try:
– wetting the wall first with the appropriate thinner to keep the wash open for longer
– using an oil-based paint wash thinned with turpentine, on an emulsion ground
– leaving bowls of water in the room overnight in dry weather to increase the level of atmospheric humidity so that a water-based wash doesn't dry so quickly.
* Experiment by putting a pale wash of one colour over the ground of another as shown opposite.
* Try using other tools to apply the wash, such as a sponge.

An early eighteenth-century room taken from Lee in New Hampshire, where the pine walls are painted in traditional paints. The blemished and dusty qualities of this paint are exquisite. In a room where panelling is already painted in modern synthetic alkyd paints, the difficulty lies in procuring the same kind of aged, bleached quality. The solution is to apply one or even two veils of colour directly over the alkyd using a thinned eggshell wash. Alternatively, a thinned water-based acrylic could be used for the wash, provided it contained whiting or fuller's earth to absorb surface grease and prevent the wash from cissing when applied.

THE ESSENTIALS OF VEILING

DERIVATION

A late twentieth-century technique using modern, synthetic materials to emulate the powdery bloom that traditional materials impart to paint surfaces.

SURFACES

Any non-absorbent, non-flaking surface such as oil-based or acrylic paint. For the wash, use emulsion on emulsion, oil-based eggshell on itself or on gloss, or acrylic on acrylic, or a wash of pigment and solvent bound with a small amount (10-15 percent) of the appropriate binder or varnish.

PREPARATION

No preparation is needed for the base coat. This is the beauty of this technique – it is readily applied to any previously painted surface. Older, painted surfaces should, however, be washed down first to remove dirt and grease.

FINISHING

Although there is no specific finish required for this technique, persistent

FINISHING (CONT)

sponging of the damp wall as it dries will result in a very textural bloom. With the right colours, this technique can be used to simulate different materials such as terracotta (opposite), lead, pewter and bare pink plaster. As with colourwashing, areas of high wear should be varnished with acrylic or oil-based matt varnish.

A pale cream wash over an orange-brown ground, lightly sponged as it dries, can fake the salty patina of terracotta. The ground should be damped down first.

White over pale blue. Note that by simply leaving the wash to settle, it forms into minute freckles.

Dark green, washed over with a pale blue. The wash was then all but removed from the panel, but it was allowed to sit in the moulding, forming a sharp line.

A fake rust finish can be perfectly achieved using several coloured washes, dabbed on and mixed when wet with a sponge. The ground here was burnt umber and the washes in other earth colours.

Oil paints

Although we like to think of oil paints as sophisticated modern coatings, since antiquity artists have used a variety of oils, resins and mastics to bind paints in surprisingly complex formulae.

Historically, nearly all oil paints contained lead compounds (lead carbonate or lead sulphate) to render them opaque and assist as a dryer, while the oil used was usually a pale, raw linseed oil. Rarely have two natural ingredients combined so well to make a product; it is tough, flexible, opaque, and handles well under the brush. For different coloured oil paints, pigments were added, ready liquefied in oil of turpentine (see page 56). The whole took considerably longer to dry than a modern-day equivalent, but the result was a paint with a charming bloom and character somewhat akin to distemper or limewash.

Over time, traditional oil paint wears thin rather than chipping or flaking off, since the oil remains elastic when dry. Modern household paints, however, tend to chip because synthetic alkyd resin binders are used in them and these break down on exposure to ultraviolet light.

The simplified recipe given below for making an oil paint doesn't call for lead and (for simple furniture and general house-painting) uses boiled linseed oil, which has a shorter drying time than raw linseed oil.

YOU WILL NEED

Mortar or old can
Boiled linseed oil
Powdered pigment (yellow ochre, ultramarine blue)
Old paintbrush
Muller
Oil of turpentine

The tools for grinding: a flexible knife, pair of mullers for grinding and an alternative, home-made pestle using a ceramic door knob. The glass sheet should ideally be painted white on the reverse to render the ground paint mix more visible, and given a rough surface by rubbing with carborundum.

1 *In a mortar or old can, mix boiled linseed oil and pigment, first with an old brush and then by grinding them with a purpose-made tool. Here I use an improvized muller, made from a ceramic door knob and hammer handle. This ensures complete blending and thorough breakdown of the coarser pigment particles.*

2 *Once the pigments and oil are well mixed, ideally to a fluid paste, add pure oil of turpentine (not substitute) to thin the paint. Mix together with a paintbrush. For a matt finish, more turpentine may be added (up to 10 times the volume of linseed oil), although exterior work requires a high level of binder and thus very little turpentine. The paint should then be strained.*

3 *As with conventional glosswork, the paint is applied over an undercoat and is usually dry in about 10 hours. Notice how the separate pigments spot through the paint layer as it dries, due to imperfect mixing; this is often desirable as it adds life and character to the paint film.*

ARTIST'S GRADE OIL PAINT

If you intend to mix your own oil paint for use in easel painting or for fine decorative work, then consider making it to artist's grade standard, the type you buy in tubes.

YOU WILL NEED

Pigments
Cold-pressed linseed oil
Piece thick glass or marble
Palette knife or spatula
Muller
Small air-tight jar

1 *Mix the pigment(s) and cold-pressed linseed oil on a piece of thick glass or marble using a flexible palette knife or spatula to your desired consistency. However, you may wish to grind your pigments separately, and then only mix on the palette.*

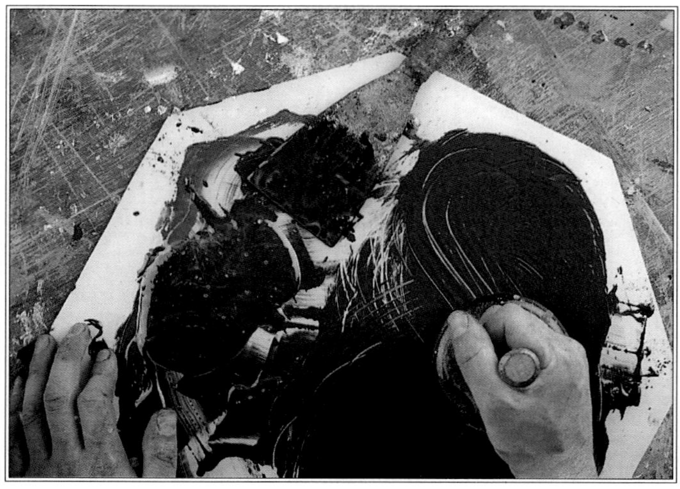

2 *Use a muller to thoroughly admix the pigment and oil in figure-of-eight motions. As soon as you feel the mix becoming more slippery under the muller, it is ready to be potted into a small, air-tight jar, or put into empty paint tubes with open rear ends that you can crimp shut.*

PAINT FROM FLAX, WALNUTS AND SOYA BEANS

Until the widespread use of synthetic petroleum-based resins and oils in the latter half of the twentieth century, most oil paints and varnishes were bound with some kind of vegetable oil. These oils are known as drying oils due to their ability to absorb oxygen quickly and subsequently form a hard film. Although linseed oil from flax was perhaps the most widely available, Cennino Cennini refers to alternatives as being superior and less liable to yellow when used in easel paintings. And an invoice of 1764 for the decoration of a grand English house, Holkham, lists 'White Lead... ground in Nut Oil'.

That most used in varnish used to be tung oil, a thick nut oil originally from China, which has excellent flow properties producing very durable coatings. Even today, some synthetic varnishes incorporate soya bean oil as a non-yellowing agent mixed with alkyd resin.

But as a binder in paint, linseed oil has the most distinguished pedigree of all. The oil is extracted either by cold pressing, producing a very pale and superior artist's-grade oil, or by steam heating to extract a cruder oil in greater volume. The latter is often refined and bleached before being sold as raw linseed oil or it is part oxygenated and sold as boiled oil. Also known as blown or bodied oil, boiled oil has a shorter drying time than raw linseed oil, but it is darker.

Stand oil is raw oil that has been heated to above 525° C (977° F) to form a thick, honey-like consistency, and is the best choice for glazing techniques since it is thick and withstands dilution, and hardly yellows at all when compared with raw or boiled oil.

RAW OR BOILED?

Most painters and decorators have opted for raw oil in the past on account of its paler colour and its better flowing properties when brushed out. When dry, it is more durable and harder than boiled oil, despite having less of a gloss. However, its drying time is longer, unless mixed with a pigment that will assist in the oxygenation such as white lead or either umber colours which contain manganese, a strong oxygenating catalyst. It also yellows over the years, especially if over-bleached.

TURPENTINE

Venice turpentine or oil of turpentine (see Common solvents on page 56) has always been considered by artists as the best drying oil as it is sympathetic to the way in which linseed oil dries. Although historically most of the commercial turpentine was produced by the Baltic states. America now grows the pine trees from which it is produced; the tree resin is distilled, producing two useful products, turpentine and rosin.

Turpentine substitute is a different animal, being (like its twin sister, white spirit) a petroleum distillate. Although almost identical in performance to pure oil of turpentine, it is less pleasant to handle, and much runnier, and so is rejected by most artists (also see Common solvents on page 57).

USING LEAD-BASED OIL PAINTS IN OLD BUILDINGS

Conservation bodies have long recognized the need for old buildings to be repaired and maintained with materials that are sympathetic to the original. However, many national and international directives now prevent lead from being added to exterior paints, despite the unique qualities of flexibility and wear that lead imparts.

The good news is that, after much campaigning, it has now become possible to buy lead-based oil paints in some countries for exterior use only, provided that you can demonstrate to your local council that your house is of sufficient historic merit.

HINTS AND TIPS

* Unlike water paints, linseed oil does not dry by evaporation but by absorbing oxygen and forming a rigid, non-soluble crust known as linoxyn. So ensure that your work is well-ventilated rather than heated if you wish to reduce drying times.
* Different pigments possess differing characteristics when mixed with oils, assisting or retarding drying, and creating paint films of differing durability. Formerly, the use of lead carbonate as the principal pigment in oil paint ensured a reliability of performance.
* You may be surprised at how well this paint covers a surface. This is because of the high pigment content, but be prepared for exceptions; certain pigments such as terra verde are quite translucent in oil.
* Unlike water-based traditional coatings, oil paints will not dry lighter or darker.
* Do not use whiting in oil, unless you want to produce your own transparent oil glaze (scumble). The refractive indices of oil and whiting are so close that, when mixed, the whiting turns a translucent grey. However, since it can be mixed in quantity, and so thickens the oil, it produces a cheap and useful extending medium for any oil paint. This allows you to apply a thin transparent glaze to a wall without it running down. Incidentally, if you continue to add more whiting you will eventually manufacture your own glazing putty.
* Brushes used for oil painting should be washed in turpentine substitute (white spirit) and then in soap and water before leaving to dry.
* Varnish brushes should be reserved for that use alone; the resins and oils in varnishes can strip dried-up particles of old paint from a brush, leaving them floating in the varnish coat.
* Wash and clean varnish brushes as for oil paint brushes, or better still, suspend them in a pot of linseed oil until they are next required.
* NEVER remove old lead-based paints with sanding materials or machinery; you will be creating a cloud of lead particles if you do.
* Equally, NEVER combine chemical paint strippers with blow torches, since the resulting fumes can be almost immediately fatal.
* Oil paints should be built in several layers, working 'lean-to-fat'. Thus a priming coat should contain slightly less oil than an undercoat, and an undercoat less than a top coat. This procedure is good practice as it creates a series of coatings that will adhere well to each other and form a hard, non-cracking topcoat. Priming coats are usually thinner to permit absorption into the surface, thereby providing better adhesion.

THE ESSENTIALS OF OIL PAINTS

DERIVATION

Used for many hundreds of years by artists, the simplest recipe for oil paint has a pedigree of at least 500 years in northern Europe, and calls for an admixture of just two ingredients. As an estimate of 1713 puts it, 'done in the best manner with Good Red and White Lead and Linseed oyl 4 times over.'

SURFACES

Usually wood surfaces require priming and undercoating first.

PREPARATION

Undercoats should contain less oil and more pigment than the top coat, working in the time-honoured manner of applying coats lean-to-fat.

FINISHING

Good housepainting follows three steps of application: brushing on, brushing out across the work (adding no more paint), and laying off by lightly stroking the work with the tips of the bristles, in the original direction of application.

Gesso

Nothing can compare with the subtle sheen of a polished gesso coat. Unlike paint, its surface assumes a life and identity of its own, a complexity that bears witness to the effort involved in its making. Its magic lies in its mirror-like polish and its exquisite smoothness; when stroked, there is not a hint of resistance under the fingers. It is the paint for traditional Italian and French furniture *par excellence*, and may be pigmented.

True gesso, as restorers and gilders know it, is a composition of glue mixed with an inert filler. The glue is an animal gelatine made from parchment for the finest work, or rabbitskin. Cheaper and darker glues such as scotch, pearl or bone glue would discolour the gesso and introduce impurities. The filler is most usually whiting. The mixture of the two gives an extremely strong and highly adhesive paint that can be re-coated as soon as it has cooled and set on a surface. This then allows the application of as many as 12 coats in one day. When properly dry it may be scraped and polished. Note that the recipe for soft distemper (see pages 76-7) calls for almost identical ingredients in a weaker combination, interesting proof of the flexibility of these traditional materials.

YOU WILL NEED
Rabbitskin glue
Water
Double boiler
Sieve
Whiting (gilder's grade)
Clean metal or wooden spoon
Soft paintbrush

This carved wooden cornice was made in our studio as a sample six years ago. Despite having been knocked around, the gesso is still as magical to the touch as it was then. A controversial technique was used for the cracking method (see page 94).

1 *Soak a cup of rabbitskin glue in 1 litre (2 pints) of water overnight (cups vary in size, but so do rabbits). The following day, warm the mixture until liquid in the double boiler. You may improvise this with two saucepans and a block of wood to space them apart. It is imperative that the glue does not boil as this will kill its adhesive power and render it useless.*

2 *When all the granules are dissolved, begin to sift in the whiting. DO NOT STIR. Instead, continue sifting, distributing the fall of whiting around the glue pan until the whiting eventually peaks above the surface of the glue. In this way you will avoid creating lumps. Stirring will interrupt the precipitation of the whiting as it moves through the glue, absorbing it as it falls.*

3 *Stir the mixture with the spoon. Do this very slowly to avoid trapping air in the mixture which could later manifest itself as bubbles in the painted surface. Now, as at all other times, gentleness and care are essential. Do not whip the mixture. At this stage it should resemble warm single cream.*

4 *Generously load the brush with paint and flow it gently onto the surface with little pressure and not brushing it out. Apply in strips without overlapping. Once a coat has cooled and developed a matt surface (3-10 minutes), it will have solidified to a jellied mass. At this point you may, with infinite care, apply another coat, moving the brush at 90° to the direction of the brush marks beneath; use too much pressure here and you will disturb the underlying coat and create a horrible, congealed mess. Use this cross-layering technique with each successive coat to build between 8 and 12 coats. Do not allow the surface to dry out completely between coats as this may result in the finished surface flaking.*

A fake gesso

Although traditionally-formulated gesso will yield quite unmatchable results, and is the correct method for the finest quality work, there are instances where you require a finish that is not half as laborious, but which produces a similar effect. This technique takes advantage of the ordinary characteristics of casein paint, which polishes easily to a finish very similar to that of gesso. At a pinch, you can even use ordinary emulsion or acrylic paint and rely on a wax polish finish to supply the required sheen.

YOU WILL NEED
Casein paint
50mm (2in)-wide paintbrush
Linen pad (optional)
Beeswax polish
Pigment (raw umber)
Sandpaper (fine grade)

2 *As an option for both polished and textured versions, the gesso can be lightly stained. Here a beeswax polish mixed with raw umber pigment (artist's oil colour is an alternative) is rubbed into the surface.*

1 *Brush casein wall paint onto the surface to be painted. Use the brush to either lay the surface off (smooth it by stroking across the brush marks) or deliberately texture it, as here, with a grain. When touch dry (2-4 hours), it may be polished with a damp linen pad, or left textured.*

3 *Rub the surface with fine sandpaper to reveal the raised areas of texture in strong contrast against the antiquing colour. It also polishes them to a lustre. This rapid technique is one often reproduced on 'antique' painted furniture, using coloured paints. Variations in effect can be achieved by rubbing the surface more or less, by applying coloured waxes of differing densities, or by passing over the fresh wax with a cloth soaked in turpentine, prior to sanding. This use of texture in the paint is a neat trick for hiding the bland surface of MDF.*

THE ESSENTIALS OF GESSO

DERIVATION

The word 'gesso' comes from the Italian for plaster and is indeed any thinly applied material that can be scraped and polished. Given that the word has such loose definitions, it is not surprising that paint manufacturers now produce acrylic gesso (in reality a thick acrylic paint). However, I find that this product bears no relationship to real gesso, either in composition or performance. Unlike a true gesso, it isn't possible to scrape and polish an acrylic gesso.

SURFACES

May be applied to any wood, once it has been sized with a weak solution of gelatine glue. It may also be applied to canvas or linen stretched over a frame or panel.

PREPARATION

Coat a timber or cloth ground with a diluted rabbitskin glue (say 1:3 with water). All gelatines when mixed with water will rot after a few days, so gesso must be made up daily. However, the glue, once mixed, may be frozen for storage.

FINISHING

Once a gessoed surface is thoroughly dry (48 hours at least, in a warm dry room), it may be polished. The laborious method is to work through finer and finer grades of sandpaper, using a block, finishing with 00 grade, or flour as it is known. Alternatively, V & R Borradaille give this intriguing method of Cennini's: dust charcoal powder onto the dry surface and gently rub it with a dry brush. Then take a large plasterer's scraper and scrape the surface with some considerable pressure in various directions, which will reveal clean white gesso where you have scraped. It may take some time to grind the surface down to one that is quite level and smooth, but is quicker than sanding. The charcoal gives the additional advantage of showing you remaining pits and hollows that need to be scraped back.

It is worth noting that a gesso made with plaster will be much tougher and therefore harder to scrape than one made with whiting.

You can then offer the gesso a final cut with flour grade paper on a block, followed by fine wire wool (0000 grade) and a polish using an old piece of linen or silk to buff it to an ivory finish.

At this stage your gesso is ready for painting on (for fine detail work in acrylic or tempera), for covering in bole clay in preparation for water gilding, or for wax polishing as a final protect-ive coat. Beeswax furniture polish is best. To take the pure whiteness out of the gesso and to stain it very lightly prior to waxing, I have also at times washed it over with turpentine thinly coloured with raw umber oil paint.

Needless to say, you should not wet polished gesso with water; gelatine, even when hundreds of years old, is water-soluble, and therefore so is gesso. Get it wet or even damp and it will be ruined.

OTHER RECIPES

* An alternative simple recipe for making up any animal glue, be it hoof, horn, scotch, rabbitskin, pearl or parchment, is to dissolve 1 part of powdered glue in 10 parts water, leave overnight and warm.
* To produce a hard and durable size for sealing plaster walls, a small amount of alum may be added to the glue. Dissolve 1 part alum in 10 parts hot water, and add a teaspoon of this mixture to 1 litre (2 pints) of glue.
* One experimental gesso we have made in the studio uses whiting sifted into a dilution of PVA glue (thinned about 1:2 with water). This is, of course, a cold mix, and layers have to dry for at least 8 hours before the next can be applied. This gesso can be polished, and if EVA glue, which is waterproof, is used, the resulting gesso could be water- resistant.
* Cennino Cennini gives a recipe that calls for fine plaster of Paris (gypsum) that has been slaked, ie hardened with water, into a solid cake and then crumbled back into water to make a thick paste. This is then strained through linen leaving a stiff 'cheese', which can be cut into flakes with a sharp knife directly into the glue. These complicated steps will have the effect of weakening the plaster, kneading it and refining it for use.
* The highest quality casein paint (see page 78) makes an excellent and quick substitute for gesso because it can be applied like conventional paint and, when dry, polished to an equally brilliant lustre. Casein paints, also known as milk paints, have a long pedigree in the USA and Scandinavia for their use on furniture, and are more flexible than gesso. The casein may even be lightly wetted once it is dry (the same day of application) and given an initial polish with a linen cloth formed into a pad. However, after several days the casein will have cured dry and no longer be susceptible to water. These qualities of casein paint have not been fully exploited in recent years. An even more inferior gesso effect can be produced with standard emulsion paints following the stages opposite.

HINTS AND TIPS

* Always paint gesso in a clean, warm and dry atmosphere. Dust will settle on a surface and consequently ruin freshly applied gesso.
* Do not overheat the warm gesso in the pot; it will skin badly and lose water through evaporation. Skin may be stirred into the pot with great diligence, and it is always a good idea to add a little water to the gesso pot throughout the day; evaporation renders it more concentrated, and if strong gesso is laid over weak gesso, it will crack off and fail.
* Overheating the glue before sifting the whiting into it will also increase the risk of air bubbles being introduced into the mixture.
* Pinholing, the opening of tiny holes in a wet surface, occurs in a water-based coating when grease or oil is present. To prevent this from happening, prior to working, dust the surface with powdered whiting to absorb grease, and/or wipe over the surface with methylated spirits (alcohol). The most overlooked source of grease is the brush, easily detectable by the presence of pinholing in gesso layers applied after the first one. Dedicate one brush to gessoing and nothing else and wash it regularly in soap and warm water.
* To apply the mixture, I find that a well-bodied but soft paintbrush is the best one to use (fine pig lily bristle or goat hair) (see photograph below). Brushes such as camel mops get too floppy with the weight of the warm gesso.

A CONTENTIOUS METHOD FOR CRACKING GESSO

The standard method for producing a cracked gesso is to apply true gesso to a linen cloth that has been stretched over a sheet of plastic and tacked down along its edges. When dry and polished, it is removed and drawn over a table edge, cracking as it goes. The more layers, the bigger the cracks; two or three coats will produce very fine cracks. The linen is then delicately glued on the reverse, to soften the gesso from behind and adhered to the surface on which it will eventually sit. When dry, a final polish is usually needed. This is the standard reliable method for panels, mouldings, picture frames and mounts, and quite a laborious one.

On page 90, the cornice illustrated was finished using quite another method that has provided me with intermittent success. A full day is needed for this technique and prior to this you will need to seal the ground with a thinned shellac or varnish. The next day, first thing, coat it with the highest quality oil gold size (the only one that seems to work is one traditionally made from heated linseed oil that has stood in the light, known as stand oil). Whereas for gilding, this product would be left for up to several hours till it is barely tacky, it is ready for gessoing when it has ceased to be fluid or gooey and has reached the point of stickiness.

Apply the gesso by brush and then massage it into the size with the fingers (strangely, a method Cennini recommends for 'pushing' the first coat of gesso into a surface to gain adhesion). Then apply subsequent gesso layers as normal throughout the course of the morning and leave it to dry. It is possible to accelerate the drying time by delicately using a hair dryer, so that within half an hour or so the gesso is bright white and completely dry. To crack the gesso, turn the heat right up. The cracking occurs as the still soft varnish beneath expands and contracts from the applied heat.

If the gesso and varnish have not bonded, and this is quite possible, then great flakes of gesso will peel off when the heat is applied. It is therefore wise to apply the gold size over a ground of previously applied gesso so that if chunks flake away, it is gesso that is revealed, not bare wood.

This decorative finish is highly effective but not reliable, and it is certainly not one for the beginner. As with most paint techniques, it requires practice and trial and error.

COLOURING GESSO

The colouring of any homemade paint is not a straightforward affair. For a start, any bought pigment is bound to be coarser than the synthetic pigments used by paint manufacturers. Consequently, in stirring and applying the coating, coarse particles break down to produce streaks. Some suppliers sell superfine pigments, already milled to a very fine grade, but there is no substitute for actually grinding a pigment into the medium in which it will be bound. For gesso, pigments should be ground in water, using a mortar and pestle, or bought already in water (see page 58).

To add the pigment to the warmed gesso on the stove, the pigment/water mixture should be diluted to a consistency slightly thinner than that of the gesso – any thicker and it may form a lump when mixed. It should be gently stirred in.

The second major problem of colouring gesso is that of tonality. A pigment will almost certainly appear darker when mixed with water than when dry. When added to gesso, the

Several layers of black gesso coloured with black pigment were built up and polished smooth. Two coats of bright red casein paint were then applied, cut back and polished in the usual way. Care was taken not to leave any texture in the black layer since this would have looked rather crude through the red. An alternative would be to use just casein paint (as in rubbed paint on pages 174-5) or gesso.

To imitate a boled and gilded gesso, a conventional surface of polished white gesso was gently coated with a thin layer of gesso tinted with yellow and red ochre pigments. This was gently rubbed back with 0000 grade wire wool, and then wax polished.

For a coarse and distressed surface, this swatch was rendered by leaving the gesso half finished rather than taking it to a full finish. To add depth, the surface was then washed with diluted raw umber artist's oil colour and wax polished when dry.

pigment mixes with the whiting to produce a lighter tint in the pot. Then when applied, the coloured gesso will lighten in colour yet again as it dries, often very markedly. Upon scraping and polishing, it will darken slightly. This is particularly so when the pigment used has strong staining power, as with cerulean or Prussian blue. Finally, a darker tone will emerge once the surface is wax polished.

This incredible chain of variations is so wildly unpredictable that the job of colour matching is almost impossible and usually requires an educated guess. Generally speaking, the colour of the gesso in the pot is not greatly removed from that when it is finally wax polished, but there are exceptions. Pigments that stain, such as those mentioned, or pigments that are coarse will break down into smaller and smaller particles and intensify the colour, not only under the brush, but particularly under the scraper and sanding block.

The whole process can be so frustrating that the only reliable method for colour mixing is to make up some test samples for which you should allow several hours. Make up small pots of liquid gesso, keep them warm, and add pigments in measured units such as teaspoons. Sample boards can be quickly gessoed with a couple of coats, dried under the hair dryer, swiftly sanded and waxed to see the results. One word of warning; wax polish contains a solvent that evaporates within about 20 minutes, and this solvent will darken the surface to a tone deeper than that of the final result. Wait for it to vanish before evaluating the final waxed colour.

Limewashing

By far the most appropriate and traditional paint for decorating the outside of the house is limewash. Its coarse structure, powdery finish and subtle translucency give the walls life and identity in just the same way that modern, synthetic coatings can make a surface appear to be shrink-wrapped in polythene.

For at least 6,000 years, lime has been used in buildings, as plaster, mortar and coating. Unfortunately, in the twentieth century it has been replaced by modern equivalents that may be harder, but which are also more brittle, and do not let old buildings breathe. Exterior acrylic masonry paints trap moisture in the walls and can eventually cause the coating to fail and fall away. Lime, on the other hand, is a very elastic material that allows moisture to pass through, such as from a wall with rising damp. It also weathers extremely well outside, gently wearing back instead of falling off in chunks. It is an ideal vehicle for pigment colours, forming an important contribution to the way we see regional colours (see pages13-15).

Lime slaking (soaking in cold water) is a dangerous process (see overleaf) and there are many excellent companies making and slaking lime so the process is best left to the experts. Lime is also best used when matured (been left to slake for at least three months) when unslaked particles of active quicklime won't explode during or after application. Pliny the Elder in his *Chapters on Chemical Subjects* describes how plasterers required lime that had been slaked for at least three years; difficult to obtain these days.

YOU WILL NEED
Protective clothing
Lime
Drill with mixer attachment or egg whisk
Bucket
Water
Pigment (yellow ochre)
Empty coffee jar
Stocking

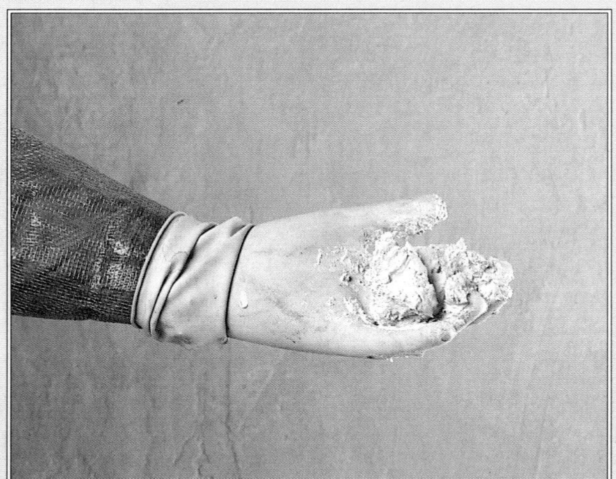

1 Lime may be bought in tubs in putty form, for masonry work or for dilution to limewash. Use a drill with mixer attachment or an egg whisk and dilute the lime to a watery wash. Wear skin and eye protection at all stages of preparation and application since lime is caustic – about as alkaline as dilute household bleach.

2 Pigment may be added at this stage, ready mixed in water. The easiest method is to shake a few tablespoons of pigment in a coffee jar half-filled with water. This crude liquid form of colorant is known simply as a suspension.

3 Before adding the colour, sieve the limewash through a piece of stocking or gauze stretched over the top of the bucket to remove any lumps. The pigment, too, should be poured through the sieve. Once added, stir well; for a patchy finish you need not stir for too long.

4 Once fully covered with protective clothing, you can begin applying the limewash, but this must be done in several thin coats. Uncoloured, it appears virtually transparent when wet, drying back to white. Thus, once pigmented, you must expect it to dramatically lighten in colour once dry. Anticipate this and dry some test samples with a hair dryer.

HOW FAR CAN A LIME CYCLE?

I am not the first person to crack this joke (the lime cycle is the cyclical process by which lime is made and used) and, sadly, I won't be the last. What is weird about lime and limewash is the way it completely changes its chemical state at every turn. It starts out quite innocuously as limestone, chalk or even as varieties of marble (all of which naturally occur as calcium carbonate) which is then vigorously heated to drive off carbon dioxide. This leaves a very unstable product, quicklime or burnt lime (calcium oxide), which can best be described as thirsty, searching constantly to absorb moisture from wherever it can. It is often sold as powder or small lumps, which should be kept dry before slaking.

The process of slaking is dramatic; the quicklime is thrown into water and reacts with it, absorbing its component gases to produce slaked lime (calcium hydroxide). In so doing, it creates fantastic heat (up to 400°C [752° F]) and violently boils the water. Exciting stuff.

Once fully slaked, and this can take months in order to completely convert every particle of unslaked lime, it is ready for use, usually in putty form, and is at this stage very alkaline and caustic. The most extraordinary thing about lime is that, once it has been applied, whether as limewash, mortar or plaster, the lime then sets by absorbing carbon dioxide from the atmosphere and thus neatly returns to its original, innocuous state, as calcium carbonate (in the case of mortar this can, in fact, take many hundreds of years to fully occur).

An example of how limewash weathers; colours on a wall in south-eastern France.

The subtlety of this last stage is that, in converting back, the calcium carbonate links together to form an integral mass, not a powder. This is why, unlike any other paint, limewash needs no binder or medium to stop it from falling off the wall.

This last point is important, because many have come to see the addition of some kind of waterproofer such as tallow or linseed oil as essential; not so. They should only be permitted where a limewash is going to be exposed to extremely heavy weather. Then, tallow must be added

THE ESSENTIALS OF LIMEWASHING

DERIVATION

Every early civilization used it except the Egyptians, who relied on gypsum and mud in their dry climate. Universally recognized as a true and traditional coating for older buildings on account of its moisture permeability (allowing walls to breathe) and its tendency to 'weather in'. Over time, coloured washes tend to fade and patch a little. This process accounts for the way in which certain

DERIVATION (CONT)

regional palettes can slowly change over the course of several centuries; the delicate pale colour known as Suffolk Pink to inhabitants of eastern England, often used to be applied as a deep red ochre in previous centuries. Whereas pink is still a popular colour for painted British houses, manufacturers of synthetic wall paints do not even make modern paint in true red ochre.

SURFACES

Requires a porous ground such as lime mortar, brick, concrete or stone, so that it can adhere.

PREPARATION

Ensure that the surface is sound and dust-free. The substrate must be wetted down before painting and during application. Must be applied thinly, allowing 24 hours drying time between coats.

FINISHING

No sealing or finishing of dry limewash is necessary or desirable. If wet weather approaches, protect the wall with plastic sheeting during the drying process. Protect the painted surface from direct sunlight too, since if the water evaporates too quickly, the hydrated lime will not have had sufficient time to absorb enough carbon dioxide and will powder away.

at the factory, but oil (Jane Schofield recommends an eggcupful per bucket) or casein in the form of skimmed milk (½ litre [1 pint] per bucket) may be added during mixing.

HINTS AND TIPS

* The action of brushing limewash helps to bond it to the substrate. However, don't overbrush it, particularly when applying many coats, as this can dissolve and loosen previously applied layers.
* Consider an unevenly coloured surface as natural; it is almost impossible to achieve a perfect finish with limewash.
* Remember that limewash must be water thin and applied in several extremely thin coats (six is not unusual). Do not cheat, as a thicker mix will inevitably craze or fall off when dry.
* Limewash may be applied to interior walls, particularly in ancient houses, but I have seen tests that demonstrate that it abrades very badly in areas of high wear such as hallways, particularly if you have children or pets. However, it may be emulated by using soft distemper (its interior equivalent) or a casein wall paint (see pages 78-9), both of which can be tinted with the same pigments, and both of which yield the same dusty finish.
* Stir limewash frequently and attempt to mix coloured limewashes in large batches; because it lightens as it dries, limewash is almost impossible to exactly colour match.
* At all times exercise extreme caution with limewash. In its wet state it can burn the skin and even cause blindness.

Here on a newly built concrete house in Mallorca, a wall displays all the depth and subtlety of freshly applied limewash.

2 Decorative techniques

Decorative techniques

The title of this chapter may seem odd – why group a small number of paint techniques under the heading 'decorative' when surely all paint finishes have a decorative value? The answer is, I suppose, that all techniques fall into some category or other according to their purpose. Thus, techniques that are imitative of specific materials, such as marbling or graining, have become known as faux, or fake, techniques. If a technique's essence is its ability to reflect light in a certain way, then I have grouped these under a heading of reflective techniques (see pages 128-39). This chapter is not placed second out of coincidence; it runs directly on from the first, in which many of the techniques were less to do with creative manipulating of the paint, and rather more concerned with the surface qualities and structure of traditional paint, which means you can apply it in a standard way and rely on the paint itself (and serendipity) to provide the effect.

This chapter contains many of the traditional techniques – dragging, stippling, broken colourwork – that have been covered countless times over in books already published. The difference that I want to point out is that these effects (now considered rather staid and uninspired) owe their invention to the very materials covered in chapter 1; distemper, size paints and traditional oil paint. The fact that distemper paints have poor covering power means that decorators historically had to invent brush techniques to disguise this fact. This was especially necessary from the middle of the eighteenth century onwards, when the decorative schemes of the rococo and chinoiserie styles demanded very crisp arrangements of colour, pattern and carving. The easiest way to handle the paint was to drag it, or stipple it quickly. Although there is little documentary evidence to support this theory, it is borne out by the limitations of the materials themselves. I strongly recommend you spend a day handling soft distemper; you will quickly discover how necessary, and basic, these brush techniques are in handling the paint.

OIL GLAZES VERSUS SCUMBLE GLAZES

Of course, since their inception, many of these techniques have developed and changed, mainly due to the widespread promotion in the 1970s and 1980s of oil glazes to produce increasingly subtle and transparent effects. With these long-drying media, effects such as stippling and dragging are very easily achieved. These oil glazes are a mid-nineteenth-century invention, originally produced to assist in the production of marbling and simple graining. It is interesting to note that, as late as the 1930s, decorating manuals were suggesting that basic decorative techniques be executed not in oil glaze, but in distemper and other water-based wall paints. If you are prepared to practise, you will discover that, for example, dragging can produce quite wild and exciting effects if executed in a semi-opaque or opaque wall paint, especially if the ground is of a contrasting colour.

The accepted canon for decorative glazework prescribes a pale ground with a darker glaze colour that is manipulated on top of it. However, very striking versions of the techniques in this chapter can be realized by using intense base colours, producing exciting twists to the standard versions.

Sponging, glazing and stippling techniques offer the historical decorator alternatives to a flat coat of paint. These techniques have a long pedigree, and their subtlety allows them to be used as very discreet additions to a decorative scheme.

Alternatively, a stippled coat of soft distemper, even on a white ground, will add to the charm and depth that such paint already possesses.

Ironically, these 'historical' techniques are now even easier to accomplish since the introduction of water-borne acrylic media such as acrylic scumble glaze and drying retarders. Their popularity is partly due to environmental and health concerns about the use of oils- and solvent-based media in decorating and they were intended to totally replace products such as oil-based transparent glaze. Of course, they are less workable than oil-glaze products and so often behave more like ordinary water-based products such as emulsion or acrylic paint.

Ironically, their limitations mean that the finished effects often more closely mimic those of traditional distemper than of oil paint. Try dragging with acrylic scumble glaze mixed with emulsion paint; the opacity and quick drying times of the mixture are quite unlike an oil glaze.

Sponging on and off

Sponging creates a soft, textural effect that is ideal for a large surface where you wish to create a light and shadow effect rather than the flat monotone of a single coat of paint. It is quick and relatively easy to work, but the key is to use a paint that will stay 'open' or wet long enough for you to be able to work it. Originally, a traditional oil glaze was used for precisely this reason, but not only does it smell strongly it also stays open far longer than is really necessary.

A far better solution is a gum arabic-based paint (effectively a home-made gouache paint), to which water is added, to thin it. It has the bonus, too, that you need only to wet it to render it workable again, which is a great help if you want to correct mistakes.

The most attractive sponged effects are made with a natural sponge (which is expensive) or with a cellulose sponge that you have doctored by removing small pieces from it to produce an irregular pattern (above). There are a number of ways of executing sponged effects – as you do it, you will discover that you start to develop your own preferred methods. The ones given here are my versions, because I like the resulting marks.

Apply the paint with a sponge (sponging on). Alternatively apply paint liberally with a brush and then remove it with a sponge and cloth (sponging off). The former gives a smaller, regular, fragmented pattern, the latter produces a diffused, irregular, blotted look.

YOU WILL NEED
Pigment (red ochre)
Gum arabic
50mm (2in)-wide flat paintbrush
Sponge
Old cloth

Sponging on

1 *Make up a thinnish paint from pigment dissolved in water and then add gum arabic binder (add approximately 15-20 percent binder to the mixture of pigment and water). Dab it over the surface using the paintbrush in a random pattern.*

2 *Using a lightly dampened sponge, start to move the paint about on the surface in light dabbing movements to achieve a random pattern.*

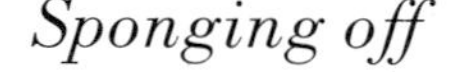

Sponging off

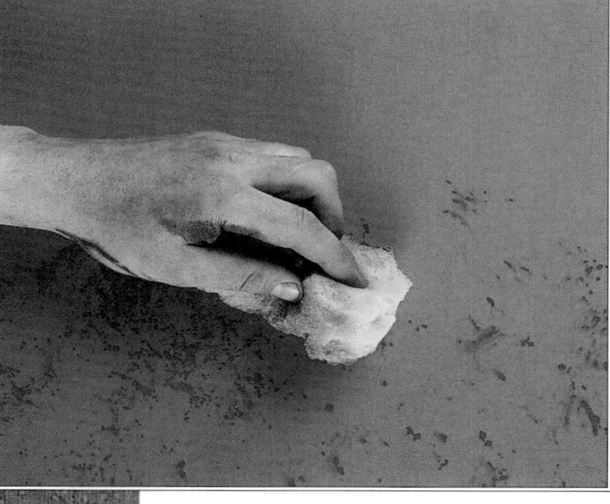

1 *Brush on a coat of gum arabic-based paint (see step 1 of Sponging on) to cover the surface. Leave it to dry completely, then with a damp sponge, lightly dab the surface of the paint to leave a crisp pattern of damp marks.*

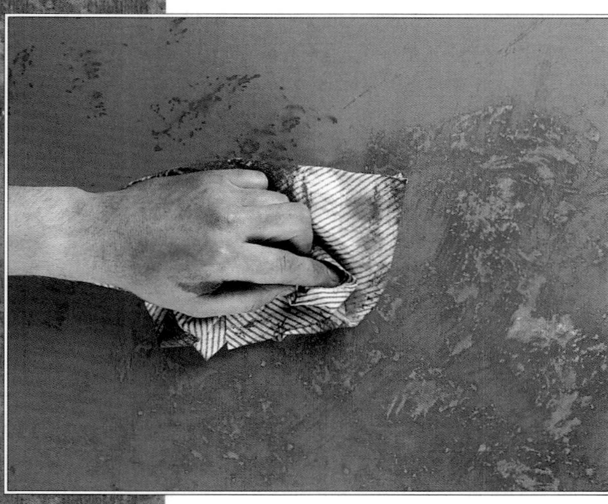

2 *With a dry cloth, lightly rub the wet areas to remove the wetted paint. The degree of pressure will determine how much paint is removed. To achieve a consistent pattern, keep presenting areas of clean, dry cloth to the surface.*

CHOOSING THE MEDIUM

Sponging is a much used paint technique which is also very adaptable. You can use it on its own, or with other techniques to soften, mottle or otherwise blend patterns and make them more subtle and subdued. You can use more than one colour, although ideally only closely toning colours should be used for this kind of effect, so that you are almost unaware of the colour difference; you simply see a tonal variation.

One aspect of the technique that many people find difficult is working into the angle of a wall or close to a cornice, for example. The best solution is to cheat and either cut a tiny piece off the sponge to use for these awkward edges, or use a narrow brush to lightly stipple and splodge the paint to achieve a similar effect.

A sponge can be employed not only for putting paint on or pulling it off, but also for moving it around a wall surface, like a brush. Such effects are similar to those produced by rag-rolling or softening glazes with a brush.

THE ESSENTIALS OF SPONGING ON AND OFF

DERIVATION

Sponged effects have been around since paint effects first became popular. In fact, it seems likely that as far back as Roman times, sponges were used to manipulate paint. One of the simplest paint effects, it is also one of the quickest to apply.

SURFACES

Any: walls, furniture or objects such as picture frames, for example, provided they have been prepared. Ideally, though, they should have a reasonably smooth, fairly water-resistant finish. Sponging on a very shiny surface is hard because the paint tends to reticulate, or ciss, on the surface. You can sponge over a water-based emulsion, but the effect may be difficult to achieve since cheap emulsions will absorb the wash too easily. The best surface is a good-quality emulsion or acrylic paint.

PREPARATION

Any surface that is clean and dry. Ideally, use a water-based ground for gum arabic washes. To make gum arabic binder (see recipe on page 60).

FINISHING

When the surface is completed, seal it with a couple of coats of varnish; if you work very speedily, you may succeed in varnishing with water-based acrylic varnish without lifting the dry paint. Otherwise, an oil-based varnish will be necessary. Many decorators simply leave the gum paint to the elements and hope for the best.

HINTS AND TIPS

* By using gum arabic paint, you can simply wipe the surface clean and start again (in sponging on) or repaint the base coat (in sponging off), if you aren't happy with the end result.
* It is important when sponging on or off to replace the cloth or wring out the sponge at frequent intervals, otherwise you will find that the marks tend to clog and lose their individuality.
* Recent tradition (from the 1970s) often stipulates the use of emulsion paints, which are far too inflexible and dry too quickly, or smelly oil glazes, which become dirty on application and take days to harden properly. Gum arabic-based paints offer a much better alternative. Being water-based, they remain flexible for a long time.
* Acrylic scumble can also be used, and stays open and workable for a reasonable time, but after it dries, mistakes cannot be corrected. If you use a scumble for sponging off techniques, do not let it dry – work on it while the glaze is still wet.

Of the various period settings which will accept sponging, the 1930s is the one with which the technique is most identified. This vaguely art deco interior is decorated with a mid-tone opaque paint that has been sponged off, and around, for an effective evocation of the period.

Dragging and stippling

Both these effects 'break' the surface of the paint in an evenly textured way, using a brush. For traditional dragging, a soft-bristled brush (known in the trade as a flogger) is pulled vertically through the wet paint to create narrow vertical lines in the surface, and in stippling, a stiff-bristled stippling brush is patted onto the wet paint to create an evenly mottled effect.

In practice, you can use a range of different tools to achieve textured effects in wet paint. Here, the dragging tool used was a comb wrapped in a piece of kitchen cloth, but anything from a pot scourer to a thistle head could conceivably be used. The effect will vary in consistency and density according to the implement chosen and the opacity and fluidity of the paint.

Dragging tends to be most effective when used in combination with opaque paints, so you could use either a 'traditional' paint or make your own from acrylic scumble or gum arabic and pigment. For a greater sheen, use a thinned oil-based eggshell paint.

The paint mixture for stippling is usually a fairly thin mixture of, say, acrylic-based emulsion mixed with acrylic scumble, to which pigment is added for colour. Alternatively, you could use an oil-based paint and stipple it with a brush soaked in white spirit to give a mottled, watermark appearance.

YOU WILL NEED

Acrylic paint
Pigments (white, ultramarine blue, yellow ochre)
Decorator's brushes
Comb
Kitchen cloths
Stippling or scrubbing brush

Dragging a comb in a cloth

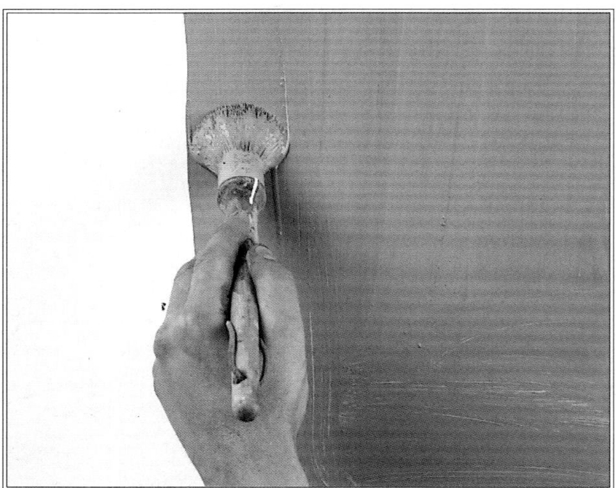

1 *Paint the base coat with a thickish paint (use either a traditional paint or an acrylic paint with pigment added).*

2 *Wrap a comb (or the chosen tool) in a piece of kitchen cloth and, holding it firmly at each end, drag it smoothly through the paint. To ensure that a clean edge is kept, replace the cloth at the end of each down stroke.*

Stippling a pilaster

1 *Paint the surface with the chosen base coat. Allow it to dry before repainting with a coat (toning in this case) of acrylic-based mix of emulsion and scumble glaze in a fairly thin consistency.*

2 *While wet, apply the stippling tool using a firm, regular patting motion over the whole surface so that it becomes lightly textured, revealing a speckled two-tone effect.*

THE ESSENTIALS OF DRAGGING AND STIPPLING

DERIVATION

These techniques are a development of the sophisticated eighteenth-century practice of manipulating translucent distemper paints on paler plaster grounds. Since the distemper could not easily be re-coated, these decorative brush marks were developed as a finishing technique.

SURFACES

Any plaster or wood surface, properly prepared and painted with a base coat of any non-absorbent ground, preferably with a mid-sheen finish. Stippling can be carried out on raised or relief surfaces.

PREPARATION

Must be smooth or flawless for dragging, but almost any texture, including quite rough plaster, for stippling.

FINISHING

Choose between several forms of finish, depending on the use to which the finished piece will be put. Normally it will be traditional oil varnish, with or without a finishing wax, but you can also use acrylic varnish, also with or without a finishing wax coat.

MATCHING TECHNIQUE AND SURFACE

Any surface can be dragged or stippled, from walls to floors to woodwork. Dragging is often chosen as a finish for doors because it helps to break up the area attractively, as the light catches the faint texture of the painted surface. For the same reason, stippling is ideal for less than perfect walls.

For either of these effects, it is usual to paint the surface in one colour and

This cupboard, an ugly lump of a piece, has been superbly repainted in, first, a layer of brown glaze or paint, and when dry, a layer of blue paint. Each layer was combed (dragged with a metal or rubber decorator's comb), in differing directions while wet.

Stippling and wiping. *This technique is an excellent treatment for furniture or any surface where relief forms an essential component. This surface was stippled with paint and glaze tinted with ultramarine green and a little raw umber and then the raised areas carefully wiped with a cloth stretched over the fingers to reveal the ground, as shown on the bottom right-hand corner. If the contrast is hard and the wiping action has left streaks of glaze, gently re-stipple the wiped areas, as shown on the bottom left-hand corner.*

Stippling and softening. *This swatch was stippled all over and then gently softened with a lily-bristle softening brush. The two actions may be alternated as long as the glaze remains workable. The third technique of 'ragging off' with a cloth may also be introduced. You may like to consider this exercise as good practice for both stippling and softening, which can be viewed as the two 'finishing' processes of a great deal of fine decorative work.*

then stipple or drag into a second colour painted over the top. This second colour should preferably tone with the first coat, often using pale tints over white. The underlying white then shows through in the finished surface, giving it a reflective quality. It is usually a mistake to use contrasting colours for either of these effects, as the aim is to be subtle rather than to surprise. But much depends on the overall effect you are aiming at – strong colour combinations can sometimes work extremely well.

With stippling, you could in theory use one, two, three or even more colours, allowing the coats to dry between each application. Dragging, however, is normally limited to one or two colours unless you change the direction of the marks to create a honeycomb effect, as opposite.

Stippling is an excellent way of imparting colour to raised or relief plasterwork to give it an authentically aged appearance, since you can create interestingly shadowed effects to throw the mouldings into greater relief. The surface is normally stippled, the highlights wiped to reveal the ground, and the surface then re-stippled, as per the sample above.

HINTS AND TIPS

* It saves a lot of time and effort if you work with a partner, one of you applying the base coat and the other working it with the tool.
* Always paint in smallish sections, about 60cm (2ft) square, so that the paint does not dry too quickly, and so that you can keep a wet edge going. This will allow the new paint to blend in with any already applied.
* Clean the dragging/stippling tool frequently to prevent paint clogging it and spoiling the marks made on the surface.
* In dragging, try not to stop half-way down a vertical surface when dragging the tool through the paint otherwise you will leave a tidemark.
* In stippling, the application of the stippling brush should be done with a firm, even, regular pressure.

Softening glazes

Pure glazes are essentially oily, or gummy, liquids that act as a vehicle for paint colour, and a glaze of some kind is the finishing touch to many paint effects – the application of a very thin coat of resin and pigment to create a delicate, light reflecting finish.

Historically, glazes were oil-based, permitting the artist to thin the paint to a thick but translucent consistency. Oil-based glazes are still the best, allowing you to produce a wonderfully soft translucent coating, but they have a very slow drying time (see page 52). Acrylic-based glazes can also be used, if they are of a brand that has a satisfactorily slow drying time. Drying retardant additives can be purchased separately, if needed.

Glazes are normally used in darker tints of the ground colour beneath. To work light on dark, an opaque pale paint may be mixed with glaze. Coloured glazes generally contain pigment or paint that is added to them to render them slightly opaque rather than clear. A good glaze recipe for softening and diffusing a surface colour is composed of raw sienna and raw umber, added to clear glaze. Mixing graded tones of glaze takes practice and patience, but if you decide to use more than one glaze colour for a graded effect, make sure you apply the second colour while the first is still wet to blur the edges.

The softening glaze featured on these pages has been used by artists for centuries to create delicate layered, graded effects on, say, areas of sky on a canvas. In house-painting, it is used for creating areas of depth and shadow and for faking an antique appearance.

As with all paint effects, there are no hard and fast rules as to how it should be done, or with what medium exactly. There is even confusion as to what constitutes 'glazing' and what should be more correctly termed 'scumbling', although the latter term seems to be given to anything which involves an opaque, as opposed to a clear, glaze. The key point is that the glaze, opaque or otherwise, is thin but not so runny that it falls off the wall. You brush it on and find various ways to remove it until you have achieved the exact amount of covering glaze that you want. Use whatever you like to remove it – soft-bristled brushes, rags, sponges or even your fingers – as long as whatever you use does not introduce dirt or dust to the surface.

YOU WILL NEED
Glaze
Pigments (raw sienna, raw umber)
Paintbrushes (round fitch, lily-bristle softener)
Lint-free rags

1 *Paint the initial glaze coat over the surface and brush it out well so that only a thin layer covers it.*

2 *Soften with the lily-bristle brush to remove any obvious brush marks, using progressively lighter and more delicate strokes of the brush.*

3 *With a rag, start to move the surface out in a light dabbing motion – a few delicate marks are acceptable on the finished surface.*

4 *Work over the surface with the softening brush, using just the tips of the bristles, very lightly and in different directions.*

5 *Wipe any surplus glaze off the brush with a dry rag at frequent intervals. Finish an oil-based glaze with a spirit-based varnish, a water-based glaze with acrylic varnish, and/or wax polish as a finishing touch in either case.*

Painted plaster

This technique is used for colouring all forms of decorative plaster: cornices, plaques, pilasters or panels, and can be carried out on both unpainted plaster and ordinary white-emulsioned surfaces. It works best on unpainted plaster, however, as the process of adding translucent colour to the plaster gives a special depth to the colour. Any plaster surface is suitable, including pieces of discarded plaster from a reclamation yard or a plasterer's workshop.

Water-based gouache paint, which has a gum arabic binding agent, produces the best effects giving both softness and depth of colour. However, you can also use acrylic paint, which produces a tougher, less diffused finish. The colours you use should be much stronger than the desired finished effect, as the rubbing down process distinctly softens them.

YOU WILL NEED

Water
100mm (4in)-wide paintbrush
Shellac
Methylated spirits
Gouache or acrylic paints
Artist's paintbrush
Liming wax (ready-made, or see recipe page 118)
Pigments (burnt sienna, burnt umber)
Turpentine
Stippling brush
Soft cloths

1 *Using one of the large paintbrushes, brush water very liberally onto the new plaster, which will drink it up as avidly as a legionnaire in the desert. The water treatment gives the plaster an appetite for the coat of shellac, which you apply next.*

2 *While the plaster is still wet and using the same paintbrush, brush on a coat of shellac, diluted 50:50 with methylated spirits. This seals and colours the plaster and gives depth to the colour, which you then apply.*

3 *The object may then be decorated with paint, using either gouache or acrylics. Thin the paint with water to the consistency of single cream. Here viridian green has been used for the leaves (with touches of vermilion on the raised parts), yellow ochre, cobalt blue and Mars violet for the coloured bands, and vermilion for the grapes.*

4 Now brush on the polishing coat of liming wax, mixed with a very small quantity of raw sienna and raw umber pigment, and diluted with turpentine to the consistency of single cream. Using the stipple brush, stipple it into the nooks and crannies of the plasterwork, covering it completely.

5 While the wax is still wet, and using a soft cloth, you may remove some of it from the highlights of the surface, as desired, to reveal the work beneath. Allow the wax to dry for about 20 minutes, and then buff up the surface with a soft cloth.

The ceiling of the entrance hall at Osterley Park is one of the many fine examples of coloured plaster which are the legacy of Robert Adam (1728-92), Britain's greatest exponent of the art. The ceiling was painted in soft distempers traditionally used to produce an even, flat finish.

CHOOSING THE MEDIUM

Painted plasterwork has a long and honourable tradition in interior decoration. The Frenchman Jean Cotelle published a series of designs for relief plaster ceilings in the seventeenth century, not all of which were plain white. Some had the details picked out in gold; others had coloured grounds, and many other ceilings were also coloured, often boldly, as were the mantles for fireplaces. At that time, soft blue, Indian red and ochre were popular colours. During the eighteenth century, however, when Robert Adam was engaged in designing Osterley Park (left), the taste was for a coloured ground with the relief plasterwork in white, often with a Grecian or Pompeian theme.

By the nineteenth century, however, a much richer colour palette had become the vogue, culminating in Victorian polychromy in which deep, rich, dark colours were combined to colour ornate designs.

To recreate a period feel, it pays to do some historical research, but for general purposes you can simply have fun playing with colours to create a range of pastiche effects. If you want the purity and clarity of the Adam look, then omit the tint from the final coat of liming wax, or leave the relief plaster white.

THE ESSENTIALS OF PAINTED PLASTER

DERIVATION

A bit of a mixed bag, this one. Incorporates elements of seventeenth-century painted plaster, with eighteenth-century Adam relief plaster and nineteenth-century polychromy. Take your pick!

SURFACES

Any plaster surface either in its natural uncured state or plaster that has been given a coat of white emulsion. The uncured plaster creates a deeper, more translucent effect, owing to its refractive index being altered by the water and shellac treatment. Literally, the surface is rendered more translucent.

PREPARATION

None, except to ensure that the surface is clean, free from dust and not flaky. Brush over lightly first to remove any surface dust, and then go straight into step 1 on unprepared plaster.

FINISHING

The wax coat, to which white pigment is added, tones down the colour but also burnishes it, giving it an attractive sheen on the parts of the plasterwork in relief. Adding a dark pigment to this coat will produce an antiqued effect.

Two shellacs were used together when wet; one standard pale brown and the other coloured by admixing raw umber pigment. This produced a random, softened patching with fine veins where the pigment ran out of the shellac with gravity. Over this I painted fine white marbling veins.

A thinned shellac produces a pale ground. Here it was stippled out as it dried to produce a mottled pattern, and waxed with white liming wax.

For an effect of old wood, two coats of shellac were applied. The surface was antiqued with a thinned liming wax coloured with raw umber pigment.

A mid-strength shellac will give warm, honeyed tones. This example is antiqued with liming wax tinted with red ochre pigment.

HINTS AND TIPS

* Experiment first with the colours on a piece of broken plaster cornice, because it is impossible to predict the final depth of the colour until you have gone through the whole process. You may need to make the initial paint colour stronger or weaker to achieve the effect you desire from it. Work your way through the whole process as the lining wax changes the colours so much.

* The addition of the raw sienna and raw umber pigments to the liming wax in step 4 gives the plasterwork an antiqued effect. The more you add, the older it will look. Experiment to work out the effect you require.

* If you are decorating a high cornice, to save a considerable amount of strain on your arms and neck, use a long handled soft-bristled broom for the buffing up element of the last step on page 115.

Combining media

Of all the techniques illustrated in this book, this one holds the key to invention; once you understand the principles, you will know how the most elegant and breathtaking finishes are performed. Although the effect emulated here is of old, coloured gesso, the colours used and even the processes described are not as important as the magical ingredient that makes this technique so effective; the use of differing materials.

YOU WILL NEED
Beeswax
Double boiler
Mixing surface
Trowel
Pigments (titanium white, red ochre)
Turpentine
Shellac
Artist's paintbrush
Casein paint
Clean soft cloths

1 *For liming wax, gently heat beeswax polish in a double boiler (see step 3, page 76) and add a small quantity of titanium white pigment (relatively harmless). While cooling, turpentine may be added to thin the mixture if it proves too stiff. For a pink wax, add some red ochre pigment to the mixture.*

2 *Paint the surface to be decorated with a coat of ordinary shellac admixed with red ochre pigment. Note how dark the colour is in shellac. When dry, apply a coat of casein paint thinned with some water to a single cream consistency. This will adhere very well to the shellac and will not ciss open on contact.*

3 When fully dry (allow a full 24 hours for casein paints) apply the liming wax, taking care to apply it fully into all the interstices. An imperfectly coloured batch will give rise to pleasing changes in colour on the surface of the object.

4 Immediately wipe off the excess wax with a clean soft cloth, leaving the wax in the recesses while vigorously removing it from projecting areas. Some of the casein paint will also be removed, revealing shellac. Leave the object for two days to allow the wax to harden and polish the surface with another soft cloth to produce a gesso-like sheen.

WHY DOES COMBINING MEDIA WORK?

The beauty of combining media is that paints of different provenances seem to perform so much more beautifully when they are brought together in particular combinations. This is precisely what happened with the example on the previous pages – a combination of shellac with water-based casein paint and beeswax (soluble in turpentine), applied one after the other. This established formula is almost identically repeated in the Painted plaster technique (see pages 114-7), and other examples of combining media appear in Dry brushing on pages 124-7 (using only shellac and acrylics), and Polite graining on pages 230-5 (another tried formula, that of alternating oil- and water-based layers).

What is most exciting about these combinations is that in every example cited above, the results defy analysis and it becomes almost impossible for the lay critic to understand how they were done. And yet the manual processes involved can often be simplicity itself and relatively unskilled, as is the case here.

The combinations seem particularly surprising since they appear to confound all popular opinion about how different media should 'not be mixed' and how 'water will not sit on oil'. But a fuller understanding of the chemistry of the materials reveals all; the best book on the subject is Ralph Mayer's *The Artist's Handbook of Materials and Techniques*. Once you have such an understanding, you will be able to develop and invent your own techniques because you will know why certain reactions take place between paint layers.

HINTS AND TIPS

* Note the specific use of colour in this technique and how the same red ochre pigment was used as a colorant in both the ground shellac and the finishing wax. The tonal progression to imitate a worn polished surface such as this is:

1 Dark ground
2 Bright mid-tone second coat
3 Pale tinted finishing coat, mainly removed.

For this effect, this formula can be repeated using any colour. Altering the tonal relationship between layers will radically change the character of the piece. Thus a process that starts light and ends as dark will appear antiqued or stained, and one where the brightest colour is applied last will appear broken and distressed. Extremely subtle effects, such as plaster, terracotta, wood and fantasy materials, can be achieved by using the different media, but in closely approximating colours.

* A full description of the chemistry and physics of different media cannot be gone into, but consult the media and solvents on pages 48-57 for a full summary. A few useful hints are as follows.

* When dry, alcohol-based products such as shellac will dissolve in alcohol again. Bear this in mind when building layers of shellac.

* Nearly all water-based media, including emulsion and acrylics, can be broken down again in alcohol (methylated spirits for example) when dry, or in products containing alcohol, such as shellac. However, the hardest acrylic varnishes resist this. The softer the binder, the easier it will dissolve.

THE ESSENTIALS OF COMBINING MEDIA

DERIVATION

It is surprising to learn that combination techniques were in use in fine and decorative painting as early as the Middle Ages. Vasari describes a form of easel tempera painting that had been developed in Flanders soon after 1400 and which often involved alternating layers of water-borne tempera with oil-or resin-based glazes. A sophisticated version of this even called for the application of egg tempera formulations directly into oil/resin glazes, a wet-on-wet technique.

SURFACES

Because combinations of materials will vary from technique to technique, it is not possible to list all the possible substrates that each technique will work on. Suffice to say that an average ground, and one that serves perfectly well for almost all experiments is a smooth non-absorbent coat of acrylic primer. This product should provide sufficient adhesion for anything and is not porous.

PREPARATION

If you are using acrylic primer, if should ideally be thinned and well brushed out to avoid brush marks. If shellac is your first coat, however, then you will be pleasantly surprised to find out just how many surfaces shellac will happily adhere to. It has excellent adhesive qualities and, for a simple natural varnish, is surprisingly resistant to abrasion when dry.

FINISHING

Oil- or water-based varnishes are popularly recognized as hardening finishes which will protect a surface, but oil-based products can severely darken other absorbent coatings such as casein paints or gesso. Beeswax polish is an excellent finishing material for dry paint, although wax will not tolerate a further coat of any material whatsoever; the latter will simply flake off.

* Water-based media that are known as 'soft' (gums and gelatine-type glues that can be used to make simple paints) will dissolve in water again when dry. Casein will do the same until such time as it has fully cured and is water-resistant.
* When dry, synthetic resin or oil-based products such as varnish and oil paint, will not dissolve in their own solvents but require much more pernicious petroleum distillates to remove them, such as toluene or xylene (highly toxic). Linoxyn, hardened and oxidized linseed oil, is, however, soluble in acetone.
* For other examples of combination techniques, look at the Ageing and Fake finishes sections of the book, particularly the following techniques: Craquelure (pages 162-5), Cracked paint (pages 166-9), Rubbed paint (pages 174-9), Peeled and chipped (pages 170-3), Polite graining (pages 230-5, Bronzing (pages 236-41) and Verdigris (pages 242-7).

SIMPLE MEDIA COMBINATIONS

These combinations are worth experimenting with; each layer should should be executed in a different colour. Many of these processes masquerade as other techniques in this book.

1 Coloured shellac – slightly thined acrylic emulsion paints rubbed or washed on – tinted liming wax.
2 Coloured or plain shellac – tinted liming wax.
3 Coloured or plain shellac – pigments in gum arabic – tinted oil varnish.
4 Flat or eggshell oil paint – beeswax polish.
5 Textured acrylic or emulsion paint – coloured beeswax polish.
6 Acrylic or emulsion paint – casein paint, rubbed back and polished when dry – beeswax polish, perhaps with colour.

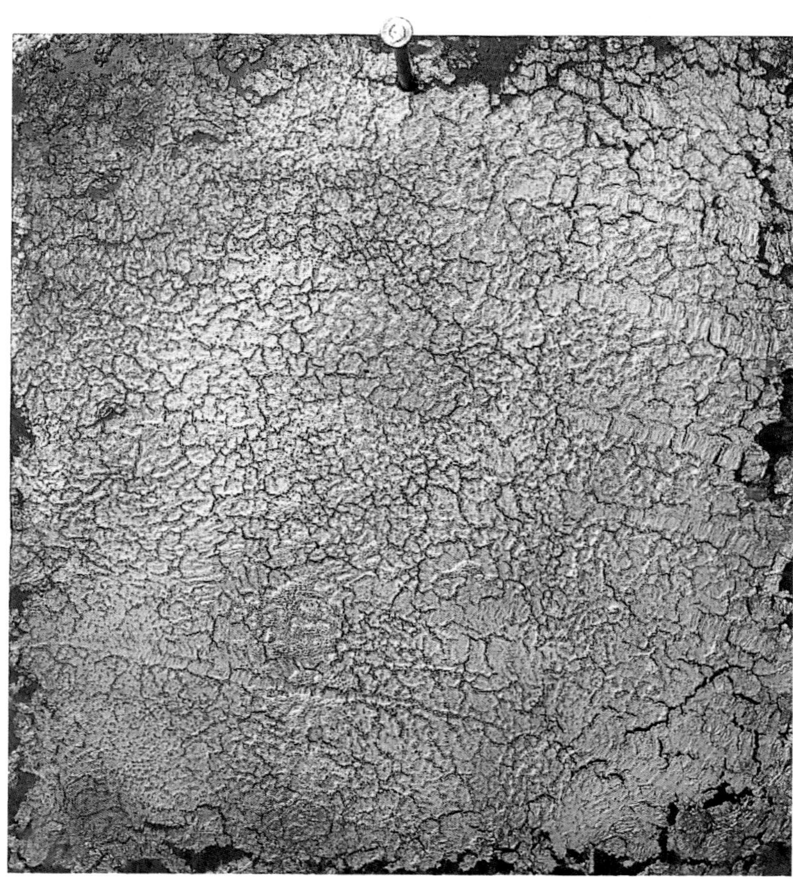

This fake cracked 'leather' panel, which appears to have been gilded, results from experimenting with the characteristics of different media that do not, at face value, like working with each other. Liquid gum arabic was generously applied over a dry dark brown emulsion paint. When fully dry, an orange-ochre emulsion paint (the colour of gilding bole) was thinned to double cream consistency, generously applied to a flat sponge and decisively and systematically sponged over the dry gum till the surface was covered. We knew that the top layer of emulsion would crack open with this process and also knew that the sponging on would yield a rough texture with good, random cracking over the next ten minutes. So, quickly, before the cracks had started to appear, the surface was sprayed with a thin layer of cellulose-based, decorative gold paint. This product was surface dry within seconds but it was sitting on an unstable coating of relatively thick, water-based paint. Since it acted as a barrier, the dried gold paint permitted the use of a dry cloth to gently dab at the surface and move the underlying layers around.

Finally, after 24 hours, when completely dry and quite stable, the entire surface was antiqued and protected with brown coloured wax. The result: a cracked gold, textured surface with occasional glimpses of bole colour and edges that had been disturbed during the drying process to appear broken and distressed.

Frottage

Although the term Frottage, meaning 'rubbing', is popularly employed for this technique, it is rather inappropriate. Strictly speaking, frottage is a taken rubbing such as a brass rubbing, and was adopted as a term by the early twentieth-century experimental artists such as the Dadaists, together with such unlikely sounding techniques as *coulage* (dripping) and *éclaboussage* (splashing and spattering). For this technique, then, I prefer the term blottage.

The effect relies simply upon the application of a layer of sheet material such as mutton cloth, newspaper, plastic sheeting or bubblewrap over an already painted or glazed surface. The end result relies on the way the blotting material is applied; this requires some experimenting. If a thinned oil paint, an acrylic scumble glaze or a coloured transparent oil glaze is used, the coating will take longer to dry and so more fluid effects can be procured.

Almost any sheet material can be used, and combination effects can be produced by double applications of the same material, or by mixing them. This is a technique where, more than any other, your own trials will produce the best results. As a tip, try paints or glaze on a non-absorbent ground. For example, red casein or gouache paint on a gold ground produces a deep and interesting effect.

Surfaces can be any non-absorbent, non-flaking surface such as oil-based or acrylic paint. The beauty of this technique is that no preparation is needed for the base coat; it is readily applied to any previously painted surface. Older, painted surfaces should, however, be washed down first to remove dirt and grease.

YOU WILL NEED

Base coat of paint
100mm (4in)-wide paintbrush
Sheeting material

1 *Begin by coating the area to be worked, ensuring that (particularly with water-based media) you are not too ambitious in this. If your blotting sheets are of a regular size, you may wish to paint an area, say half a wall, corresponding to an exact number of sheets. Since there will be joints in the pattern, these may as well also be the overlaps where painted areas meet.*

If an absorbent material is chosen for this technique, it is as well to slightly dampen it first with water or the appropriate solvent for the paint. This will aid its ability to blot the paint.

2 A damp piece of newspaper was laid over this wall which was first coated in casein-based red ochre water paint thinned to a milk-like consistency. The vertical line was left where two sheets had been applied separately. The effect on the left-hand side of the photograph, which appears less wildly textured, is produced by a second application of a clean damp sheet of paper, to blot more loose paint. The effect on the right resembles the pattern left by plastic sheeting.

3 A quite extraordinary effect can be produced with corrugated cardboard. Dampened slightly to increase their absorbency of the paint, sheets of the material are pressed firmly against the wet paint layer. The same red ochre casein paint was employed here as for the other effect; when dry, this paint takes on a dusty matt quality that when employed in this technique can appear as deep as velvet.

Dry brushing

No other paint technique has such a theatrical background as dry brushing; it is frequently used by prop makers. Perhaps it is for this reason that most decorators never consider using it in interior decoration. And yet the effects produced by it can be as subtle as any. The main charm of dry brushing derives from the chalky dryness it can render, or from the exaggerated depth of texture it can produce.

The technique featured on these pages illustrates how dry brushing can be employed as a purely decorative finish for objects in low relief such as wood carvings or plaster castings. The resultant effect suggests modelling of a much deeper nature and a clean scrubbed finish. This is due to the natural modelling of the item being exaggerated; full, deep colours are applied to the recesses and pale colours lightly applied to the projections. A poorly cast or made item can often be disguised in this manner, appearing as something quite delicate. It is for this reason that the technique has found such a home in the theatre, where textures need to be exaggerated to be visible from the back row, and poor-quality carving tricked up. I once painted a whole street of sham clapboard houses in this way.

Although well recognized for its use in theatre, film and television, this technique has also crudely made its way into shop displays and exhibition design. This debases one of its more noble provenances as a distemper-style decorative finish used on carving in the Baroque churches of Italy. There is no indication of when it was first used in this context, but sixteenth-century treatises on Italian theatre design make reference to the similarity between the structures and designs of scenery and florid church carvings of the period.

YOU WILL NEED

Shellac varnish
Pigments (yellow ochre, red ochre)
Artist's paintbrushes (medium, small)
Acrylic paint
Tissue paper or rag (optional)

1 *Quickly prime the item to be dry brushed (here, a resin casting) with shellac varnish to give a quick-drying coating. In this photograph, yellow ochre pigment has been mixed into the shellac. When this coat is dry, colourwash it with a thinned acrylic paint (this colour was produced by mixing red and yellow ochres together).*

2 *Delicately brush a second, paler but thicker coat (the consistency of single cream) of acrylic paint onto the raised and flat areas of the casting. It is imperative not to load the brush too heavily for this step. To make sure that only the minimum amount of paint is on the brush, work the bristles on a piece of newspaper before applying the paintbrush to the object.*

3 *Immediately soften this coat with your fingers, tissue paper or a rag. As the paints are water-based, don't work too large an area at a time, otherwise layers will dry too quickly and cannot be easily manipulated.*

4 *Finally, and with great delicacy, use a small brush to highlight the extreme edges of the object with a very pale colour. These additions must be applied with discretion; too much and the item may appear to have frostbite. For finishing, see The Essentials, overleaf.*

HINTS AND TIPS

* The technique demonstrated here is not absolutely traditional in that it employs coloured shellac as the first coat; this permits further coats to be more easily manipulated. To create a true, dry distemper quality, use casein or gouache paints.

* The effect shown appears powdery due to the gradual lightening of successive coats. For a charred effect, gradually darken the successive coats.

* We have successfully adapted this technique for exterior use on painted window surrounds to suggest stone using conventional exterior masonry paints. Three suitable colours are best, varying in tone from off-white to a dark stone colour representative of your area. Apply all three colours at once with separate brushes as a solid covering coat and wet-mix slightly once applied to the surface. When completely dry, two colours (the mid-tone and the light tone) are then re-used, but this time by very lightly dry-brushing them over lighter or darker underlying areas, as appropriate, using two separately loaded brushes. I have found this to provide an excellent imitation stone. But only use on concrete or stone items such as windows where the removal of previous coats of paint is either impossible or undesirable, and where a stone finish is appropriate or original. Do not be tempted to apply this method to old stone surfaces that you feel need renewing (see also Stone, pages 152-5).

* Equally, dry brushing can be effectively used to emphasize the grain of wood in a coarse variation of the technique that relies on a water-based first coat being applied to raise the grain. This can subsequently be delicately dry-brushed; a silvery grey ground with the dry brushing executed in a paler tint will emulate driftwood in a highly theatrical way.

* A development of dry brushing is that shown in Combining media (pages 118-21) where the first stages of dry brushing are repeated and then followed with other media.

Artificial texture can be produced on a smooth surface by dragging, or by manipulating a brush through a thick base coat. When dry, this paint will take dry brushing extremely effectively, emulating woodgrain or a distressed finish. In the case of linear dragged marks like these, always drag the bristles across the texture, only touching the raised areas of paint.

THE ESSENTIALS OF DRY BRUSHING

DERIVATION

Bernini adopted a great number of life-size models as trial structures in the decoration of St Peter's in Rome, including low-relief sculptures modelled onto wooden profiles and painted to simulate depth when viewed from a distance. Since until the last century the use of scenery was not restricted to the theatre but extended to festivals, pageants and even temporary buildings for the marking of state occasions (the first Arc de Triomphe was built from plaster and canvas in 1810 for the entrance of Napoleon and his second wife), it is reasonable to assume that such decorative painting techniques were viewed in much wider contexts than they are now. The use of dry brushing was certainly widespread in Italian rural church decoration by the nineteenth century, where it was employed mainly for reasons of economy.

SURFACES

Can be applied to any surface, whether it be prepared walls, bare plaster, metals or timber.

PREPARATION

Since the technique can be performed in virtually any medium, it suffices that each medium will require its own primer/undercoat. Most importantly, the primer/undercoat should be correct for the substrate; shellac for bare plaster, suitable oil or cellulose primers for metals, and a non water-based primer for timber. A water-based primer will raise the grain and so add more to the finished effect, if desired.

FINISHING

Generally, for authentic work, no finish is required. However, a coat of water-based matt acrylic varnish will seal the surface without changing its reflective quality and will harden the top paint layers. For a more delicate, cherished effect, beeswax polish may be applied and buffed up.

Reduced to its simplest form, dry brushing is simply the skill of laying on a delicate layer of paint with the side of a brush that has been lightly loaded, on a surface that ideally has some raised texture or form. I originally came across it in the theatre, where it is a widely used stock technique for exaggerating the textures of surfaces such as wood and plaster. All these swatches are entirely executed in dry brush.

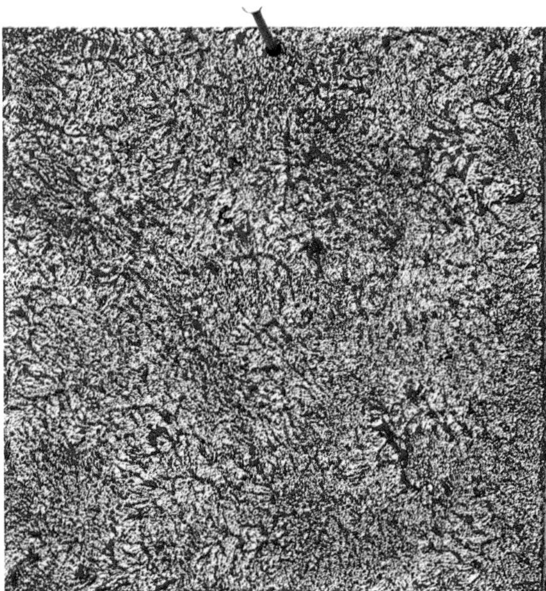

A stippled brown acrylic paint was left to dry and then several metallic paints (bronze, gold and copper) were lightly dry brushed over the surface, one at a time.

A similar brown surface was gilded with Dutch metal and dry brushed with red, black and beige acrylics. Beige was applied first and more heavily than the other colours.

We heavily painted this sludge blue sample, dragging the brush through the wet paint to ridge it. When dry, I then lightly dry brushed it with a red acrylic paint.

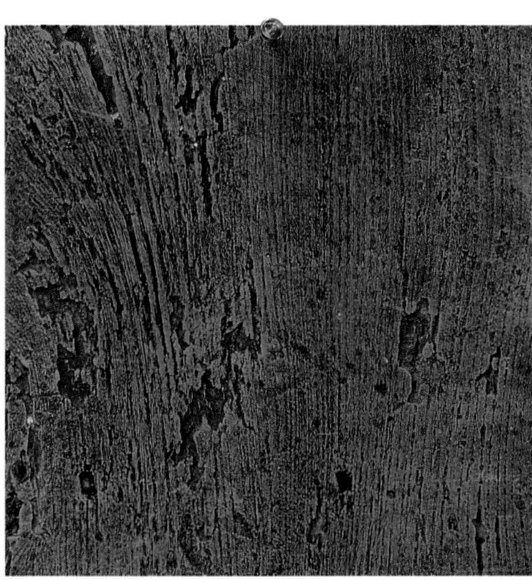

This ancient piece of elm board was dry brushed in grey and beige acrylic paint to deliberately emphasize the grain. This is a useful technique for artificially 'weathering' timber.

3 Reflective techniques

Reflective techniques

There is no doubt that paint effects that have extra, unusual qualities, such as added depth, transparency, texture or reflective sheen, exercise powerful effects on us. The combination of the pattern in the paint, both with colour and with aspects of the coating's surface, is a beguiling one, and this impact should be borne in mind when attempting to create new effects.

For a truly complex and successful paint effect, you should exploit the surface texture of your object or wall (even perhaps creating a texture) and think about the reflectiveness of the finished surface. Should the reflectiveness be gloss, matt or mid-sheen, or should it instead be wax that has been polished for an inscrutable depth and shine quite unlike that imparted by a varnish?

Reflectance has hitherto only been viewed as the last element of paint finishing – the quality of the final surface – and has never been considered as something that could form the essence of a technique. But it is high time we thoroughly exploited this innate quality of our materials; if nothing else, the few techniques in this chapter can form the starting point for a new area of experimentation.

EXAMPLES OF REFLECTANCE

Of course, experiments can be very simple. One of the easiest and most effective techniques that we developed using reflectance was for a shop down the road from Harrods in London. The brief was to do something inexpensive (as usual) but chic (also usual) in paint on the walls. We considered the standard choices, colourwashing, distressing, polished plaster, fresco work and so on, but they were all too costly or too hackneyed. Because the client was a wedding gift shop, we hit upon the idea of striping the walls to suggest a marquee interior, but this had to be done subtly. The obvious solution was to paint stripes, not in paint but in gloss varnish, onto a coat of dead matt colour.

The ground chosen was a warm, pale, yellowish-grey emulsion paint onto which 25cm (10in)-wide stripes were marked precisely out using a large ruler, spirit level and white chalk. The stripes were then painted

A simple and almost obvious advantage of highly reflective surfaces is that they can move the boundaries of a room. When faced with the challenge of a large restaurant in France that had a low, 20m (22yd)-long ceiling, we finished the entire place in a glossy nicotine-coloured glaze. The full-height windows are reflected in the ceiling, suggesting a much higher space.

freehand using an alkyd resin varnish. The wavy edging to the stripes added to their charm, and the choice of an oil-based varnish meant that the chalk guidelines, once varnished over, disappeared.

This story only goes to show how simple the invention of an effect can sometimes be. Indeed, there are some effects that rely simply on the inherent qualities of the basic materials used. Polished plaster, whether it be conventional sirapite or lime plaster, or a more sophisticated, coloured form such as stucco lustro, provides one such effect. Its attractiveness stems from the fact that the material is not totally opaque, like paint. Instead, it is microscopically crystalline, a feature that allows light hitting the plaster surface to be refracted through, as well as reflected off, the surface. When you look at a polished plaster wall, you are, in fact, looking through the top half millimetre of the surface. This optical effect is akin to that of looking at a wall on which several transparent glazes have been built up, but is more attractive because of the integrity of the material and the naturally occurring impurities and faults in the surface.

Limewash behaves in a similar fashion. Although it apparently dries back to a dense white, as it converts to calcium carbonate (on contact with the air), its surface is forming into a matrix of calcium carbonate crystals. The resultant effect is a surface with incredible sparkle and life because, again, the crystals are permitting the light to pass through them as well as bounce off them.

These simple effects are appropriate in the right context, but lend themselves little to classically decorated interiors. One of the more interesting (and very complex) effects using reflectance can be found on page 142 (top picture). At first sight, the gessoed walls seem to have been executed rather carelessly. In fact, the thickly brushed texture has been exploited to the full; the areas of low relief are a dusty pink, resulting from the mixture of pigment and chalk in the gesso, and matt. The raised areas, on the other hand, are polished and highly reflective, and as a result the gesso is much darker in these areas.

It would be fatuous to suggest that the decorator had meticulously planned this effect or even analysed it in terms of the interplay between reflection, texture and colour. He or she had probably seen it somewhere and felt compelled to reproduce it for its beauty. But it is interesting to analyse it in retrospect. Once we know how a paint effect is done, and what makes it work, we can reproduce it, and once we have mastered that, begin to play with it. You can't be a magician without first learning the tricks and then practising them hard.

Polished plaster pretends to be a natural and honest finish, but, of course, serves the role of 'covering-up' the really honest materials. Its true charm derives from its surface translucency. Note how the plasterer's trowel marks have been organized and incorporated into the design.

Lacquer

Nowadays the term lacquer is often used to describe an oil-based varnish, but traditionally it defines a much more painstaking process of building a succession of fine layers to create a completely smooth, sheeny finish. Shellac varnish (made from resin with a methylated spirit base) is traditionally used for the job because it allows you to work very fast. It dries quickly, taking only 15 to 20 minutes for each coat to dry, so you can apply the coats of varnish in rapid succession. It is the smoothness of the varnish and the number of the layers – normally about eight to ten of them – which gives lacquerwork its distinctive depth. Shellac varnish has the other distinct advantage of not discolouring with age, unlike linseed oil varnish.

A picture frame (ideally one without too much moulding), or some other small wooden object, makes the ideal starter project. The picture frame to the right, has been lacquered over a ground of Chinese red (vermilion casein paint to which red ochre powder pigment is added to produce just the right shade) decorated with gold bamboo and cloud pattern to resemble the original Chinese lacquerwork introduced into the West in the seventeenth century. The red ground was built by applying three coats of the Chinese red mix, each sanded with flour-grade sandpaper and the final coat polished with a linen cloth before the lacquering proper was begun. It is important that the surface on which you lacquer is as smooth and fine as possible. Original lacquerwork is sometimes done on a polished gesso base (see pages 90-5) for just that reason.

YOU WILL NEED

Casein paint
Pigment (red ochre)
Sandpaper (fine flour grade)
Linen cloth
Shellac varnish
Rubber (see Hints and tips, overleaf)
Linseed oil
Gold pen
Dipping pen
Gold ink
Rags
Methylated spirits

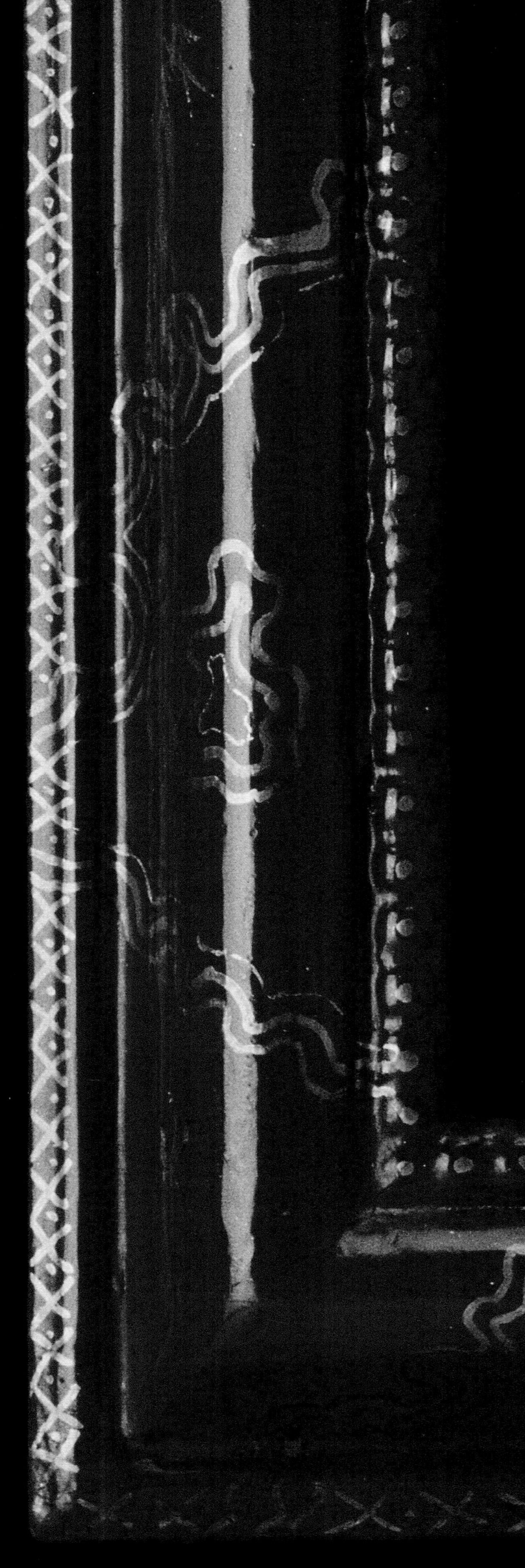

1 *Apply a thin layer of shellac with the rubber to seal the surface before decorating it. Using the flat of the rubber, dip it in the shellac and smooth it gently onto the frame. Use a very light pressure only, to avoid dragging up the surface; you are seeking a completely smooth, even finish with no marks.*

2 *Using the gold pen, decorate the ground with a chinoiserie-style pattern of grasses, bamboos or clouds. Any Chinese or Japanese book of ornament will give you inspiration for these patterns, or use simple geometric shapes such as lattice and dot patterns.*

3 *With the dipping pen and gold ink, add the finer details as required.*

4 *When the goldwork is completely dry, cover the ground with shellac, applied as in step 1, using as many coats as necessary (8 to 10 is quite normal) to create a completely smooth, lustrous finish.*

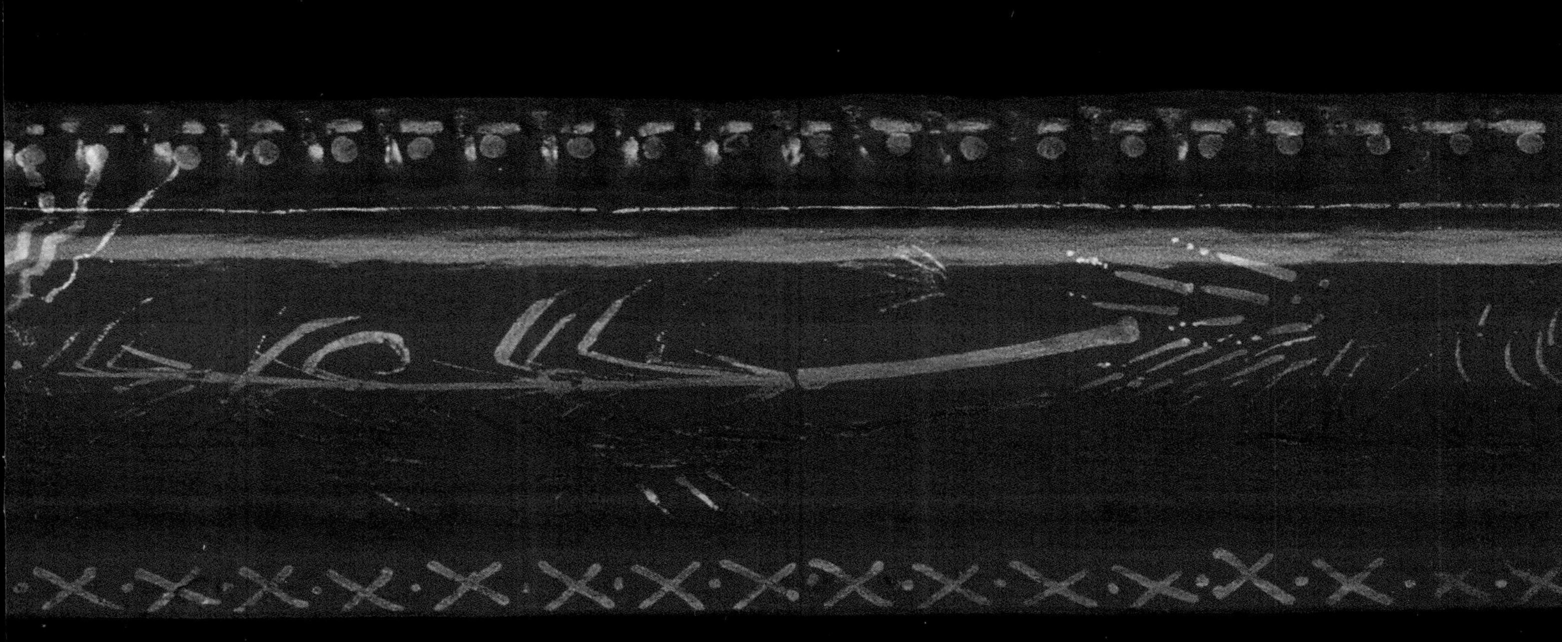

The rubber used for lacquering – it must form a smooth, round ball so that no marks are left when the shellac is applied to the surface. Normally, a small pad of cotton wool is enclosed in a piece of lint-free cloth (a piece of old sheeting is ideal), with the ends tucked in.

HINTS AND TIPS

* To make your rubber, fold a small square of the lint-free cloth around a small cotton wool ball. The rubber needs to be sufficiently small such that you can hold it between your thumb and forefinger, as shown above.
* A little linseed oil applied to the base of the rubber beforehand will help the shellac to flow.
* If you start to feel resistance to the rubber, you are overworking the shellac, which means the surface will streak and break up. In this case, gently, and extremely carefully, remove the current layer using a rag soaked in methylated spirits. If you wipe it quickly and lightly, it will not touch the already dried and hardened coats of shellac beneath.
* To get the right Oriental feel for the decoration, experiment first on a piece of card. This will help you not only to perfect the design but also to discover how the solvent on which the pen is based reacts with the shellac. If it is methylated spirit-based, it will dissolve in the shellac. If this happens, seal the goldwork with acrylic varnish before lacquering it.
* To perfect your lacquerwork, you can go over the ground very lightly with a linen cloth moistened with methylated spirits to remove any minor marks and blemishes. In the trade, this is known as flashing off.
* To create a particularly fine sheen, once the lacquer is bone dry, give it a coat of beeswax polish, applied with very fine grade wire wool. Buff up when thoroughly dry.

CHOOSING THE MEDIUM

Lacquerwork has a long and illustrious, let alone lustrous, history. It comes from the East, and the first examples were created using the resin of the sumach tree, to which cinnabar was added to create the traditional red colour, or charred bone meal to create the black versions. Normally, up to 12 base coats were required, the decoration would be added to this, and a further half-dozen or so layers

(RIGHT) *Original lacquerwork – nineteenth-century versions, and modern copies – all combine the techniques of both drawing or gilding straight onto a coloured ground (here black) and of building up the design in base-relief using gesso. Although painstaking, this is easy to do; build your gesso (following the technique on pages 90-5) by applying several coats to the areas you wish to be raised, such as the rocks and the bird in this example. When quite dry, it can be scraped, polished and gilded before the lacquering process is continued. Note that in every traditional case, the gilding is executed with gold or metal leaf, applied over some form of size to adhere it.*

THE ESSENTIALS OF LACQUER

DERIVATION

From the early seventeenth century, lacquerwork was imported from the Far East, and subsequently adapted in the eighteenth and nineteenth centuries to a less highly finished form.

SURFACES

Any very smooth surface that has been carefully prepared – polished gesso is ideal.

PREPARATION

Apply several coats of paint, each sandpapered smooth before the next is applied, to achieve the smoothest possible finish.

FINISHING

Polish with wax, using a lint-free cloth, to produce the maximum sheen on the finish.

of varnish would finish the piece. By building up the surface in this way, layer by layer, it acquired great depth and translucency, and, of course, great beauty. Needless to say, because it was so time-consuming, it was expensive and highly prized.

Lacquerwork imported from the East became all the rage in Europe from the seventeenth century right through to the end of the nineteenth century, and was often known as japanning (the technique having been refined and perfected in Japan in the seventeenth century but recreated in Europe in the eighteenth and nineteenth centuries with home-produced paints and varnishes). Boxes, chests, cupboards and wardrobes were all given the japanning treatment, often in black with a gold Chinese-style design. In the nineteenth century, japanned chests were extremely popular – one even plays a key role in the plot of Jane Austen's Gothic burlesque, *Northanger Abbey*. The term 'japanning' is used today to distinguish the European product, made from synthetic resin varnishes, from the original.

Cissed paint

Like so many other techniques, this is one that I developed from an accident. It relies on the play of light between a matt and a glossy surface and exploits the reaction known as cissing, the splitting and breaking action of thinned water-based paints when applied to a glossy, oily surface such as household gloss. You may use wildly radical colours or prefer, as I do, very similar colours that deceive the eye into perceiving just one paint colour with interesting modulations. Suitable as a wall finish (provided your walls are not of historic value, or are damp and need to breathe), it is also eminently suitable as a ceiling finish, as shown here, where the play of reflectance can be used to best advantage.

YOU WILL NEED

Emulsion or acrylic paint
Water
Container for mixing
Paintbrush
Rag or dry sponge (optional)

THE ESSENTIALS OF CISSED PAINT

DERIVATION

Technique exploiting the reaction of thinned water-based paints applied to a glossy, oily surface.

SURFACES

Walls and ceilings treated with a coat of gloss paint.

PREPARATION

If the surface is painted with water-based paint rather than gloss, rub linseed oil over the top and leave it to dry before cissing. Alternatively, coat with a gloss varnish.

FINISHING

Either leave wash to dry naturally or enhance the effect with a rag or dry sponge as described in step 3 (right). Do not varnish or wax polish as this negates the effect.

1 On a dry coat of gloss paint, brush out an emulsion or acrylic paint thinned to single cream consistency. Wait for the paint to ciss, or split open.

2 The consequent marks may be crude and show obvious brush marks, so experiment with the thickness of the paint. After a few minutes, you might also try re-brushing (but without loading any more of the paint onto the brush).

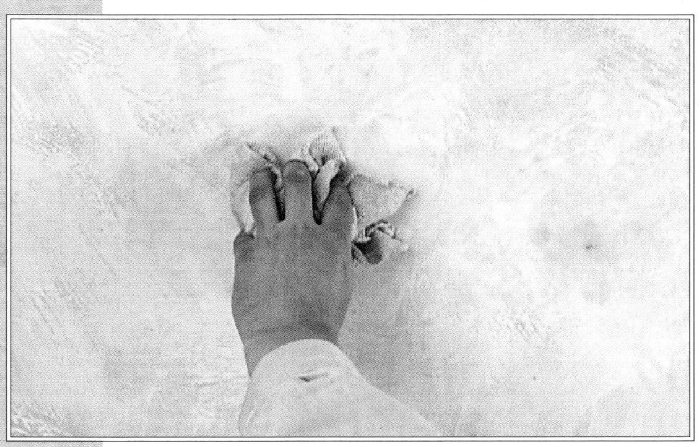

3 An extremely subtle finish can be obtained with a rag or dry sponge, used to move the paint around and blur brush marks. Again, this should be done a few minutes after the paint is applied. Surprisingly, when dry, the water-based paint will adhere extremely well.

Wax polishing

Waxing with a coating of burnished beeswax utterly transforms a painted surface, and this result cannot be underrated when compared to the finish obtained by mere varnishing. The process of applying and polishing wax adds depth and character to a paint film by rendering its surface slightly translucent and producing a soft reflective sheen that is quite seductive to the eye and to the touch.

Most surfaces will benefit from an application of beeswax polish, including plaster walls, decorative objects and painted furniture coated in gesso, oil paint, casein paint, acrylics or emulsion paints. The exceptions are soft paints such as distempers or gouaches that contain whiting which would be rendered transparent in the wax. It should also not be considered for surfaces that will receive regular re-coatings, such as plain walls, since the wax will almost permanently repel any attempts to coat it. Arguably, in this case, you should employ an acrylic wax: a non-buffing formulation of polymers and silicone waxes which will accept further paint layers once washed down and keyed back. Wax polish is also considered the *de rigueur* finish for French polished furniture, and lacquer and varnish coats that imitate these finishes.

Modern waxes are usually formulated as blends of beeswax (notable as a soft and flexible wax with an extremely pleasant smell), and small amounts of carnauba wax. The resultant mix is a wax that resists filming and cracking but that dries to a hard and permanent shine. In order to satisfactorily dissolve the waxes into a paste, some manufacturers have incorporated toluene as a solvent as well as the more conventional turpentine substitute (real turpentine has the strange effect of swelling and crystallizing beeswax). You should avoid any product that contains toluene; it is known to be a carcinogen.

YOU WILL NEED

Beeswax
Fine wire wool (grade 0000)
Clean, lint-free cloth

PREPARATION

The oak table top illustrated was given two coats of thinned shellac, applied with a tight cloth pad, or rubber (really a short-cut version of French polishing, where the shellac is built up in many layers), as a traditional preparation for waxing. An alternative and harder finish would be three coats of oil-based varnish prior to waxing, each of them systematically cut back with sandpaper when fully hardened, washed to remove dust produced during

1 *Most surfaces will be durable enough to accept an application of beeswax, not on a cloth but on a small pad of very fine wire wool. Apply sustained and firm pressure, working in figure-of-eight or circular patterns. The wire wool presses and integrates the wax into the top coat of varnish or paint and also serves to remove any remaining nibs in the surface.*

2 *Aim for the thinnest possible coating to avoid smearing; sadly, the best waxed effects on polished furniture result from many successive applications over months and years. Do not imagine that you will achieve similar results by larding on one single application! Instead, wipe off any excess with the lint-free cloth.*

3 Several days later, when the wax is completely dry and hard, polish it off. The longer you leave it, the more elbow grease is required, but equally the more impressive the finish. If polished too soon, wax will smear and mark. After several days, apply a second coat, but only with a cloth. Do not hasten this; dry wax on a surface still containing minute proportions of solvent is quickly broken down in a fresh application.

sanding, and then thoroughly dried before re-coating. When applying wax over varnish, ensure the latter is thoroughly hard; oil-based varnishes that are not fully cured will dissolve in the wax's solvents.

Do not be tempted to skip this preparation by substituting the use of wire wool for a good rubbing down with abrasive paper. The use of paper on a block ensures that a surface is rendered quite flat and faultless; wire wool under the fingers tends to ride the surface like a roller coaster and should only be considered as an abrasive in the smallest crevices and mouldings.

4 Textural techniques

Historically, architects and house owners have preferred not to use paint as a texturing medium on the interior of buildings. Interior decorative coatings such as distemper and even modern synthetic emulsions have always been perceived as friable and too weak to withstand heavy build-up. Besides, an interestingly textured surface has always been possible with other, more alluring, materials such as tapestries, silks and carpets (employed in early seventeenth-century Europe as tablecloths and chair coverings), and carved ornamentation in wood or modelled in stucco, cast plasterwork and composition.

However, on the exterior of buildings, paint, stucco and plaster have contrived for many centuries to provide textural surfaces. For example, columns at Herculaneum, although structurally of brick, are dressed with stucco to resemble a variety of materials, chiefly marble and stone, and this tradition has persisted into the twentieth century. Traditional and modern buildings in the centre of Paris are often coated with a pale brown-grey strengthened *platre*, or gypsum plaster. This simulates stone in the form of blockwork, courses or simple large areas that are scraped with a steel-toothed trowel to resemble the texture of limestone. A whole industry has now grown up in France dedicated to manufacturing and applying cement-based renders to simulate stone. They are sprayed onto the external shell walls of buildings, whether constructed of blockwork or poured concrete, and then scraped to a variety of desired finishes.

Contemporary interiors accept textured walls particularly well. This example was stippled and scraped over most of its surface. The intaglio design was executed in plaster that had been very thickly applied in that area.

Gesso requires that it is applied warm, making it cumbersome to use. However, as a textural finish it is unsurpassable, particularly if rubbed and polished on the highlights to create a variety of reflective surfaces and changes in colour.

THE VALUE OF TEXTURAL COATINGS

Here it is worth mentioning the role of such coatings, not least because, with care, they may be translated and usefully exploited for indoor use. The first (and most important use outside) is to protect the building against the ravages of weather and to prevent softer surfaces beneath from being damaged. This principle is now adopted by conservationists, who, for example, may apply a coat of limewash to the exterior of a building or even statue as a 'sacrificial coating' to wear the worst of the weather and gently erode away.

Second, texturing materials have always served to hide cheap construction methods. Just as a coat of plaster tricks us into believing that a room is of immaculate construction, so a coat of render on the outside of a Palladian eighteenth-century mansion often conceals shoddy brickwork that may be of such poor material that it is very often highly porous. Of course, not only does the coating hide the construction method and allow for an inexpensive building, it can also be made to look like yet something else again, often stone. On some East Anglian buildings, a more honest approach was not to fake another material but to model the material into low-relief patterns and lettering.

Third, the use of a texturing material on the outside of a building strikes up a relationship between it and directional light. The effect of sunlight on a textured surface is infinitely more interesting than that on a smooth one, and as the sun wheels around during the day, so the shadows it creates on texture bring a surface to life. This is nowhere more so than on a coating that is self-coloured; one where individual particles of pigment or sand, for example, are clearly visible, and the material is already granted some surface interest.

TEXTURAL COATINGS IN INTERIORS

This last characteristic is perhaps the most interesting in interior decoration. Two of the illustrations on these pages (above left and right) clearly demonstrate the play of light on texture. In the case of the red gesso wall, the material when rubbed takes on a polish it does not possess in the rough, thus combining shadow and relief with tricks of reflectance.

What is also especially satisfying about these two interiors is how much the textural effects contribute to the character of the rooms, and how effortless it all seems. Neither technique has any real historical antecedent, yet merely the use of traditional materials such as gesso or plaster to texture a wall suggests the technique may have a full pedigree. It is as though the natural and venerated qualities of these materials help to impart character.

This is perhaps the secret of texture; that when executed in 'real materials', plaster, stucco, papier mâché, gesso or even lime mortar, it is possible to see and feel the qualities of the material used. Plastered surfaces, when waxed, are not entirely opaque and so refract the light in a subtle translucency. When textured, gesso preserves its character as a powdery, chalky material, while taking a burnish on its highlights. And yet these same materials can appear dead and dull when coated with a flat paint, particularly if the coating is a synthetic one of absolute perfection and even colouring.

Texture is the most underrated tool in interior decoration. Our forebears used it madly, on leather panels, in stonework and rough interior renders, in flock wallpaper and even in graining (English Heritage have discovered 'textured' patterns as part of some late seventeenth-century woodgraining techniques at Cogges Manor farm in Oxfordshire). Today, its use has sadly been reduced to puffy vinyl wall coverings and plastic leatherette car dashboards, and so proper interior decoration is crying out for greater use of texture. If paint techniques are to develop anywhere at all, it must be in this direction.

Textural techniques need not be coarse. Subtle marks left by the plasterer's trowel can be emphasized with a colourwash afterwards. However, the trowel marks left by a cowboy plasterer somehow don't look the same.

Texturing

The illustrations on these pages are not intended as step-by-step stages but as variations on how to introduce textural effects as part of decoration on both walls and furniture. Further, coloured, effects are shown overleaf, and the successive two techniques of Leather and Stone (on pages 148-51 and 152-5) illustrate successful and more formal applications of texture in paint techniques imitating other materials.

Although raised and moulded patterns ought to be modelled in a material fit for the job, such as plaster or gesso, low-relief texture is quite possible using paint alone (see also Leather, Rubbed paint [pages 174-9] and Bronzing [pages 236-41]) or paint admixed with a neutral filler or extender such as talcum powder or powdered rottenstone to provide the paint with more body.

Experiment with materials and tools used to make the marks; many of those used in Frottage (see pages 122-3) can be transferred to this technique.

Be extremely cautious about applying texturing media to walls of old houses, since their strong adhesive power could damage any underlying paint coats of historical interest. Also, such coatings are usually quite aesthetically unsuitable for historic interiors. Remember, that unlike paint, texturing coats are very difficult to remove. If in doubt about the historical value of your house, consult your local historic buildings officer.

If you worry about having to indefinitely retain textured walls, consider making canvas wall hangings upon which you can apply the texture. Equally, polished, valuable furniture and originally painted furniture should never be coated as the process will inevitably destroy what has gone before.

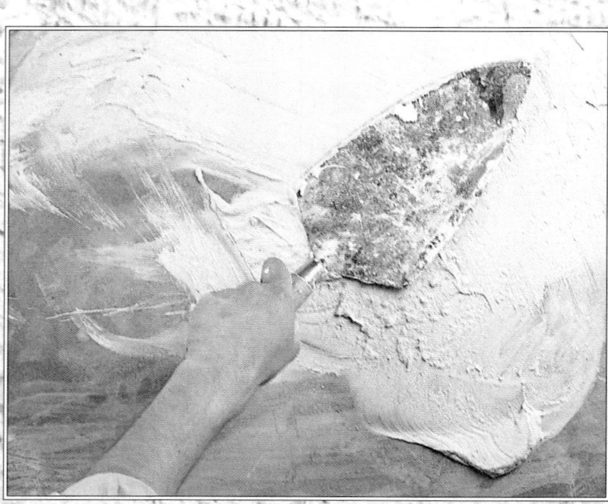

1 *THE TEXTURING MEDIUM*
On a suitably prepared surface (see The Essentials, overleaf), apply the texturing medium. Here I used decorator's white plaster (not plaster of Paris, which sets too quickly) mixed with a little PVA glue to both strengthen it and extend the working time. An alternative would be a proprietary smooth texturing medium from a DIY store.

STIPPLING AND SCRAPING
Fascinating and subtle effects can be produced by using more than one tool on the surface. Try a combination of stippling and scraping: the brush first textures the surface, which, when barely touch dry, is then carefully scraped with a wetted trowel to smooth out the peaks. This forms the basis of fake stonework.

CRUDE STIPPLING
Much cruder effects are obtainable with proprietary tools such as this rubber stippler intended for use with brand-name texturing media – the kind of things builders put on ceilings. However, if the surface is repeatedly gone over as it dries, interesting random effects result.

RUBBER ROLLING
A rubber roller is a tool that in the wrong hands can produce very tame work. If used on a wall or ceiling, allow yourself to make the largest possible marks with it, and plan the layout of such patterns beforehand. There is great potential for psychedelic work.

DRAGGING AND SCRAPING
In this combination technique, the roller is dragged over the medium to produce long, striated peaks. When almost dry, I scraped the surface with a wetted trowel and then incized lines to produce an effect quite similar to coarse woodgraining.

MARRYING THE SURFACE AND THE MEDIUM

It is important that the correct coating is applied to each type of substrate, as follows:

Bare wood

Gesso, modern proprietary texturing media from DIY stores, PVA gesso (see pages 90-5)

Painted wood or walls

PVA gesso, plaster strengthened with PVA, proprietary texture coatings. If the paint is water-based and it is also particularly absorbent, you may find it will receive gesso.

Bare walls

All of the above plus plaster, provided the surface is well keyed.

HINTS AND TIPS

* If employing paint thickened with a powder such as talcum, always coat the substrate first with a layer of the unthickened paint and allow to dry, since the addition of powdery extenders can affect a paint's penetrating and adhesive properties.

* I have always found the use of gesso-type texturing media to be the most satisfactory, partly because they are easier to handle and partly because they are tough when dry and will polish well. Standard gesso is good for furniture, but clumsy to prepare for large areas, which can be covered with a mixture of whiting sifted into dilute PVA to form a thick paste. Alternatively, plaster may be mixed with water containing anything from 10 to 30 percent PVA or acrylic binder. The addition strengthens the plaster considerably but also slows down the hardening rate, so permitting a longer working time. This recipe is not that much different from Cennini's recipe for gesso, which did not call for whiting but for gypsum plaster (plaster of Paris) that had been repeatedly soaked in water and ground up to 'take the heat out of it' and render it much less powerful as a plaster.

* You may also consider using papier mâché for texturing media,or chewed paper as one eighteenth-century gentleman disparagingly called it. Papier mâché's chief advantages are its cheapness and its light weight when dry. Traditionally, either a mashed-up paper and glue mix was pressed into a mould or the paper was pasted into the mould in strips. It is a surprisingly undervalued technique, since much of the eighteenth- and nineteenth-century decoration that we see in grand houses is made from papier mâché masquerading as plaster or stucco. We have had a bit of fun modelling the material for simple sculptural shapes, especially on walls where it is useful to mix together plaster and glue (preferably hot size or gelatine glue) to make a creamy paste before adding the wet pulp. The resultant mix should be well blended and sticky. In this way, the mixture will adhere better and not run down the wall so easily when applied.

THE ESSENTIALS OF TEXTURING

DERIVATION

Decorators and architects have relied upon textural techniques for thousands of years. On the exterior of buildings it is worth noting two unusual examples; the seventeenth-century practice of flinging tiny crystals of cobalt blue glass onto wet paint to produce a sparkling finish for metalwork known as smalt blue; and the venerable tradition of sprinkling sand and stone dust onto wet paint to fake real stonework, as practised in eighteenth-century Europe.

Cennini describes how easel painters have from the earliest times, carved and modelled their gesso grounds before painting and gilding in a process known as pastiglia, and early Renaissance panel paintings demonstrate how often this was done beneath haloes, jewellery and, in the case of some paintings, over the entire surface to include figures and drapery to suggest depth.

SURFACES

Any surface will do for this technique and it need not be of perfect smoothness. All that is required is that the substrate is clean, grease-free, strong enough to bear the weight of the coating, and that it will provide enough adhesion.

PREPARATION

Any ground that is going to receive a heavy coating will need a lot of preparation. Smooth, non-absorbent surface should be scraped or incized to provide a key and then coated with an intervening layer of the binder present in the texturing coat such as PVA or a gelatine-type glue if you are using gesso (see pages 90-5), at near-to-full strength. If you had planned to use pure plaster, then mix it with PVA to aid adhesion and plasticity. Absorbent surfaces should be first coated with a much more dilute coat of the binder present in the texturing coat or, in the case of plaster, water.

FINISHING

Bare plaster may be beeswaxed and polished, varnished or shellacked. Each will produce a different tint, and the easiest solution is to part-seal the plaster with a very dilute PVA and then beeswax. Plaster may also be stained, pre-coloured with pigment, washed over with paint or coloured with a tinted wax (this is particularly controllable if the surface is partly pre-sealed).

Gesso may be waxed, and generally most texturing media benefit from the application of polish or a dilute plastic coating such as PVA or thinned acrylic varnish to seal the surface and keep them clean.

Gesso can provide excellent and subtle effects. Here, a tinted cream gesso was dragged through with a metal comb (a saw blade will do). When dry it was sanded and then washed over with thinned yellow ochre and raw sienna paints. We executed this technique on a 1950s' panelled room to great effect.

A popular effect is that of stucco lustro, where coloured gessos are built up on a wall before polishing and waxing. The result is beautiful, but laborious. This poor imitation relied on trowelling on a thin layer of plaster, mixed with dilute PVA and powder pigments, which was worked into a part-dried coat of white plaster.

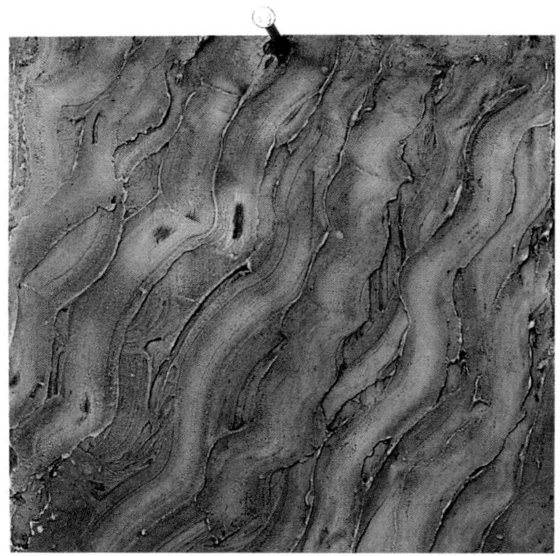

A wildly combed white plaster was stained with ink, which was absorbed at different rates, according to how dry the plaster was when the ink was applied. Use inks that are lightfast and which will resist the alkaline plaster. Or use alkali-resistant stains.

To achieve a fresco-like quality that is particularly beautiful when waxed, two or three batches of texturing medium were mixed, each a slightly different colour. They were then applied and trowelled together on the surface.

Leather

This textural technique is one in which the look of old leather is recreated with paint, and could be used successfully to imitate the surface of an old leather screen, for example. The base paint required for it is a water-based emulsion or casein paint (see page 78) tinted with raw or burnt umber to achieve a chocolate brown shade, or use an acrylic paint.

It is important to use a water-based paint because it creates the cracked finish that is essential to the look. The cracking occurs when you apply a water-based paint over a layer of gum arabic, as part of a physical reaction between the two. The layer of gum arabic absorbs the water from the paint, causing the paint to shrink while the gum expands.

To obtain the effect illustrated here, I sprayed the paint through a piece of damask-woven (and rather expensive) lace, which is stretched tightly across the surface and fixed in position to keep it taut. As you can reuse the lace time and again, it is worth spending a bit more for a really attractive fabric. This technique was worked over a wooden surface.

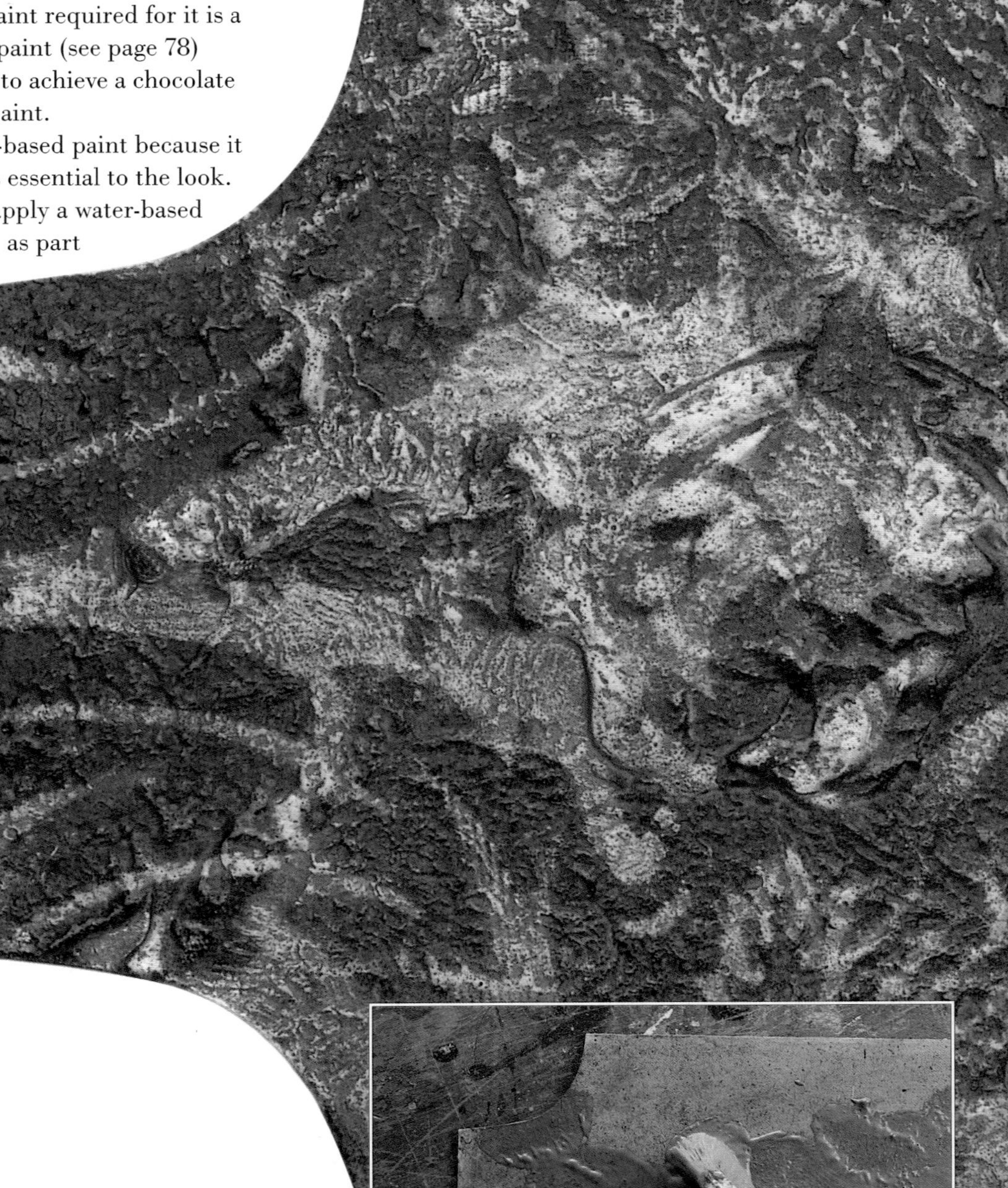

YOU WILL NEED
50mm (2in)-wide paintbrush
Shellac
Methylated spirits
Gum arabic
Emulsion paint
Piece of lace
Tacks or repositionable adhesive
Gold aerosol paint
Beeswax polish
Pigments (yellow ochre, raw sienna, burnt umber)
Sandpaper

1 *First seal the wood by painting on a coat of shellac thinned with methylated spirits to a runny consistency. Leave to dry and then thickly coat with liquid gum arabic. Allow to dry again before applying a thick coat of emulsion in rough swirls to form a relief pattern.*

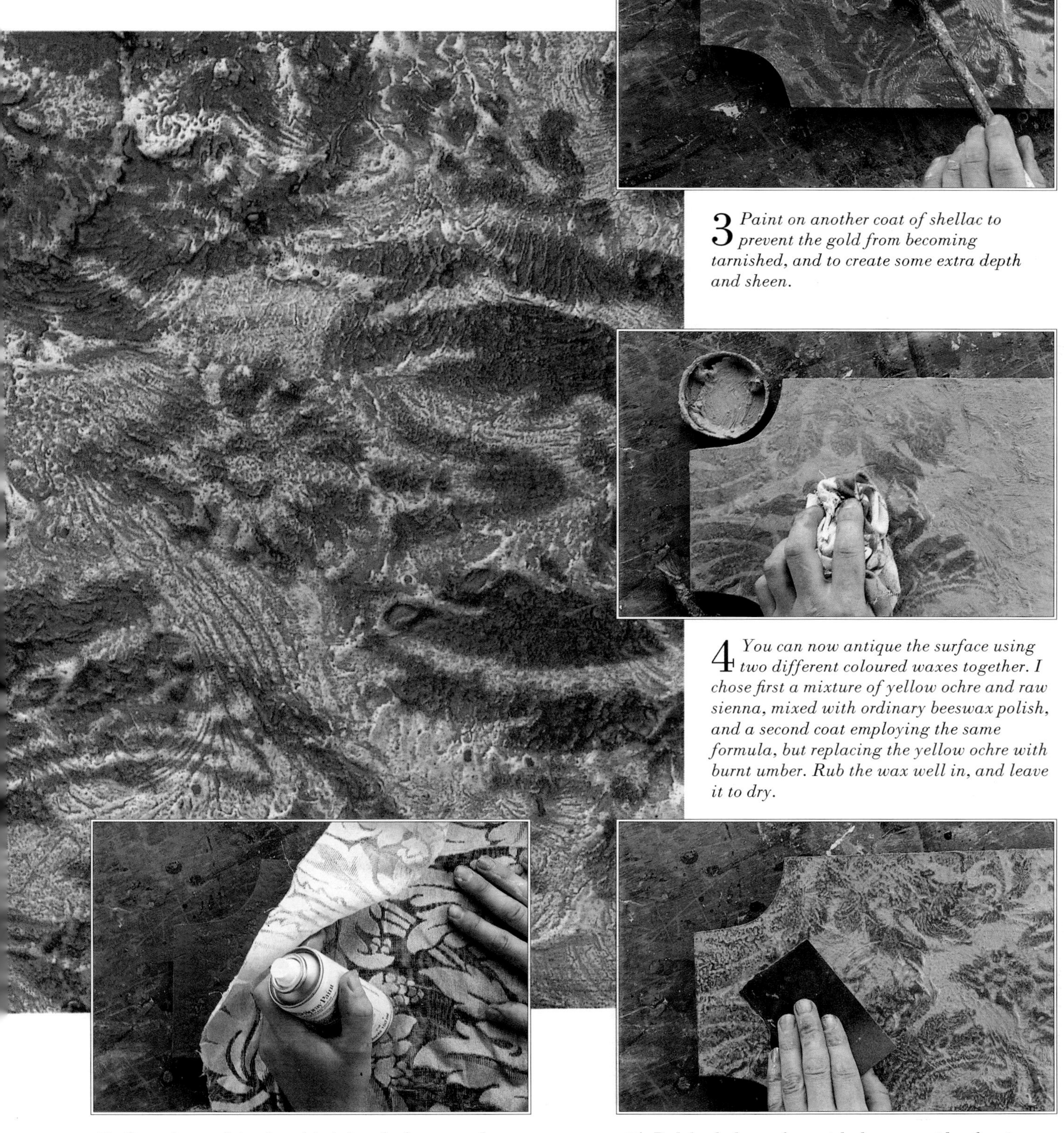

3 *Paint on another coat of shellac to prevent the gold from becoming tarnished, and to create some extra depth and sheen.*

4 *You can now antique the surface using two different coloured waxes together. I chose first a mixture of yellow ochre and raw sienna, mixed with ordinary beeswax polish, and a second coat employing the same formula, but replacing the yellow ochre with burnt umber. Rub the wax well in, and leave it to dry.*

2 *Once the emulsion has dried, lay the lace over the surface and hold it in place with tacks or repositionable adhesive. With the aerosol of gold paint, spray the surface through the lace. Reposition the lace as necessary until all the surface is covered. Allow to dry.*

5 *Rub back the surface with the paper side of a piece of sandpaper (ie very fine blotting paper), which will highlight the surface of the texture, leaving the wax in the grooves. This will give it a naturally worn and polished appearance.*

CHOOSING THE MEDIUM

The colours used in the technique on the previous page will create the rich nutty appearance of old leather of the kind found on old Victorian sofas and screens. If you want a different colour, there is nothing to stop you from creating a deep green or wine red ground instead, but make sure that the colour you use as the base has some yellowish and dark browns added to it, to give it the naturally aged and weathered look of old leather.

By swirling the base coat of paint on the surface (the paint must be sufficiently thick to keep its shape when used in this way), you create the texture of leather. This is important, because, without the raised areas of paint, the wax won't adhere to the interstices – the crannies – an important element in the 'tanned' appearance. Using an attractive piece of lace as a mask to spray through is another vital part of the process.

Painted leather finishes create an amazingly effective alternative to the real thing, at a fraction of the price. Paintings of Dutch interiors in the seventeenth century illustrate the popularity of gilt leather hangings and furnishings, often with wonderful embossed patterns in gold leaf. In Italy in the early eighteenth century, chairs were often covered in damask leather which was leather stamped with a scorched pattern achieved using a wood block and a hot iron plate applied under pressure. Modern damask fabrics (and the damask pattern lace I used on the previous page) reproduce these old designs and are ideal for the purpose of recreating damask leather.

Alternatively, you can copy the Italian idea using any attractive relief pattern (such as an old wood block for textile printing) pressed into the wet paint (in Step 1) and then gilded as opposite. This could form a one-off central motif on a panel, or a more complete general pattern.

This Dutch interior of 1631 clearly shows a leather-clad wall gilded and stamped with large-scale repeat patterns. This expensive and exclusive form of decoration made its way through Europe in the seventeenth century to be imitated in the early eighteenth century by handblocked wallpapers.

HINTS AND TIPS

* Make sure the paint is really thick for the base coat, so that you can create small peaks and troughs as you swirl it over the base surface, with generous sweeps of the brush.
* If your paint is too thin, sift some whiting into it, stirring to thicken.

THE ESSENTIALS OF LEATHER

DERIVATION

This technique derives from seventeenth- and eighteenth-century gilt leather, whether Dutch or Italian in origin. It was used for wall hangings, screens and for furniture, such as leather armchairs. The gold used then was far more costly gold leaf: today gold spray paint is a much cheaper alternative.

SURFACES

Use this technique for panels and screens. In theory, you could also apply it to a fairly thick cloth stretched tightly over a frame. But don't apply any pressure on it (such as trying to sit on it, for example) as this would cause the paint to crack. Leather is not a particularly durable finish, so use it for decoration only.

PREPARATION

Any wooden surface may be used, provided it has been primed before you apply the paint. You could also work the technique on sized canvas for, say, a screen.

FINISHING

Since you have applied wax to the surface, you cannot varnish it with an acrylic water-based varnish. Ideally, however, simply rewax the surface from time to time. For a tougher finish, substitute varnish, coloured with pigment, for the wax in step 4.

This texture was built up with gesso after the cast detail had been glued onto the panel with gelatine glue. It was then painted green and coated with oil-based varnish. The design was gilded using Dutch metal and a water-based acrylic size and the gilding then distressed by rubbing with methylated spirit. Finally, the surface was antiqued with beeswax mixed with raw umber pigment.

This is a variant of the standard technique shown on the previous pages, but using much darker paint. The surface was also highly polished with wax when the oil paint was completely dry (normally takes one week).

Exactly the same colours and process was used for this swatch, but the paint was stippled on and not 'swirled' in such a thick impasto. The result is a much more subtle effect, suitable for small objects or surfaces with relief patterns or mouldings.

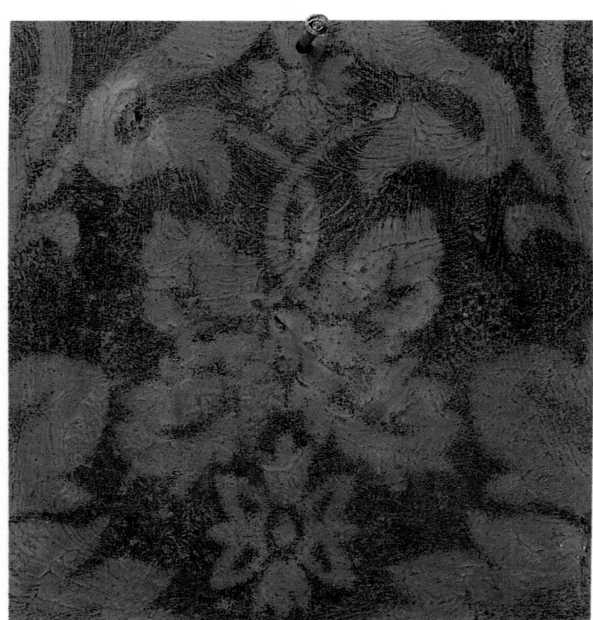

The pattern has been reversed here, and the image sprayed on in dark blue-green paint over an ochre-textured ground. So that the effect did not become muddied, no antiquing oil paint was applied, but the surface was abraded with sandpaper to disguise the spray marks.

Stone

Stone as an effect relies on some of the texturing techniques outlined earlier in this chapter allied with ordinary colourwashing skills. Although this is a finish which has often been taught and written about, there are developments and subtleties of the process that have not been discussed before and these deserve looking at.

Importantly, the colour and texture of the stone you may produce yourself is entirely variable, according to whim and what finished effect you are looking for. I have chosen here a heavy texture and medium colouring to simulate fossil limestone; a lighter stipple would suggest a stone with a much more dressed surface.

1 *On a suitably prepared and primed surface (see Stippling on pages 108-9), brush out a texturing coat of your preferred material as in Texturing (pages 144-7). Stipple roughly with a tool or coarse brush.*

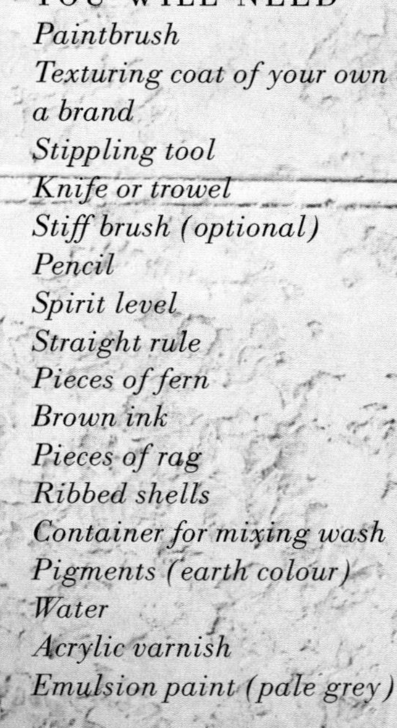

YOU WILL NEED
Paintbrush
Texturing coat of your own or a brand
Stippling tool
Knife or trowel
Stiff brush (optional)
Pencil
Spirit level
Straight rule
Pieces of fern
Brown ink
Pieces of rag
Ribbed shells
Container for mixing wash
Pigments (earth colour)
Water
Acrylic varnish
Emulsion paint (pale grey)

2 *Before the coat has dried, but while it is still damp and crumbly, scrape a knife or trowel over the whole surface. This flattens the peaks and establishes a large area of planed material that resembles rough-cut stone. It may then, optionally, be re-stippled with a stiff, coarse brush.*

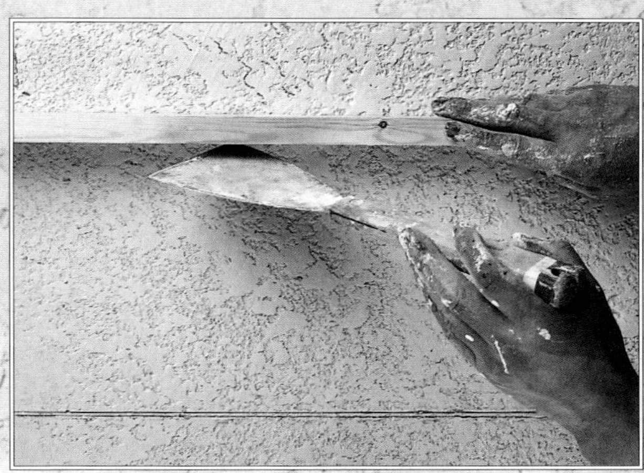

3 *Using the pencil and spirit level, mark out lines onto the damp surface to simulate blockwork, making the blocks as large or as small as you wish (horizontal lines alone provide a graphic and rather interesting Egyptian design). Then, using the trowel and straight rule, incise the lines into the surface.*

4 *To imprint the marks of ferns to fake fossil limestone, take a real fern (the more feathery the better) and dip it in brown ink. Then blot it between two pieces of rag to remove excess ink, and press firmly onto the damp surface. Blot the fern again with the paper, this time on the surface, before removing it. The print may be washed out with water or sanded half-away when dry.*

5 *Another conceit is to roll real shells (any well-ribbed variety) into the damp surface to create a fossil-like impression. Since these prints need not be specially coloured afterwards, you may throw caution to the wind and print as many as you want.*

(ABOVE LEFT) *In contrast to the photo-graph opposite, this blockwork was execut-ed with total precision and delicacy. Note how the tonal range of blockwork, high-lights and shadows is very narrow, almost pastel. This counters the strong, almost brutal, architectural nature of the design.*

(ABOVE RIGHT) *In this decorative scheme by Christophe Gollut, the stone blocking has been simply executed in softening glazes, but then theatrically*

THE ESSENTIALS OF STONE

DERIVATION

A modern invention with little historical antecedent. In the eighteenth and nineteenth centuries, stone or blockwork was internally executed in a variety of media, employing several techniques such as frottage, spattering and softening. In all cases, these produced a surface without texture.

SURFACES

Any surface will do for this technique and it need not be of perfect smoothness. All that is required is that the substrate is clean, grease-free, strong enough to bear the weight of the coating, and that it will provide enough adhesion.

PREPARATION

Any ground that is going to receive a heavy coating will need a lot of preparation. Smooth, non-absorbent surfaces, should be scraped or incized to provide a key and then coated with an intervening layer of the binder present in the texturing coat, such as PVA. Absorbent surfaces should be first coated with a much more dilute coat of the binder present in the texturing coat or, in the case of plaster, water.

FINISHING

When dry, paint the surface with washes of earth pigments (raw umber and raw sienna make two good, separate washes) bound with acrylic water-based varnish or binder (about 10 percent). Consider also picking out the joints between the blocks in a pale grey acrylic or emulsion paint to simulate mortar.

exaggerated by tinting the blocks with different coloured glazes. The theatricality is furthered by the choice of a big repeat.

HINTS AND TIPS

* A variety of tools can help you draw vertical and horizontal lines such as a plumbline, rule and a spirit level. I prefer to use a long spirit level, or a short one firmly taped onto a long rule or stick.
* It may also pay to mark out the walls first, just roughly, to gauge an idea of how large your blocks should be and where the problem areas might be, such as around doorcases.
* Look at the Dry brushing technique on pages 124-7 for further ideas on how you might colour your work once it has dried. By combining the two techniques you will get away with applying a much less thick coat of texturing medium.
* Traditionally, interior walls were not decorated with this technique, but by using glazes and paints in a trompe l'oeil fashion. Techniques that were used included Frottage (see pages 122-3) whereby sheets of paper or fabric were laid against the wet paint producing a mottled effect. Experiment with different media – plastic sheeting laid against water glazes will produce effects similar to fossilstone.
* Softening glazes (see pages 112-13) and spattering techniques were also adopted to simulate stone, sometimes in a crude and vague form.
* Both on painted and textural examples, the lines can not only be incized but also coloured. Anything from paint to felt-tipped pens can be used, but avoid black. Pencil crayons provide fine broken lines on flat, painted work that are very pleasing, and very pale grey paint looks excellent, suggesting lime mortar, and transforming the stonework effect quite radically.
* This particular technique does have one or two eighteenth-century precedents, but only on the outside of buildings. For a long time it has been common to texture and delineate render in imitation of stonework, but at Mount Vernon, Washington's home, Ian Bristow has noted that the exterior carved and heavily chamfered 'fake' stone blocks, made from timber, were painted and then strewn with sand while the paint was wet. Worth trying, it is an obvious antecedent for pebbledash.

5 Ageing techniques

Ageing techniques

This chapter, above all others, reflects the incredible surge of interest in this kind of painting that has taken place over the last eight to ten years. It seems strange that so many people feel they need to own battered and beaten-up pieces of painted furniture. I suspect that beneath our progressive exteriors we hanker for our heritage and need to be able to place ourselves, whether in a family tree, a place or a class. Antique possessions help this process of identification, and painted furniture particularly so, since it offers such a wide variety of finishes and colours that the pieces can easily be placed in our decorative schemes. So, the acquisitive message is clear; if you can't inherit any, buy it; and if you can't buy it, fake it.

Moreover, there are one or two practical advantages to be gained from employing these forms of decorative paint techniques. The shortest route to obtaining an 'historical' effect is to choose from a traditional palette of colours such as those employed in this book, and intermix them. Off-white inevitably looks older than brilliant white, and most colours can be 'broken' by the admixture of an earth colour or two, such as raw umber (most widely used) or raw sienna. Similar effects can be achieved by the addition of a small amount of a colour's complementary shade. Such softened or dirty colours are intrinsically pleasing because of their complexity and the fact that they tend to the neutral. The inclusion of more than one pigment in a paint often means that it will appear to change colour under different light sources such as tungsten lamps, full sunlight or

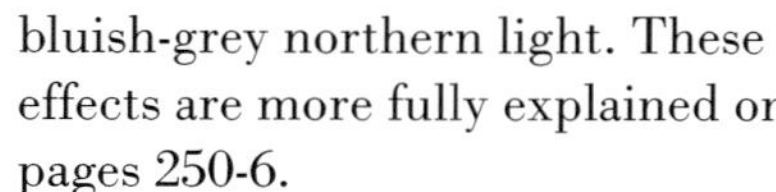

bluish-grey northern light. These effects are more fully explained on pages 250-6.

Another exciting use of these techniques is as a platform for a more adventurous use of colour and colour combinations. The unifying effect of bare old wood grinning through multi-coloured paint layers on an old dresser helps to harmonize those colours and permit their inclusion in a room's decoration. It is as though the crude wood layer pulls everything back to it and roots the colours in the object's homogeneity. Using and revealing underlying substrates like wood, plaster and metal will allow bolder and stronger arrangements of colour. Applying final antiquing solutions to different colours will perform the same kind of effect.

THE ETHICS OF AGEING

If you have ever attempted these techniques, you will know that adding a few centuries here and there to a wall or a cupboard is particularly satisfying work. The years just seem to roll off the brush. But there is no doubt that while most decorators will happily age and distress until the clients come home, some do wonder if it is all going too far and whether the techniques now adopted are so accurate that we run the risk of deceiving future generations; whether we are producing purely decorative effects that deceive the eye, or fakery that one day could deceive the wallet.

In building conservation circles, the whole idea of faking age and covering everything with imitation dirt sits uneasily on many people's conscience. The arguments against such pretence and deception of the eye are based on the fear that they may distort history; both the history

Ageing techniques are often employed just for their theatrical impact. It is obvious that this cracked paint effect is just that; it is not a convincing fake at all.

More often than not, ageing techniques are used to disguise new (and even old) pieces of furniture to accommodate them into a scheme. This cupboard has been antiqued ('dirtied') a little too enthusiastically with the result that it rather overpowers the elegant antique Swedish painted furniture.

of our forebears that we see around us, and the history for our descendants, who may be confused by the wealth of fakery that could abound.

But these arguments seem to me ill-informed; furniture makers of the nineteenth century excelled in producing reproduction furniture of many periods, some of it almost indistinguishable from the original. Yet we recognize the vast majority of it as being false.

It is as though each age will determinedly inject something of its spirit into the fakes it produces, no matter how faithful a fake it thinks it is. Only the tiniest minority of reproduction furniture and buildings has ever been so successfully constructed and finished as to be truly called fake. The phenomenon is very rare.

The late twentieth century has seen different strands of taste emerge in architecture and decoration. On either side of the middle ground, representing a gentle progression, lie the avant-garde and the traditionalists. The former state a case for honesty and truth in

This small dresser in a cottage in New South Wales has been knackered beyond belief. This is literally so; the distressing and dirtying that time has imposed are more dramatic than any paint effects an expert would fake. The result is that we can't quite believe it and suspect the hand of a faker.

materials, rejecting the fussiness of wallpaper and the dirtiness of paint effects. The latter are keen to promote simple vernacular taste for traditional paints and colours, another honest approach to buildings and their decoration. (I admit to belonging to the latter camp, but adopt the former as my hobby.) Both movements consider that distressing pieces of furniture or antiquing walls is dishonest and untruthful. My response is that if that is so, then so is any coat of flat paint or plaster, since the history of decoration is about the covering up of rather crude structures with superficial layers that serve little or no practical use, but which we find pleasing and sophisticated. A blue-stained concrete wall can be as satisfying for the modernist as a distressed and grained cupboard can be for me. Neither can occupy the higher moral ground.

TYING-IN CONTEMPORARY WORK TO THE PAST

At a practical level, the building conservation industry is much less purist than it likes to think. William Morris, who founded the Society for the Protection of Ancient Buildings, emphasized in his manifesto for that esteemed body how important it is to 'treat our ancient buildings as monuments of a bygone art created by bygone manners, that modern art cannot meddle with without destroying'. He was opposed to fakery and felt that older buildings need to be respected for their original fabric, and gently and conservatively repaired in discreet but obvious ways, so that such repairs cannot be confused with what was past. This formula for treating old buildings has now been adopted as the accepted canon in building conservation.

Yet in the repainting of historic rooms, the question is often not what was there originally, but what colour should be put back that will happily sit with the battered furniture that remains from the period? There is a respected tradition among gilders that when gold leaf has been applied to the carefully prepared gesso and bole surface, it is perfectly legitimate to lightly distress the surface by polishing it back with fine wire wool and powdered rottenstone to reveal a little of the bole colour underneath. This 'ties back the leaf' into the surface, an expression which neatly conveys the solution to the problem of how superimposed layers of paint, leaf, etc. can often appear to be disconcertingly separated from each other and obviously applied one by one. Tying back, by rubbing or distressing, visually fuses those layers and effectively makes it much more difficult to discern the separate, different applications. It is a much undervalued aspect of decoration, especially where many translucent or broken coatings are applied.

In London, at Spencer House, restorers have gone further, in applying an 'antiquing' coating to gilded picture frames, a layer of umber pigment in a thin gelatine glue to tone the gilding and render it more acceptable when the frames are hung next to those with original gilding. Not only is the gelatine glue a familiar and traditional material in gilding, the pigment itself is composed mainly of powdered clay, real dust...

The reason for this tying-in (or faking, perhaps) is that a finish had to be achieved in order that the sparkling new gilding did not unbalance the decoration in the room; the new frames should not have overpowered their antique partners in the general context of the room's decoration. A mile or so to the east, at the John Soane museum, newly gilded frames surrounding the collection of Hogarth paintings have NOT been distressed, or antiqued, and ironically they have received much criticism for looking too new!

The general conclusion that one is tempted to reach is that for centuries, where new gilding has been added to old, it has probably been at least rubbed back a little in order to help it settle into its new surroundings, to tie it in; good commonsense and traditional workshop practice dictate that this should be so.

JUSTIFYING AGEING TECHNIQUES

So the hard-and-fast rules that govern how our old buildings and furniture are maintained are not so fast and hard after all. It is clear that, very often, the aesthetics of an item or the context in which it sits demand that the overlapping borders of restoration, conservation and faking are smudged together. In *Authentic Decor*, Peter Thornton writes how Pugin's original scheme of London's Houses of Parliament included staining of all the oak to make it look old; 'the fields between Gothic ribbing and colonettes could then be treated with boldly coloured effects ... it was only when the original colouring was restored recently that the intended balance became evident once again.' So we need not feel too guilty at what we get up to on our repro pine furniture. Morally, our distressed pine TV cabinet has every right to be dressed up in this way, since such deception of age is nearly always short-lived and harmless.

There are other justifications for faking and ageing that are very appealing. The whole art of fine decorative painting relies on the ability of the painter to hide his brush marks, and weave spells with the paint. Herein lies the magic and the ability to delight and mystify. Ageing, distressing and antiquing are finishes that form part of this magic circle. They too can procure admiration and fascination; and the more complex the pattern and surface, the greater is this wonder.

These techniques are hardly ever used to fake, rather they are there to be exploited for their theatricality and for introducing some fantasy into our lives. The results they produce should be thought of as pure pastiche and gossamer-thin pieces of nonsense.

By contrast to the picture opposite, this exterior of another cottage in Australia, at Mulgoa, shows the gentler hand of time at work. The paint has been dulled, has crazed and is worn and chipped in a random, subtle way. These effects are all but impossible to fake. Note the use of colour: an earth umber brown and forms of copper-type green paint.

Craquelure

This highly attractive, transparent technique has been thoroughly written about before, but here I am including several new refinements which my studio has developed over the last few years. These improvements should allow you to achieve the perfect, faultless finish, but remember that this is not an easy technique to master; it requires endless practice. In particular, read the hints and tips overleaf concerned with atmospheric conditions.

YOU WILL NEED
Varnishing brush
Goldsize
Turpentine (optional)
Liquid gum arabic
Soft round paintbrush
Artist's oil paint
Rag or paper towel
Cotton bud or scalpel blade
Varnish

1 *Using a varnishing brush, apply a thin coat of goldsize to the prepared ground (see The Essentials, overleaf). Apply it sparingly and extremely well brushed out; this guarantees a layer of approximately even thickness, necessary for cracks of a consistent size. You may thin the goldsize with turpentine to help you in this, but only by 10 percent.*

2 *Wait for the goldsize to become tacky (beyond sticky); the longer you leave it, the tinier the cracks will be. Then apply a generous layer of liquid gum arabic using a soft brush. A recipe for liquid gum arabic is given on page 60.*

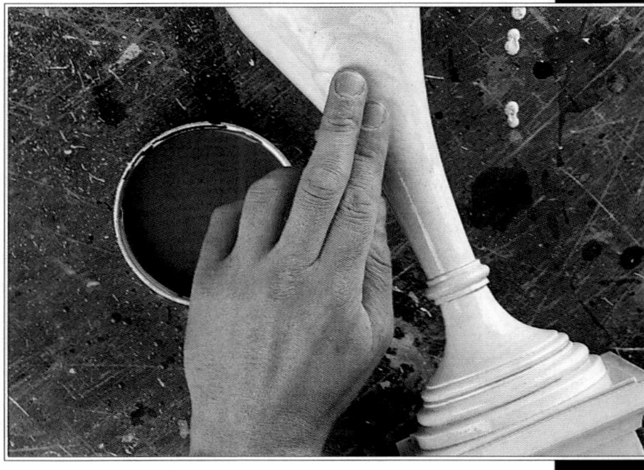

3 *Don't worry about brushing out this layer as fastidiously because the liquid gum arabic will almost certainly begin to ciss on such an oily surface as the goldsize. Wait a minute or so to allow some of the water content of the gum to evaporate and then massage the surface quickly. If the surface splits again, wait a further minute and repeat, and so on.*

4 *Leave the object in a moderately warm place, such as in an airing cupboard, to dry for a couple of days. The heat will assist the cracking process. Alternatively, when touch dry, heat the object under a hair dryer to produce cracks. Then vigorously rub artist's oil paint of any dark colour (to make your own, see page 88) well into all the cracks.*

5 *Immediately remove the oil colour from the surface with a rag or paper towel to reveal the pattern of cracks. These are made visible by the oil paint trapped within them. Stubborn recesses may be cleaned with a cotton bud or gently with a scalpel blade. For finishing, see The Essentials, overleaf.*

CRAQUELURE: HOW IT WORKS

When a paint film cracks, there may be several explanations. It can be due to the paint being applied in too thick a layer; a skin forms which contracts as it dries and so splits open to reveal softer paint beneath. Alternatively, a paint film can be inherently unstable, causing the surface to break down, crack or crocodile (as in crocodile skin). The nineteenth-century artist's habit of employing cheap bitumen-based paints in oil paintings produced this phenomenon, and Leonardo da Vinci, experimenting with bitumastic or pitch binders, produced several works that perished soon afterwards. A more stable and decorative use is shown in Cracked paint on pages 166-9.

The physical process of cracking employed in the craquelure technique featured here, relies on the superimposition of a brittle water-based varnish over a hard, flexible, oil-based coating before the latter is completely dry. Oil-based coatings dry by absorbing oxygen from the atmosphere, not by relinquishing their solvent, and so rely on oxygen to complete the hardening process.

As with the tradition of oil gilding, the second coat of craquelure has to be applied at a point where the oil has already absorbed sufficient oxygen to complete its hardening process, and so is at a point where further hardening will occur. The second, water-based, coating is quick-drying and brittle and swiftly hardens before the oil is fully oxygenated. Being water-based it will also not interfere with the processes going on beneath.

As it hardens, the oil-based coat flexes, splitting the brittle top coating. This process is aided by gentle heat, which has two effects; it speeds the oxygenation of the oil-based coat and it prevents the gum arabic (now dry) from absorbing any moisture in the atmosphere and becoming fluid or mobile again.

INGREDIENTS

The ingredients employed here are the results of tests that my studio carried out in the late 1980s in an attempt to eliminate the need to buy ready-made crackle kits.

OIL-BASED COATS

**Goldsize* A traditional varnish-like product used as an adhesive for gold or metal leaf in exterior (or cheaper) gilding. In our tests, different oil-based products were tried for the first coat and only the finest quality goldsizes containing traditional linseed and tung oils produced a crackle effect. Cheaper products failed in the trials because they were adulterated. So look for a good quality, traditional goldsize made from stand oil or linseed oil preferably containing a drying agent such as cobalt. Available with different drying times to suit the size of job, a 4 to 8-hour goldsize is ideal.

**Varnish* A synthetic, polyurethane structure. Some decorators prefer to use a high-quality polyurethane varnish for the first coat, maintaining that it procures a more even and reliable crackle. I have found the opposite, which only serves to illustrate how important it is to experiment and practise a technique.

THE ESSENTIALS OF CRAQUELURE

DERIVATION

The recipe is taken from an eighteenth-century invention that was patented in France by the Martin brothers. This was in response to fashionable taste for decorative finishes in imitation of Oriental finishes on objects such as Raku decorative pottery and lacquerwork. Interestingly, the significance of cracked patterns in Buddhism and Shintoism is religious and symbolic rather than representing objects as simply being old or decorative.

SURFACES

Any surface to be crackled must be without blemish since any defect will show later through the effect. Ideally, it will also be free from any texture since this impedes the cracking.

PREPARATION

The best substrate is a water- or oil-based ground that is grease-free and has been lightly rubbed down with fine grade sandpaper and then washed and dried to remove any dust. It cannot be too heavily stressed that any dust in the atmosphere or present on the applicating brush will mar the finish of the first, oil-based coat.

FINISHING

Two options are available. Either wait for the last coat of artist's oil paint to dry (two days minimum) and then varnish it with a good oil-based varnish to protect the effect and prevent the gum from coming into contact with any more moisture. Or wait for two days and then wash off the gum under a tap or use a sponge and water. This leaves behind the cracks simply as a pattern of oil paint stuck on the first oil-based layer. The finish is much smoother and has the added advantage of returning the object to a colour much nearer the original. However, the surface should still be varnished to protect the pattern, or at the very least, waxed.

A coarse craquelure finish. Large cracks resulted from a thick coat of oil and from applying the second coat too early. The oil coat tends to wrinkle, producing blemishes in the surface.

Delicate effects can be achieved by under crackling; applying the second coat a little late.

A perfect eggshell cracking depends on the conjunction of timing, weather and correct coating thicknesses.

TOPCOATS

**Gum arabic* Water-soluble resinous crystals available from paint and polish suppliers at economical prices. The crystals should be soaked overnight just covered with cold water, resulting in a pale liquid with a gravy-like consistency. For a full description of gum arabic as a medium see page 48 and for a recipe see page 60.

**Dextrine* A realistic and under-used alternative to gum arabic. In tests, we found that dextrine actually performed better due to its inherently weaker structure. It is widely used in industry, is also the main ingredient of library paste, and is commonly available as brown gum. Dextrine powder varies in colour from white to yellow and is used by dissolving in water and leaving to stand before use.

HINTS AND TIPS

* Do not massage the gum arabic into the first coat with anything other than the lightest pressure. Heavy rubbing tends to dissolve surface particles of the oil-based coat and creates a suspension of oil in the gum layer. Such oil-in-water suspensions are employed by manufacturers for imparting strength and resilience to water-based products, and so are the last things needed here. The result will be that not only will the surface fail to crackle, but that the gum layer will also prove very difficult to dissolve later.

* An alternative, or additional, step to the massaging of the gum, is to rub the tacky oil-based coating all over with fine powdered whiting, French chalk or fuller's earth. These materials will absorb surface grease, preventing the second coat from cissing open. They should be applied with the lightest of touches and all but completely dusted off with a soft brush before the gum is applied.

* Both dextrine and gum arabic are soluble in water even once they have been applied as coatings. You may recognize this from the behaviour of artist's watercolours and gouache, both of which they bind. Gum arabic is hygroscopic, absorbing moisture from a damp atmosphere, so do not attempt this technique in a damp environment or in an unheated room during damp weather.

* The best results are obtained if the object is left to dry in a very warm, dry space such as by a boiler. Extremes of heat, such as that produced by a hot hair dryer, may be detrimental and should be applied with great caution.

* If the cracks, when they come, come too large, leave the object in a warm, dry area for a few days. On closer examination, you will notice many more minute cracks that have appeared between the larger ones.

* If cracking does not occur, a last-ditch drastic measure is to apply heat from a hair dryer and then leave the object overnight. Failing this, wash off the gum and start again.

* Use only artist's oil colours to rub into the cracks. Water-based paints will re-dissolve the gum arabic, while synthetic oil paints become sticky almost immediately once in use and leave a trace film behind.

* On light grounds, a mixture of raw umber and raw sienna oil colours gives a convincing neutrality to the cracks. On dark grounds, add white to lighten the oil; a golden mixture of yellow ochre and raw sienna is particularly attractive against black.

Cracked paint

By contrast to the technique of craquelure, which uses varnishes, this effect for cracking opaque layers of paint is quite simple, requiring little practice to master. It relies on the application of a layer of gum arabic between two layers of water-based paint; the gum is hygroscopic and when dry absorbs water from any water-based coating applied over it, shrinking the top coat, and cracking it.

Until now this technique has been given little coverage, mainly because the resultant effect has never been quite as pleasing or subtle as that obtained with the craquelure varnishes. In fact, in all its published incarnations to date, this finish has always been portrayed as decidedly rustic and coarse. However, the reason for repeating it in this volume is that in the studio we have developed several refined versions; the steps shown on these pages illustrate a new use to produce a subtler finish by applying several layers of paint and double cracking.

Equally, the swatches shown overleaf illustrate completely new developments of this technique to give the appearance of cracked leather, old gilding, and paint that has chipped or peeled away. All these finishes are richly decorative and should perhaps be employed with moderation, at least initially. However, the simplicity and reliability of this technique ensures that you can confidently consider it for furniture and large items that are begging for a theatrical approach.

YOU WILL NEED

Medium-sized round paintbrush
Liquid gum arabic
50mm (2in)-wide flat paintbrush
Emulsion paint
Sponge
Water
Varnish or wax

(LEFT) *Materials used for cracked paint (from left to right): lumps of dextrine, larger lumps of gum arabic, and gum arabic in solution.*

1 *On a water-based ground such as emulsion or acrylic, brush on a coat of liquid gum arabic and leave it to dry (approximately 1-2 hours) in a moisture-free atmosphere.*

2 *With a well-loaded brush, apply water-based paint over the gum arabic. Do not brush over the same area more than three times in quick succession as the gum arabic will congeal, producing an area that refuses to crack.*

3 *The cracking process begins after about 30 seconds. But leave this coat to dry thoroughly, for at least half a day. Meanwhile, smaller areas may be picked out in other colours.*

4 *Even when thoroughly dry, gum arabic still remains actively soluble in water. Try sponging the surface of smaller mouldings with water and leaving for a minute to allow the water to creep under the top layer of paint. When touched again, shards of dry paint should fall away on the sponge.*

5 *For a subtler cracked effect, a second coat of paint may be applied. This also allows you to cover and repair any gross messes that you created the first time round. Finally, you may wish to antique your work with a coloured wax, oil paint or tinted varnish (see Antiquing on pages 180-3).*

ABOUT GUM ARABIC

Gum arabic is the dried resin of the acacia tree as grown in quantity, especially in Nigeria, Sudan, Senegal and Australia. It is produced as water-soluble resinous crystals of varying colour from translucent black to pale amber and may be dissolved in water again and again after drying out. Gum arabic is also used as a food additive in confectionery, and in pharmaceuticals.

The finest coloured crystals are employed as the binder for artist's watercolours and in gouache paints and, more unusually, as the binders in television studio floor paints since the gum imparts a hard, shiny surface to the paint, which can be easily washed off the floor with water at any subsequent point.

Gum arabic crystals are available from paint and polish suppliers at economical prices; artist's suppliers sell only the finest and most expensive grades in small quantities.

The crystals should be soaked overnight just covered with cold water, resulting in a pale liquid with a gravy-like consistency. Dextrine may also be used for this technique (see page 165 for a description).

HINTS AND TIPS

* The single knack involved in this technique is that of applying the second coat of paint. It must be laid on thickly enough to cover the gum arabic without too much brushing out but not so thickly that it seems badly applied. You will have about 5 seconds to work the paint after applying it before the gum starts to congeal. The best way of finding out what badly applied cracked paint looks like is by testing the materials and deliberately failing.
* Because of the problem of congealing, it is impossible to cover a large area, such as a wall, with this technique unless you work in a loose chequerboard pattern. Patches of paint must be left to completely dry on the gum arabic before the intermediary areas are filled in.
* Cracks will almost always appear in the direction of the brush marks of the top layer. Experiment with media such as casein paint and acrylic primers to see how results differ.
* Other tools will procure different effects in the top layer; a roller produces almost indiscernible random cracks and a great deal of texture; spraying water-based paints creates dramatic cracks of wildly differing sizes in completely random patterns; a flat household sponge, when fully loaded, produces texture and strong cracking (as opposite).

Old linseed oil paint often crocodiles, reticulating into cube-like lumps and producing a hard, resinous skin known as linoxyn. This technique can be well employed to fake such cruddy effects.

THE ESSENTIALS OF CRACKED PAINT

DERIVATION

This technique comes really from the theatre, film and display industries where it has been used to dramatic effect for over half a century. The techniques on these pages have been refined for domestic use.

SURFACES

Any water-based painted surface will suffice and need not be of any particular quality, but should be grease and dirt free to enable the gum to adhere. There should be no damp since it will prevent the gum from drying. A shellacked surface will also accept gum arabic.

PREPARATION

Ensure the surface is grease and dirt free – lightly wash it if necessary, but let the surface dry thoroughly before painting on the gum arabic.

FINISHING

Since gum arabic remains water-soluble, any finished surface should ideally be varnished, or at least waxed to protect it from water.

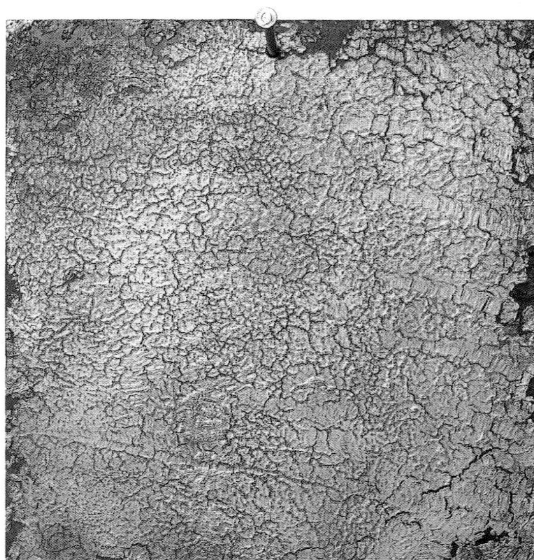

An interesting distressed gold, produced by heavily sponging brown-orange emulsion over gum arabic on a brown base. The emulsion was immediately sprayed with decorative gold spray prior to any cracks forming. Once the gold has skinned, the soft paint beneath can be manipulated with a rag, as at the edges.

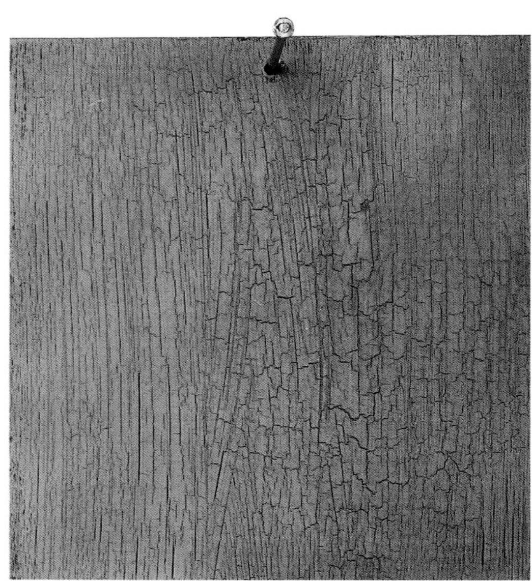

Pale brown cracked paint was antiqued with raw umber oil paint and then sanded to accentuate the depth of texture. This technique effectively emulates leather (see pages 148-51).

Thin washes of colour will crack more densely and much more in line with the direction of the brush strokes.

This is step 4 of the technique as applied to a flat surface. Once the cracking process was complete and the work dry, this sample board was literally held under the tap to lift shards of paint. Larger items of furniture may be hosed down.

Peeled and chipped paint

Strictly speaking this is a resist technique where a coating of a resist medium such as wax or rubber inhibits a paint from adhering to the ground. This is quite different to Cracked paint (see pages 166-9) which relies more on the interference of an intervening medium between two paint coats.

The choice of resist medium will greatly affect the result of peeled and chipped paint. Candle wax under a water-based paint yields a soft, rubbed effect, while latex rubber glue produces sharply-edged, chipped marks.

If used carefully, this technique can be used to great effect to imitate antique paint that has been worn and dented, especially on furniture and painted panelling. The essential knack is to apply the resist rubber glue in as random a way as possible, continuously changing the size, shape and the spacing between the resist blobs.

YOU WILL NEED
Wax candles
Paper towels or sponge
Latex rubber glue
Emulsion, casein or acrylic paint
Paintbrush
Scouring pad
Beeswax polish

1 *On large flat areas, use wax candles of various sizes, corresponding to the size of area to be covered, and rub vigorously over the surface. The result should not be a 100 percent coverage but a mottled deposit rather like colouring with a wax crayon.*

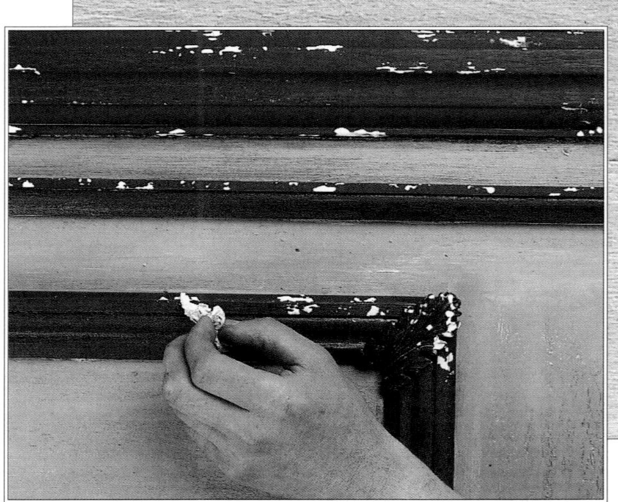

2 *For mouldings and areas of high wear, dip a small and crumpled piece of torn paper towel or, even better, a ripped piece of sponge, into household latex rubber glue and generously apply to the surface in a random and uneven way.*

3 *Let the rubber dry (it will turn translucent) and apply one coat of emulsion, casein or acrylic paint over the wax and rubber. Allow to dry, but do not use any applied heat as this will simply melt the wax beneath and stain the paint layer.*

4 *With a scourer, rub at the dried paint. This removes the soft paint sitting on the wax and starts to pull at the rubber. You may need to rub with your fingers to lift the rubber; callouses are invaluable for this. For finishing, see The Essentials, overleaf.*

The use of this technique need not be just limited to plain decorative paintwork. With judicious use and care, you can use it in conjunction with formal painting techniques, as this naive scene, painted on a door, illustrates. Remember a very important trick; that distressing or breaking down a surface will camouflage even the poorest brush work and give it the air of venerable age and naivety. This almost applies even if you can't paint at all!

HINTS AND TIPS

* Only apply rubber glue on areas of high wear, such as the edges of furniture, mouldings, and cupboard cills. Pay particular attention to the areas around handles, corners and keyholes for a fully convincing fake. Chips that appear in recesses or in the middle of panels will not appear at all convincing and will betray the overall effect.

* As an alternative to candle wax, beeswax polish can be used over large areas as a resist. However, its relative softness means that subsequent paint layers may continue to rub away over an indefinite period.

* Although water-based media are preferable because of their softness when dry, we have experimented with oil-based paints. They work moderately well over rubber, but require a lot of energy to rub back. Over candle wax, they will hardly rub away at all. Petroleum jelly can be sparingly used as a clumsy resist, producing its own blotchy effect.

* This technique can be employed on its own to superb decorative effect in quite abstract ways. But if it is to be used to fake age, peeled and chipped paint it is always best used in combination with other techniques such as Craquelure (see pages 162-5) and Antiquing (see pages 180-3).

THE ESSENTIALS OF PEELED AND CHIPPED PAINT

DERIVATION

This technique, like many in this chapter, has an unscrupulous provenance; the unacceptable but highly lucrative trade in faked antiques. More recently, reproduction furniture manufacturers have adopted it to distress painted furniture.

SURFACES

Almost any surface can be coated, including bare wood. However, the more absorbent a substrate is, the more difficult it will be to remove the rubber glue.

PREPARATION

To make timber easier to work on, stain it first and then give it a light coat of shellac to isolate it and reduce its porosity.

FINISHING

In this technique, all the resist media are, theoretically, either isolated beneath paint layers, or removed. Consequently, the finished surface should be hard and quite durable. However, any further finishing should be approached with care since when using candle wax as a resist, wax is brought to the surface during the rubbing process. This often imparts an attractive sheen to the surface and in itself offers a durable protective coating. But any solvent-based varnish or wax that is

FINISHING (CONT)

subsequently applied could dissolve the candle wax if applied with too much force, and either fail as a result when dry, or dissolve underlying layers of wax causing the whole effect to be ruined.

Equally, a water-based varnish would sit very unhappily on such a waxy surface, ciss open and probably fail when dry. The best compromise is a thin coat of beeswax polish applied with a very light pressure and allowed to thoroughly harden (24-48 hours) before buffing

Broad and bold markings were made by applying large areas of rubber glue resist and then ultramarine blue paint applied over a pale blue ground. Once rubbed back, the whole process was repeated using larger areas of rubber followed by a green paint.

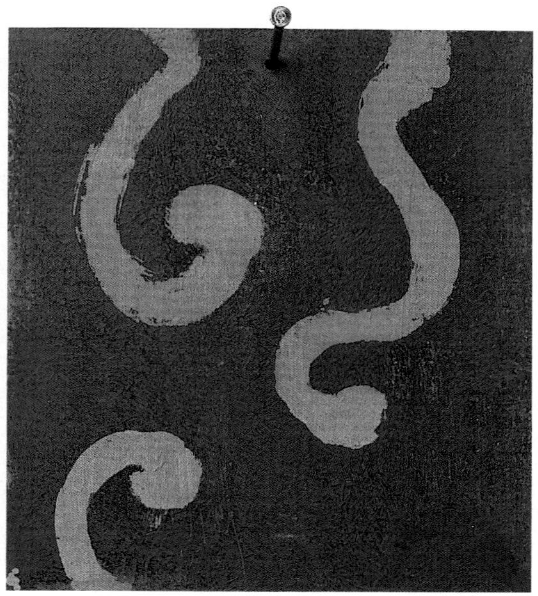

It is easy to draw patterns with a rubber or wax. Patterns made with rubber glue are best left simple since the only method of removing the glue is by hand, whereas waxed areas can be sanded back by machine.

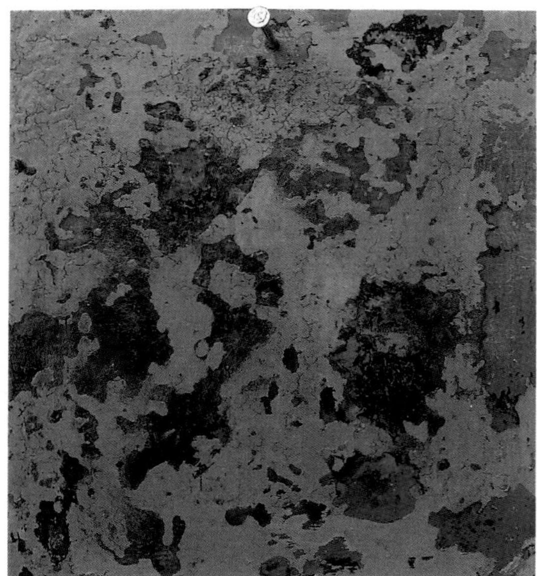

An intricate pattern is the result of laying on rubber glue very finely. The coat of paint follows the outlines of the rubber glue beneath, procuring very delicate effects. This board was painted green, coated with large areas of rubber and then painted purple. A delicate application of rubber followed before a final coat of orange paint. Only then was it rubbed back.

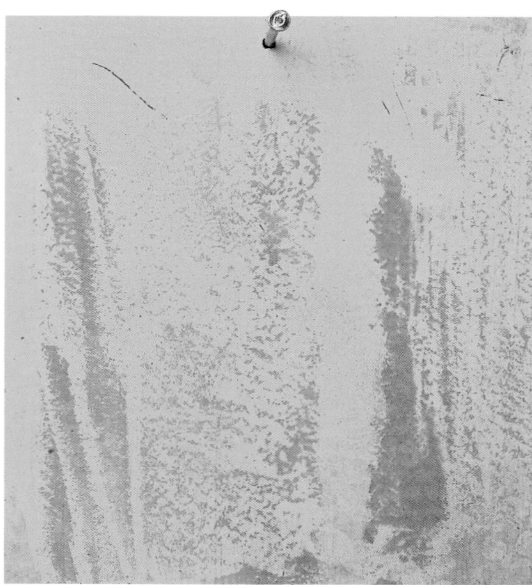

A very different effect results from using candle wax. Depending on the pressure used, different marks emerge. If the candle's edge is used, long scraped shapes emerge in the final paint layer, whereas if the side is used like a large colouring crayon, the resultant effect is like a soft puckered clouding. The top coat on this board was yellow over a mustard ground.

Rubbed paint

Like every other ageing or distressing technique, rubbing down is equally simple. It relies on colour being built in ever-softer layers (softer in the sense of toughness) which are then rubbed back to reveal those layers. Since rubbed paint is a very simple technique, its hybrids are many and its uses myriad; so it has become a useful secret weapon in the decorator's armoury. This technique may be used decoratively entirely by itself, and even over large areas such as walls (see overleaf), but to convincingly portray the effects of age, it must, as usual, be combined with other techniques for best effect.

For work on flat surfaces, a sanding block is essential, since fingers alone will never create a flat and smooth finish.

The paint used here is a ready-coloured casein formula to which more and more pigment has been added for each successive layer. The resultant glow in the surface is entirely due to the quantity of pigment present, while the quality of polish on the surface, rather like that of gesso, is a peculiarity of casein paints; it cannot be beaten.

The physical effect of weakening the binder through adding increasing quantities of pigment to each successive layer means that, when sanded, the top stratum wears more than that beneath it and so on. It should be possible to see the separate coats as coloured margins around the areas of wear.

YOU WILL NEED

Ground paint
Sandpapers (coarse, medium, fine grades)
Wet and dry papers (100, 220, 440 grit)
Pigments
35mm (1½ in)-wide flat paintbrush
Sanding block
Wire wool (00, 0000 grades)
(for mouldings only)

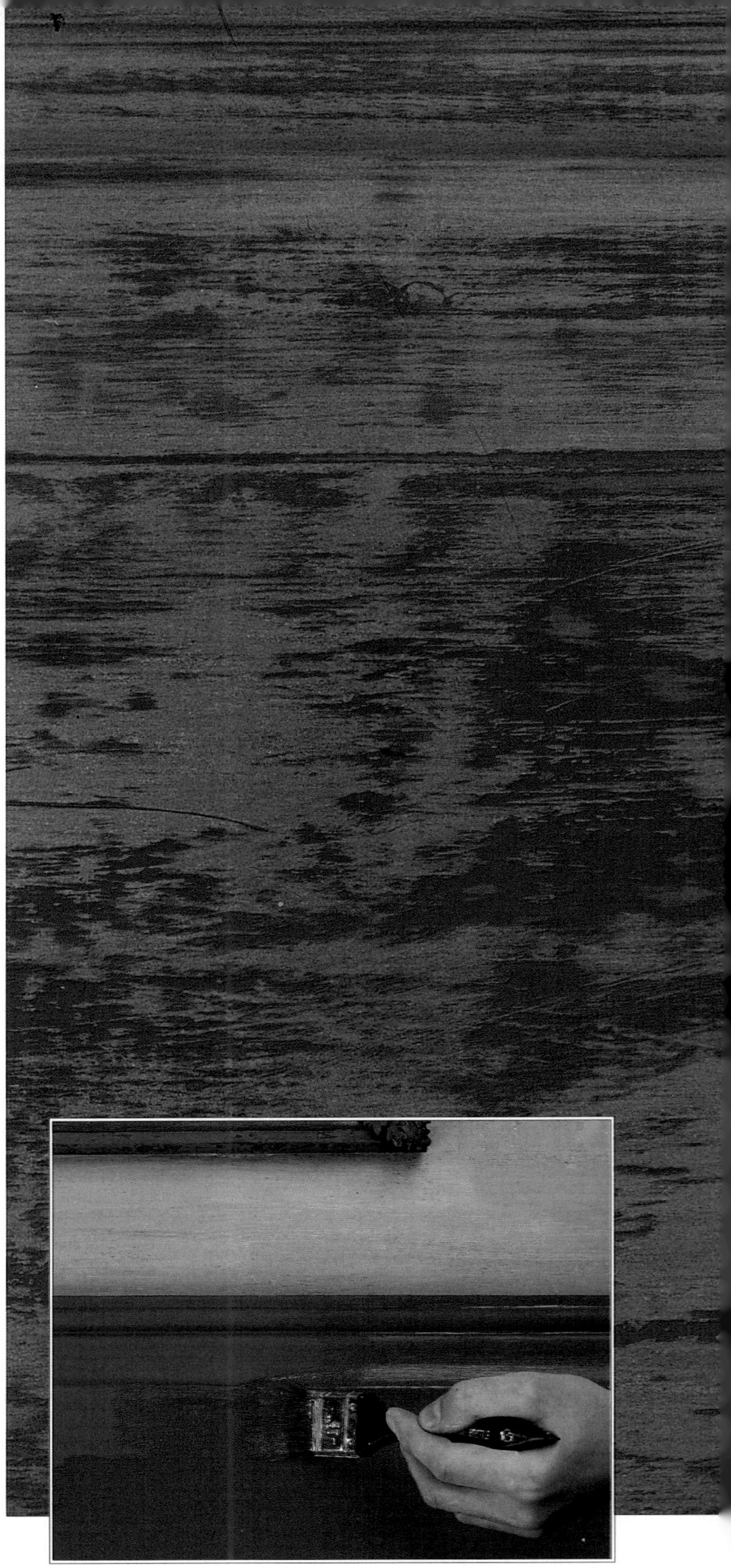

1 *Ensure that your first ground coat is tough and quite dry; you may wish to sand it smooth first. Make the next coat softer by adding some pigment to the paint and apply it in a relatively even thickness. Any coarse brush marks or texture will show up later when rubbed, so attempt as smooth a finish as possible.*

2 *If a smooth and inscrutable finish is your aim, then rub down the paint between coats, progressing from coarse to fine sandpaper. Mix even more pigment into the top coat (here a blend of ultramarine blue and yellow ochre) and apply over the previous coats, again as smoothly as possible.*

3 *When dry, rub the topcoat beginning with, say, 220 grit paper and then 440 grit. On larger areas, where occasional scratch marks are unimportant, begin with 100 grit. Use wire wool for mouldings, starting with 00 grade, followed by 0000 for a final polish. For finishing,* *see The Essentials, overleaf.*

Rubbing the surface with a dry, lint-free cloth after softening it with a solvent.

THE SOLVENT METHOD

Since most paints remain soluble in at least one solvent when dry, this may be exploited as a replacement technique for rubbing with abrasives.

The paint film is first softened by brushing on solvent and leaving for a minute or so. It is then rubbed with a dry, lint-free cloth. Care must be taken not to grind the paint and solvent together on the surface, and so make a new, sticky paint. Instead, a clean cloth must constantly be presented to the surface to absorb any mess.

The surface may be finally cleaned by quickly passing over the top with a cloth dampened with solvent. In view of the danger and high toxicity of many solvents, only methylated spirits (used for small projects) and water (for larger areas) can be recommended.

The solvent method is useful for large areas such as walls, particularly if casein paint is the choice and water can be used as the solvent. On a painted ground, brush out casein paint in all directions and then soften with the brush. Next day, dampen the surface with water and rub with a clean cloth.

HINTS AND TIPS

* The term 'soft' indicates that a paint has a weak or insubstantial quantity of binder and so is likely to be removed easily by washing or rubbing. In emergencies, excessively soft coatings can be remedied when dry by coating the work with acrylic or oil varnish; brushing the binder into the paint.
* Ground coats may be strengthened by the addition of extra binder; alkyd varnish in oil-based paints, and acrylic varnish in water-based paints. Very tough paints can be made from water-based acrylic varnish and pigment.
* When combining pigments, test the mix first, let it dry and then rub it. The green paint mixed for this technique turned oily blue in the later stages due to the ultramarine blue pigment, which broke down into finer particles upon being rubbed.
* If the solvent method is used, remember that alcohols like methylated spirits will dissolve acrylic binders (including PVA and EVA) when they

(BELOW) *The effects of rubbing can be applied to walls, furniture and accessories. Generally speaking, the smaller the object, the more pleasing and natural the effect will appear, partly because it appears more natural that way and partly because the rubbing process creates small and delicate marks in the surface. As a result, even a simple mirror frame such as this can be imbued with a value greater than its real worth.*

(RIGHT) *Rubbing goes a long way in pulling all kinds of painted objects together, especially if they share a common identity underneath. This Scandinavian room is built and furnished almost entirely with wood, and the strong presence of this material emerging through painted layers, unifies the room.*

THE ESSENTIALS OF RUBBED PAINT

DERIVATION

Although time-honoured as a method for preparing work, rubbing down has only developed as a decorative technique in the last twenty years. However, used in conjunction with textured surfaces, it has

DERIVATION (CONT)

been employed as a furniture painting technique for more than 100 years.

SURFACES

Plaster, wood or any inert substrate.

PREPARATION

The first coat of the technique may effectively be the correct primer for that substrate, coloured-up as required. But any texture or grain in the ground will make itself apparent in the rubbing down.

FINISHING

Since the process of rubbing can create an exquisitely smooth finish, it is sacrilegious to varnish over the top. A wax polish is the obvious finish on objects and furniture if they are to be highly polished. Walls can be polished to a quite extraordinary effect, or left matt.

are dry. Casein, however, is unusually friendly in that it remains water-soluble for a few days after applying.
* Never use wet and dry papers with solvents; their action is far too heavy.
* For some alternative rubbed and sanded effects with paint, see also the techniques of Texturing (pages 144-7), Leather (pages 148-51) and Stone (pages 152-5).

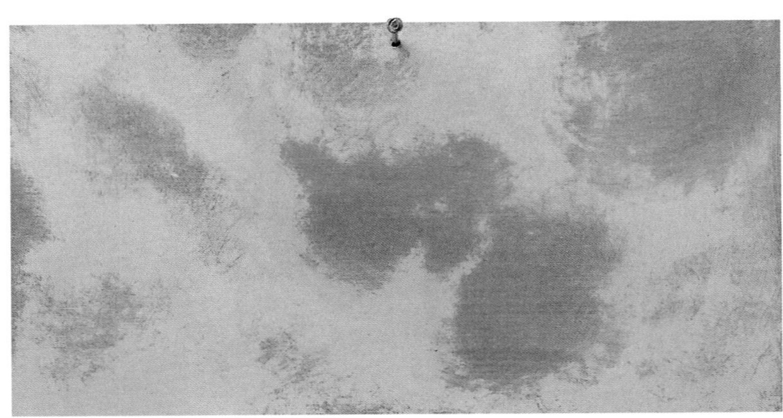

The solvent method is useful for large areas such as walls, particularly if casein paint is the choice and water can be used as the solvent. On a terracotta ground, cream casein paint (yellow ochre and white) was brushed out in all directions and softened with the brush. Next day, the surface was dampened with water and rubbed with a clean cloth.

This room is decorated with a removed, rather than applied, technique. Layers of paint and paper have been stripped off to reveal coloured plaster beneath. This can be effectively simulated by applying thinned paint to bare plaster (a casein, gum or gelatine-based paint is ideal). When completely dry, the paint can be partly removed by sponging over it with water, leaving traces of paint and stained plaster behind.

This is a more subtle variant of the Sponging off technique illustrated on pages104-7. A soft paint, such as one bound with gum arabic, casein or gelatine glue, was allowed to dry and then tamped lightly with a damp sponge. The surface was then immediately rubbed with a dry cloth to expose areas of ground.

The use of a textured ground in an underlying layer. A tough orange ground was stippled and allowed to dry, and then subsequent coats of purple and dark green were rubbed through to establish a subtle, mottled effect.

A nineteenth-century technique found on a trunk repaired in our studio was to grain the ground coat with a coarse brush to introduce linear texture (here executed in dark red ochre). When top-coated and rubbed back, the effect is remarkably similar to rustic graining of the period.

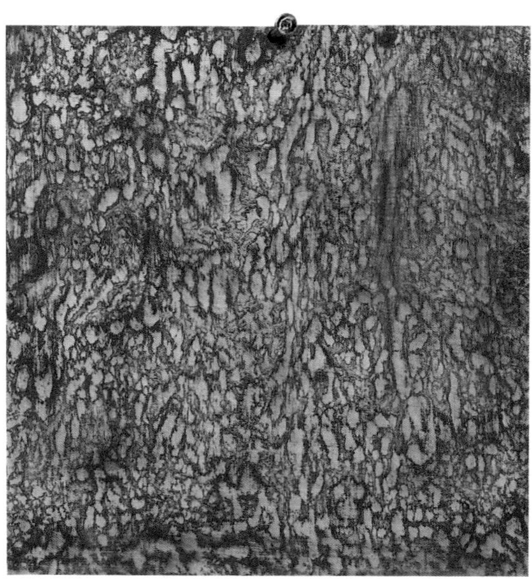

A more unusual method similar to the blue example. A thin paint of stale beer and pigment (glutinous in consistency) was painted onto a non-absorbent (oil-based) ground that had been dusted with whiting. When dry, it was delicately patterned with a damp sponge and then lightly wiped. The resultant effect is almost of vermicular stone.

Antiquing

A coy explanation for antiquing might be that it is a means of giving a surface extra depth by passing a translucent coloured varnish or glaze over it. In practice, as its name suggests, it is a coating that is intended to deceive the eye and give a surface the appearance of instant age, tying together all the devious techniques of fakery that have been employed on the piece of furniture or object.

In the antiques trade, especially on so-called restored French polished furniture, such a coating often consists of a mixture of beeswax polish, turpentine and fuller's earth or powdered rottenstone, or pigment bound in a wash of weak gelatine. When dry, these products are chemically indistinguishable from the dirt and polish that can build up over centuries on antique furniture. In conservation conditions, where fresh work must be tied-in to existing examples (such as replacement mouldings in an historical painted scheme), the preference will always be for such reversible antiquing media that can easily be removed.

The technique illustrated here is the traditional one employing beeswax and rottenstone powder. It is worth demonstrating for its ease of use and also because, on such deep mouldings as shown on the cupboard photographed, it need only sit in the deepest recesses. The paint is already quite well aged and requires no more help; all that is needed is a final tie-in.

However, in most decorative painting, requirements for an antiquing coat are frequently for a more durable and tough material, and one that has to perform as a tinting glaze over a painted surface. It must therefore often comprise finely ground pigments in a medium that can be stippled out with a brush. Tinted varnishes or thinned paints are the most appropriate, and the variations of these are listed overleaf.

YOU WILL NEED

Beeswax
Turpentine
Plastic container
Rottenstone powder
Round paintbrush
Old cotton cloth
Clean soft cloth

1 *Make the antiquing solution by diluting beeswax with turpentine to a slop and then thickening it with rottenstone. Then, using a firm brush, apply it into the mouldings. Take great care that you fill every single pore, hole, crack and recess for a fully convincing finish.*

2 *Using an old cotton cloth, wipe off all the excess solution almost immediately, taking care not to over-wipe areas that have strong wood grain markings; the solution can all too easily be lifted from these. Check that all crevices and cracks have been fully filled and that they look correct.*

3 *When the beeswax has fully hardened (4 hours plus) polish with a soft cloth to bring the wax up to a shine. Depending on the medium and material used, the resultant finish may vary in colour from when wet. Once the turpentine has evaporated from beeswax, fuller's earth or rottenstone will revert to their paler, dry colours.*

Various media used for antiquing. (TOP ROW, LEFT TO RIGHT) *Transparent oil glaze, fuller's earth, beeswax polish, rottenstone powder, white casein paint containing raw umber pigment.* (BOTTOM ROW, LEFT TO RIGHT) *Oil-based varnish with raw sienna pigment partially admixed, raw sienna pigment, raw umber pigment, liming wax.*

SOME ANTIQUING SOLUTIONS AND THEIR USES

* The addition of white pigment such as titanium white to any antiquing solution will render the mix more neutral and dusty in appearance. If you intend using liming wax, you may buy it ready-tinted white.
* Transparent oil glaze makes an excellent antiquing solution for glazing over fine decorative painting. It may be softened out with a lily-bristle softener (see brushes, page 46), finely stippled or pounced, that is, dabbed gently and repeatedly with a ball of fine, lint-free gauze.
* On timber that has been painted in flat colour, coloured varnish produces excellent antiquing results, especially if lightly tinted with a brown such as raw or burnt umber. For maximum transparency, don't add any white.
* Thinned oil-bound household paint will also suffice for a hard, durable antiquing coat (useful for treating plastic drainpipes outside). It is, in fact, nothing more than a well-controlled coat of thinned paint.
* On silver and gold spray paint or metal leaf, shellac is brilliant for enriching the colour without dampening the metallic effect.
* On metallics, emulsion or casein paints may equally be applied and then rubbed off.
* Artist's oil colours (for a homemade variety, see page 88) may be used either neat or diluted. The linseed oil provides a perfect antiquing medium that remains open for a long time. Examples of its use are seen in Leather (pages 148-51) and Craquelure (pages 162-5).

HINTS AND TIPS

* To produce emulsion or casein paint dust colours for antiquing, mix earth colours with white.
* Veiling, as described on pages 82-5, is an extended form of antiquing for large areas of paintwork. It is a variation of the light on dark principle shown opposite.
* Double antiquing is possible and produces quite staggering results, especially if it exploits the relationships thrown up when Combining media (see pages 118-21). An easy example is to antique a carved or modelled object with liming wax tinted say to a cream, leaving a light film of wax remaining. The object is then antiqued with a mid-tone emulsion or casein paint (eg raw umber and white) that is repelled by the waxy surface and shrinks back into interstices in the carving. With persistent rubbing, the water paint emulsifies slightly in the wax and doesn't move. During this stage, more paint can be loaded onto the object or wiped off, to suit. The result is often a highly complex finish.

THE ESSENTIALS OF ANTIQUING

DERIVATION

The last stage of ageing a surface, antiquing is nothing more than artificially applied dirt.

SURFACES

It is essential that any surface to be antiqued be totally non-absorbent. If at all porous, it will absorb the fluid, and prevent easy manipulation of the antiquing solution.

PREPARATION

To seal a surface, use thinned shellac, acrylic varnishes or gelatine glue prior to antiquing. Conventionally, casein, acrylic, gesso and emulsion paints require no sealing.

FINISHING

Antiquing is usually seen as the final stage in the finishing process and as such requires no further protective coatings. However, if transparent oil glaze is lightly stippled as an antiquing solution, a varnish will be needed to render it durable.

Each of these shells has the same coloured ground, but different antiquing solutions have been applied over the top. If a dark antiquing mix is applied over a lighter ground, the result is usually a dirty feel, unless applied extremely lightly.

Conversely, an antiquing solution of a lighter tone will give a dusty, cleaner appearance to the surface. You will find that the subtlest antiquing effects are achieved with solutions whose tonality most closely approximates that of the ground.

Raw umber and burnt umber pigments mixed into an oil varnish and heavily applied.

Raw sienna and raw umber pigments mixed into a thinned white casein paint.

Raw sienna mixed into white liming wax (for recipe, see page 118).

Fuller's earth (note the translucency) mixed into beeswax polish.

6 Patterning techniques

Patterning techniques

Why have pattern at all? In the late twentieth century, popular taste for it is limited; colour, surface, texture and plainness are the current buzzwords that constitute our design ethos. This is partly due to the modernist aesthetic of reduction, which underlines much of contemporary design and has dominated our palates and sensibilities for at least four decades. As a result, we are better practised and equipped to deal with the larger architectural canvas, to confront simple bold arrangements of surfaces and colours in our lives. We have spurned the clutter and mess of complex wallpapers and fabrics that could, if left unchecked, clog the freedom and sense of space that we all strive to create in our interiors. Where we do accept pattern and colour, it is controlled, by either generous portions of plain colour and area around it or by a simplicity of design and colouring within the pattern. At the very least, colours should complement each other, and pattern should gently move in and out of plainness.

All this is perhaps at the expense of our more subtle and sophisticated sensibilities. Such simplistic handling of form and colour would have seemed rather basic and crude to the decorator of 200 years ago.

Fashionable and sophisticated taste of the early 1800s extended to combining not only different patterns but also different colours on a variety of scales in a variety of manipulations. It was not unusual to find a green floral border floridly decorating a room covered in a lilac patterned wallpaper.

Yet, when we look at such odd historical arrangements, they can seem strangely pleasing. It is as though we have inherited the shadow of our forebears' taste. Although we recognize it, we don't know what to do with it, perhaps because so many of our own aesthetic sensibilities have been stripped bare by a century of thought that, in the name of simplicity, has given us crudity. Many of us no longer have the tools to exercise sophisticated good taste.

One of the major design catastrophes that led to this sorry state occurred in the late nineteenth century which saw an explosion of the decorative arts onto the popular market. Never before had design and decoration been so widely available, mechanically reproduced in factories by companies who very often exercised little taste of their own, and who plundered and mixed historical styles in a marketing quest for the novel. No wonder so much architecture and design of the period appears horrific to us now; it represents design Armageddon, and we are the post design-holocaust age.

OWEN JONES AND DEVELOPING PATTERN

Owen Jones, the noted architectural historian of that period, is now popularly viewed as having published the reference material that fuelled this phenomenon (which, presciently, he feared). Yet, in the preface to his most famous work, *The Grammar of Ornament* of 1856, he states the intention of the book as a properly researched guide that should reverse this unpalatable trend. He vilifies the commercial exploitation of historical styles and begs that manufacturers respect the independent characters of the different languages of decoration. 'I have ventured to hope that...I might aid in arresting that unfortunate tendency of our time to be content with copying...without attempting to ascertain, generally completely ignoring, the peculiar circumstances which rendered an ornament beautiful, because it was appropriate, and which, as expressive of other wants, when thus transplanted entirely fails.'

What Jones prescribed was a thorough study of historical ornament and pattern. But such study was, to Jones' mind, merely the first step in developing new architectural languages; he radically suggested free adaptation and development of designs and patterns to suit the spirit of his modern age.

Painted decoration in interiors and on furniture of the Arts and Crafts movement, was often laid onto a gilded ground. This latterday example was painted first and the gilding applied around the design. Even simple painted designs will assume much greater significance if placed on a gilded panel.

The materials of the artist determine in very strong ways the way in which he designs. This is sgraffito work, made by scratching through one coat of plaster to another coloured coat beneath. The designs therefore have to be simple and graphic. This work was executed in 1954 on the walls of the Schwarzenberg Palace in Prague.

Clearly, what he said then is as valid 150 years later; in order to develop new creative languages we should not sweep aside what has gone before, but learn the best principles from it. Interestingly, Jones distilled a number of tenets which he believed could be applied to any decoration of any period.

IN SEARCH OF A LANGUAGE OF PATTERN

There are two camps among decorators and architects that have been identified in other parts of this book and which we can caricature for the sake of convenience; the die-hard traditionalists and conservators on the one hand, and the reductionists or modernists on the other. The latters' criticisms revolve around the argument that any decoration per se is not honest or relevant to our time, or at least if decoration is to persist, it should spring directly from the function of architecture (and not its forms). The traditionalist will argue that historical examples will always remain superior to any common contemporary invention by dint of the fact that, historically, designers were much more fluent in a variety of languages on a common daily basis and that such fluency led to a more profound expression of those languages. There is also a band of extreme classicists who maintain that the principles of classical architecture were handed to Moses on Mount Sinai and represent God's true language of building. I am, er, sort of sceptical about that.

What I do believe, however (and this extends the metaphor of language even further), is that pattern and colour together form a large component of the grammar of any architectural style. They are inextricably bound up with it, whatever its period or type, be it Tudor fantasy or strict Neo-classicism. It is also our responsibility in every age to take our language forward and develop new forms of pattern and design to suit new buildings.

In the case of older buildings, the form and style of the architecture often demand a sympathetic approach such that any new decoration is appropriate and in a language that the building's architect would have recognized, even if he couldn't understand every word.

Where new additions are made to old buildings, we can allow ourselves a freer attitude and develop their architectural language, articulating it in new ways so as to be understandable to the old building but also to reflect our own time.

The new buildings of the twentieth century offer the most exciting challenge, for it is in these that we can let our imaginations run free. We should be doing as Jones proscribes; learning from our past of the intricacies and the subtle psychology that the best architecture, ornament and decoration teaches, and developing our own complex languages. If we can do this and become fluent in them, we can even invent the odd joke; always good for pricking the balloon of architectural pretentiousness.

This decorative essay is a contemporary triumph. The artist has understood the meaning of division on a wall and laid out his pattern according to the layout of the mouldings. The visual vocabulary is unusual but vigorous and represents a real knowledge of what decorative language is all about; how shapes and designs suggest different meaning and how their scale and colour must always stem from the architectural context.

Stencilling

Scores of books have been written about stencilling, each extolling the virtue of the craft as a decorative finish in its own right. But few pay any attention to the use of the stencil as a lowly tool involved on other decorative processes such as freehand painting or the manufacture of wallpaper. Any repeat pattern that is executed by hand will almost always call for stencil work.

However, at its simplest, stencilling is a convenient way of applying repeated patterns or a design onto a surface with paint. The stencil is only a guide or margin for the technique used, and the resultant effect will always bear the mark of that process; sprayed marks will have blurred edges and stippled patterns will show the marks of the brush. These simple, appealing qualities are what mark out American stencilling, on walls and furniture, which has not changed in its directness for nearly 300 years. It is this simple tradition of stencilling which has been promoted over the last 20 years.

METHOD 1 Using powder on size. Paint an oil-based goldsize all over the surface and leave it until it is almost completely dry before applying the stencil (any tackier and the stencil card or plastic will stick to it and the work will be ruined). Alternatively, use water-based acrylic size, but this gives a much cruder effect. Apply the stencil, lightly *dip cotton wool in bronze powder and then shake it out before gently applying through the stencil with small and delicate circular movements. Use the cotton wool to blend the powder into the black background while keeping the stencil firmly in place. This should produce a delicate three-dimensional effect, but requires considerable practice. By sizing the whole surface you will see the pattern you are making as you go along, and build it by varying the use of the stencil, employing individual motifs from it and so on.*

Given that the stencil is just a tool and not a process, it is not surprising that there are many ways of using it and three standard procedures are illustrated below. Overleaf you will find examples of how the use of stencils can be disguised and how they are incorporated into freehand work.

METHOD 2 Spraying. This is probably the easiest method of using a stencil. Mask the area surrounding the stencil, even temporarily, with paper to prevent any drifting spray from settling on the surface (I am always surprised at how far the drift can go). Lyn Le Grice is the undisputed mistress of the sprayed stencil and has developed extremely sophisticated techniques for blending the colours. This method can be used with discretion and is invaluable when working over difficult textured surfaces such as the fake leather panel illustrated on pages 148-9. The drawbacks to this technique are the health and environmental implications of using spray cans – always work in a well-ventilated room and wear a mask over your mouth.

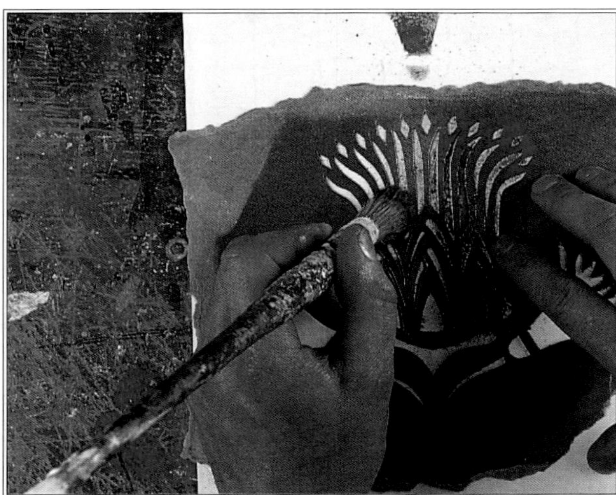

METHOD 3 Stippling. This is the oldest American technique, appearing on walls, floors and floorcloths in the early eighteenth century. Very little paint needs to be loaded

onto a stencilling brush, which should be firm and short-bristled to prevent the pattern from creeping under the edge of the profile. Check your progress with this technique by lifting the corner of the stencil; a surprisingly light application will appear as a strongly defined mark. Note also one of the most underrated advantages of stencilling; that you can use just a portion of the stencil as an individual motif in an overall design. Just above the hands, the side shoot of this Egyptian flower has been applied by itself.

(ABOVE) *Large and complicated patterned stencils will require extra support. Traditionally, stencils have been cut to include bridges or ties that link the cut card across the holes – the Japanese used human hairs delicately placed across their early stencils. On a large and complicated pattern such as this, the delicacy of the pattern would be destroyed by the clumsy inclusion of card bridges. Here a coarse dressmaker's netting was pasted over the back to retain the integrity of the design. It leaves hardly a trace of its existence on the finished pattern.*

HINTS AND TIPS

* Bought card stencils have a limited life, so look after them; you may wish to use them as a pattern for cutting your own, particularly if you wish to expand a design or integrate your own designs into an existing one. This latter approach is an ideal way to begin designing your own stencils.

* Historical references describe stencils as being made of a variety of materials, including tin, iron and stout card oiled and shellacked. For the latter material, the better of the two sealants is boiled linseed oil, which should be well rubbed into the card and then rubbed off. The card is then left for several days while the oil oxidizes and hardens to produce a tough, leather-like material which can be easily cut, used and re-used. Shellac tends to produce a brittle card, but it may be used as an 'isolator', brushed onto a card that has been oiled the same day and is still sticky. The shellac will serve as a temporary and quick-drying (30 minutes) sealant.

* These recipes for making your own stencils are invaluable, particularly when you discover that your art shop has sold out of stencil paper or when you need to re-cut a dead stencil at short notice.

* Modern synthetic acetates are a more sophisticated equivalent. Since they are transparent, they permit the work to be viewed under the stencil, enabling much better registration (the lining up of the stencil with the pattern already laid). Acetate sheeting is easy to cut but you may find it flimsy in use.

* Remember that even the smallest part of a stencil can be used on its own and that separate components can be assembled in different ways to provide many interesting variants. This is precisely the method used by early itinerant American stencillers, who composed designs from many different small emblem stencils that they carried with them. For your own project, you may wish to cut the separate designs and then tape them together to form a larger repeating pattern. Remember also that a stencil may be reversed and used upside down to effectively increase the size and variation of your design.

* A stencil can, with care, be employed with texturing media such as plaster and gesso to build low-relief patterns.

* At its simplest, a stencil can merely be a piece of card with a few guide marks cut out of it to help you mark a regular pattern over a surface. The 'ermine' on the trunk (overleaf) took its form from a stencil with five equally spaced holes on it that made registration easy. By placing the stencil partly over areas which have previously been drawn with it, it was easy to draw a precisely spaced repeat over a large surface.

* Stencils must be stored carefully; horizontally and between sheets of paper or card so that they do not tangle each other.

THE HISTORY OF STENCILLING

From looking at the wall paintings of the early Egyptians, it seems that stencils or similar templates were in use as early as 5000 BC. There is also much of Greek and Roman decoration that appears to have been executed with similar drawing aids. By the Middle Ages, the use of pattern templates was necessary to reproduce the complex repeating designs of church and secular decoration alike.

The early nineteenth-century American tradition of stencilling on

This early American bedroom at Joshua la Salle house in Windham, Connecticut, dates from 1830 and demonstrates both the lightness of touch and the variety of Colonial stencilwork. Note how the decorator has employed three different border designs plus individual motifs to emulate bordered wall hangings of the period.

furniture involved the repeated use of several different stencils over the same area to build up a picture. This was often of a cornucopia theme, involving leaves, fruit and flowers. Such stencils were known to middle-class ladies as theorems and the results often resembled delicately executed watercolours. They were usually undertaken by travelling decorators. Commercially, Lambert Hitchcock of Connecticut exploited this technique's simplicity and mass-produced decorated 'fancy chairs' that were either coloured or painted black and the patterns applied by pouncing bronze powder through a stencil onto tacky varnish (see Method 1 on page 188).

This use should not be examined in total isolation. Stencilling is a legitimate form of printing and the immediate descendant of the stencil is the silk-screen print, whereby inks are squeezed through a fine mesh that has been masked out to create a pattern – a refined version, in fact, of the large stencil featured on page 189. Although silk screening was not invented until the early twentieth century, there is ample evidence to suggest the use of sophisticated cut stencils as a form of industrialized printing as early as 1730, when English wallpaper manufacturers were applying glue through stencils and then dusting them with fine wool shearings to produce flocked papers. These were sold in imitation of fashionable silk and velvet wall hangings. Once again the lowly stencil had made its entrance as a short-cut tool.

The early Colonial interior shown here has a pattern imitative of wallpaper executed by stencilling on a boarded wall. The room is from the Joshua La Salle house in Windham, Connecticut, and was executed around 1830.

The decoration of this painted chest was a meticulous reconstruction of the wall paintings at Muchelney Abbey in Somerset. Three stencils were used as simple aids in its execution, one for the chevrons, one for the strawberry leaf repeat and one for the grey ovals that form the background to the ermine pattern. I painted the pattern directly through the stencils, tidying up the lines freehand afterwards. Further embellishments such as the loosely curving stems, the strawberry pips, the ermine hairs and the leaf details were also added freehand.

Four clear and identifiable treatments for stencilling that will dress up the technique. Initially, each sample

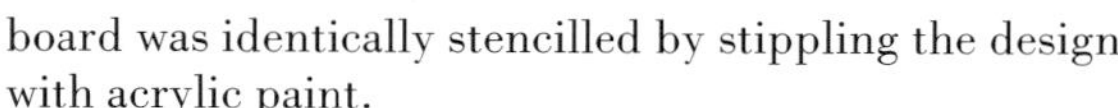
board was identically stencilled by stippling the design with acrylic paint.

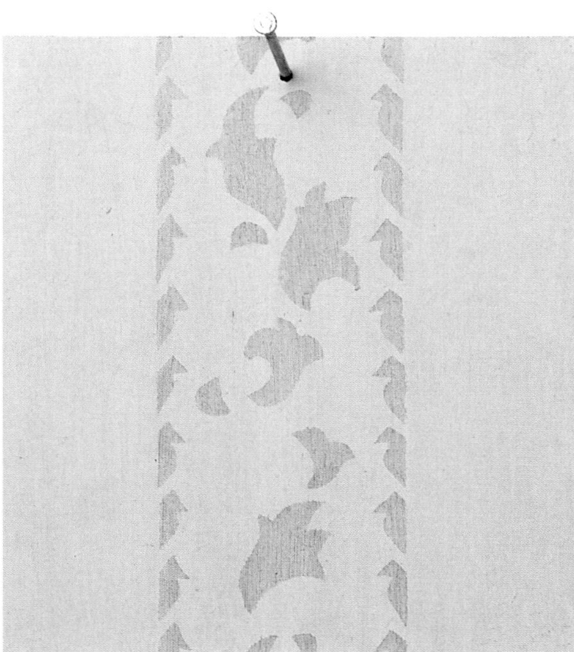

The dry stencilwork was given a thin wash of dilute white acrylic to veil the pattern and disguise the technique under another effect (see Veiling, pages 82-5).

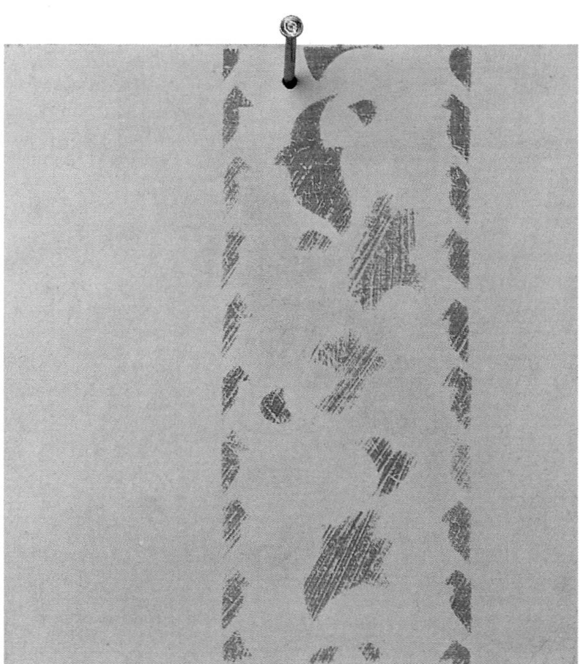

The stencilled pattern was coarsely sanded to distress it once dry. The scratch marks cleverly camouflage the original stipple marks.

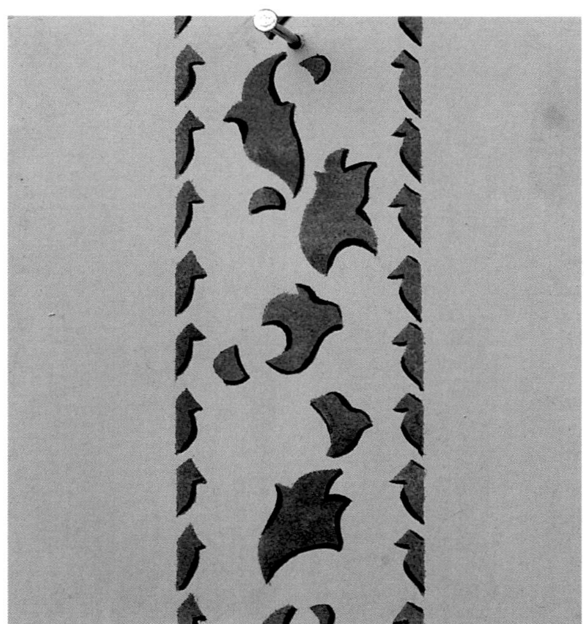

To add base relief, the pattern was shaded. On larger, more figurative stencils this can be artfully done, in the manner of trompe l'oeil painting.

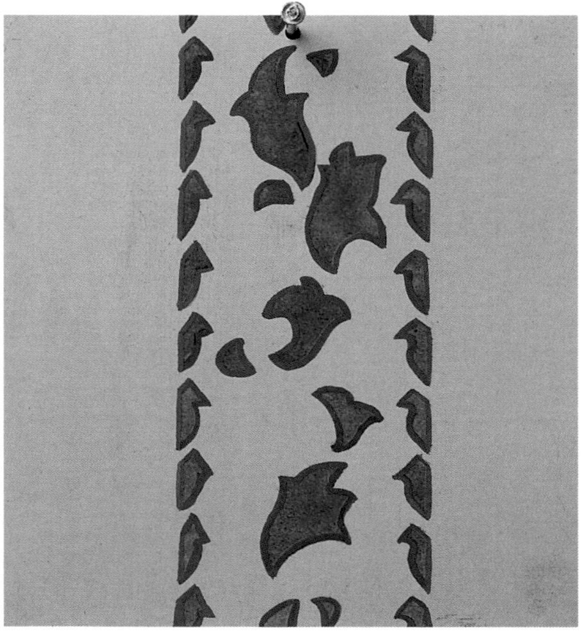

A total transformation is effected by outlining the pattern. The result is like a stylized flat wall painting. Any amount of additional freehand work may be added.

Wallpapers and borders

The popularity of paint effects over the past 20 years has led to fewer books being written on the subject of decorating with paper. This is a shame and warrants some attention in this volume, not least because wallpapers form a very important part of the history of decoration, and especially because wallpapers have historically been used much more imaginatively than today.

Without doubt, wallpapers are the most instant method of introducing colour and pattern to a room; by putting up a giant paisley pattern in the toilet you are immediately making a miniature kasbah, and this is perhaps wallpaper's most magical aspect. Like paint and paintbrushes, wallpapers are also decorating tools and at the same time form a library of reference and ideas for decorative schemes. This point is always underrated because most of us have decided what we want the wallpaper to do for us, even before we have bought it. In fact, you should look at wallpaper shopping as research for higher inspiration. I am always amazed at the variety of ideas that looking through the racks of a good stockist will provide, especially if they carry a good body of historical papers, such as those that are manufactured by Brunschwig, Coles, Sanderson or Zuber.

Many of these 'document' papers are still produced from copies of the original wood blocks and offer an incredible and direct link with the past. It is impossible to know exactly what decorative paint schemes were like in the eighteenth century, but by buying a reproduction paper that has been printed to a recipe dating from that period, it is possible to decorate with brand new eighteenth-century wallpaper and take advantage of the wealth of resource that designers and craftsmen of the past have handed down to us. It is as though wallpapers, and historical fabrics too, offer us the chance to look at design through our forebears' eyes and glean something of their taste and sophistication. As a method of researching historical taste it should not be underrated.

DERIVATION AND HISTORICAL USES

The history of wallpapers is one of rags to riches, and all during one century, since the eighteenth century is the age of wallpaper for historians. Earliest examples are English and date from the sixteenth century, but the wholesale manufacture of it did not grow before the end of the seventeenth century, when trade with the East led to the introduction by the East India Company of hand-painted Chinese wallpapers.

These were clearly expensive items and their popularity continued well

(LEFT) *We think of borders as suitable for imitating a dado or for strengthening a frieze. But used with style, a paper border can add great weight and originality to an interior. This example combines a painted ground with prints which could be pasted directly onto the wall.*

(RIGHT) *By the mid-nineteenth century, both the designs and execution of distemper papers had reached a point of perfection; registration was impeccable and inks could be formulated that did not blur or run. This fine Gothic revival paper was designed by Pugin for the Houses of Parliament in London and is still produced to order by the John Perry wallpaper factory in North London from the original blocks.*

into the nineteenth century. They were glued to canvas, which was stretched over wooden batten frames on the wall, and often the canvas was given a preparatory coat of lining paper first. This habit prevented damp from entering the paper through the wall and provided a perfectly flat surface for viewing, in exactly the same way that canvases and leather were being hung at the time. It remained the standard method of hanging printed papers throughout the century both in Europe and America, where a frame was sometimes discarded and the canvas was directly pasted onto wallboards. In America, the papers usually had to be imported and so were used in only the wealthiest homes, while in more modest dwellings paper was imitated with stencilling (see pages 188-93).

Early printed papers were not only copied as wall stencils but were themselves imitative of other, even more expensive, materials; stamped and gilded leather, damask silk hangings and tapestries. Such early products were supplied in individual sheet form, but by the turn of the eighteenth century they were being glued together to form 12-yard lengths which could then be printed with large repeating patterns, usually in monochrome. They were intended to be coloured once hung.

By 1712, trade in Britain was successful enough for the government to impose a 1d per yard tax on all printed and stained papers and over the next 20 years the market for this new product grew until it received the stamp of official approval when in the 1730s the Offices of the Privy Council were hung in crimson flock paper. This was a new invention whereby fine wool shearings were sprinkled onto glue or varnish that had been applied through a patterned stencil. By varying the colour of background and wool, it was possible to produce very rich and textural effects redolent of Venetian gauffrage velvets, but now on a massive scale; the repeat of this paper was 2m (2yd) high.

By now, perversely and inevitably, wallpaper had grown to supplant the very materials it had sought to emulate; the historian Steven Parissien describes how Lady de Grey removed her 'expensive and prestigious but now sadly old-fashioned stamped leather hangings...and hung wallpaper in their place'. Mme de Pompadour also hung 'English paper' in her *cabinet de bain* at Château de Champs in the late 1750s, indicating the supremacy of the English manufacturers at this time. And as early as 1737, a London firm had advertised papers imitating chintzes and even needlework.

But the Seven Years War interrupted trade between England and France and gave French manufacturers the crucial opportunity to develop their own factories and styles. The great house of Reveillon was founded then, receiving its Royal Warrant in 1784, followed by Zuber and Dufour. Their products were strikingly fresh and delicately patterned, innovations that resulted from increasingly high levels of craftsmanship and a refined approach to design never seen before.

By the 1780s, papers were still being hand blocked using carved wooden printing blocks coated with water-based distemper inks, but patterns were now being produced of incredible lightness, with many more colours being applied to the same

Strong and vibrant papers and patterns can be incorporated into a decorative scheme by using them selectively. This room is heavily panelled but the presence of a dado is sufficient to divide the wall space into manageable areas. Note that the vertical corner timbers, painted white, separate the areas of papering, so that the upper wall is not continuous but appears as a set of panels, containing and controlling the paper.

paper. The results were subtle and included complex renderings of Lyons silks and chintzes, where even the highlights and reflectance of the materials were being printed in. By now, designers had started to develop a decorative language belonging to this new form of wallhanging, producing Gothic stone-coloured papers and grisaille architectural compositions. Zuber could even provide entire full-coloured landscapes (many of which are still available today).

Meanwhile, in England, other developments had taken place, not least the explosion of interest in Chiaro Oscuro papers, an invention of John Baptist Jackson, who had travelled classical Europe and in 1746 began manufacturing black and white prints of landscapes and statuary, and even reproducing great paintings of the masters. These could be bought in kit form with borders, garlands and frames that were all to be pasted onto the walls and then hand coloured. A great self-promoter, Jackson produced a book in 1754 as a publicity vehicle for his own range, which enjoyed huge popularity throughout the remainder of the century. It is his work which almost entirely constitutes what we now know as eighteenth-century print rooms, which became popular in England, Ireland and even America, where a South Carolina merchant proclaimed that 'the expense of papering a room does not amount to more than a middling set of prints'.

The manufacturing techniques developed in the eighteenth century have been supplanted to a large extent by modern commercial processes. Roller surface printing, first developed in the nineteenth century, and modern screen printing have led to mass production of cheap papers and fabrics with huge ranges of patterns and colours. And yet, not surprisingly this is at the expense of the charm and craftsman qualities of the earlier papers. Many of us would not stop to look at a hand-blocked paper, but were we to compare it against its machine-made equivalent, we would find within the small marks, wrinkles and bubbles in the paint that tell exactly how the image was produced and even allows us to gauge the thickness of the ink.

The impact of this hand-blocked damask is furthered by the painted decoration of the room, which is all red (including the floor). The paper has a truly astonishing presence in the room and appears to gently hover in front of the wall. It is not a flock paper, but an even cheaper mock flock, printed in deep crimson distemper inks on a brighter ground. The ground colour backs the slightly translucent inks and causes them to glow.

As in the red room (left), the weight of this paper is emphasized by the wood-work, painted to match the ground. The pattern, however, is printed in a light ink on a darker ground for a delicate effect, redolent of lace. With modern inks, light on dark most closely approximates the character of distemper inks giving a decorative short-cut for historic rooms where traditional papers would not survive the demands of modern living.

DISTEMPER INKS

One other reason why hand-blocked papers seem to have a life of their own is because their colours are not synthetic process colours but hand-mixed distemper inks coloured with pigments. Distemper and limewash glint in the light because the minute pigment particles are unevenly dispersed over the surface (see pages 250-6), and the same effect is true of distemper inks, which have traditionally been formulated using either gelatine or, more popularly, casein binders.

The effect is hardly discernible when looking at a small sample or swatch of the paper, but can be immensely powerful when the paper is viewed on the wall. The red damask shown on this page is an example which, sadly, the camera cannot capture; it appears in real life less like paper and more like velvet. This feature of traditionally printed paper is not to be underrated, and goes some way to explain why you will only find modern synthetic flock papers in curry houses.

HINTS AND TIPS

* Although the practical guides to hanging paper are excellent aids for helping you to calculate quantities and carry out the work, they offer no aesthetic help. Remember that you can design with wallpapers and borders, using them as tools.
* An example is to use part of a wallpaper pattern as a border, chopping up the paper, and perhaps bordering the walls with the same design but in a different colour.
* Papers may be employed in the time-honoured tradition of lining cupboards and boxes, but also use them to cover the outsides. Once dry it may be coated with several coats of

If we fail at all in using borders, it is in not using enough of them in any one room. This particular example has been chosen to pick up the stripes in the wallpaper that falls below it.

acrylic varnish to render it durable.
* Similarly, it is possible to produce decorative panels by pasting wallpaper to boards that can be framed and hung.

We have produced panelling for an entire wall in a French château, gluing Reveillon patterns onto timber boards and then varnishing with water-based lacquers to seal them when dry; the synthetic inks used to print the papers are waterproof and will not be affected. Moreover, once protected, we were able to crackle varnish each panel over the paper, producing an effect similar to an ancient hand-painted panel.
* Note that papers printed with synthetic inks will not smudge when coated with water or most oil-based lacquers. But, if the paper is exposed, it may absorb oil-based coatings and darken considerably. If in doubt, always seal the surface with a water-based coating first.
* Papers printed with distemper inks can be treated with a manufacturer's glaze to render them more durable and wipeable; however, this inevitably mars the dusty quality of the inks.
* Giant striped patterns, particularly effective in large spaces, can be attempted by the bold. Simply order half your wallpaper requirements in a different colourway and alternate colours around the room. This is in direct imitation of a mid-sixteenth-century trend of alternating silk hangings of different colours and even different patterns.
* Look for the occasional large patterns that possess a double repeat, whereby two pieces of paper can be lined up with the pattern matching and then one moved up or down exactly half way to provide a staggered pattern that still joins in all the right places. Surprisingly, historical examples exist where the paper was thrown up with no regard for whether the pattern matched!
* In direct imitation of Jackson's Chiaro Oscuro papers, photocopy engravings and designs and paste them up. The photocopier is the descendant of the copper engraving plate. Equally, colour photocopies provide surprisingly convincing prints for decoration; the inks used are remarkably lightfast.

The patterns and colours of this eighteenth-century Scandinavian interior are typical of the period; a mixture of designs of different scales and the use of complementary colours, or at least completely unrelated colours!

7 Fakery

Fakery

There is a view held by those sceptics of 'paint finishes' that of all the things you can do with paint, faking another material is perhaps the most immoral. This view is one held by many craftsmen who, influenced by the great crafts theories of the past 100 or so years, those of the Arts and Crafts movement and of the Bauhaus, consider it dishonest to hide the true materials of our homes and furniture. They prefer to polish wood and not paint it, to display their dovetail joints and not hide them. The net result is that, in the art market, terrific emphasis is placed on the value and worth of furniture and sculpture that is made from what it says it is, while a natural suspicion falls on those pieces that pretend to be other things. For example, a modern bronze sculpture with a small amount of permitted artificial patination is acceptable; a carved wood, gesso and paint sculpture in imitation of bronze is not.

In the process of adapting imagery and references for interior decoration, it is usual to find that they undergo some kind of transformation. This fakery is quite obviously in paint, indeed it is executed in a very 'painterly' way, with all the fluid and spontaneous brush marks visible.

This viewpoint is flawed for two reasons. First, it grossly underestimates and insults the painter's skills as a craftsman. Second, it is self-contradictory, since there are many exceptions to the rule. For example, as mentioned, fine art bronzes are nearly always chemically patinated to instantly add age and depth. Likewise, although a modern item that has been woodgrained is not considered collectable, a piece that may have been inlaid with veneer is; yet both items may display an equal level of skill and the same intention to hide the true materials used for the structure of the piece. The most mistaken stance of the modern minimalist decorator or architect is that polished plaster represents an honest finish when, in fact, a truly honest surface would be bare brick or an earth floor.

INTEGRATING SPIRIT WITH ARTIFICE

The big problem is that we have made the mistake of introducing morality into our art and architecture and as a result decorative painting has been sidelined. This was not a problem for our forebears who managed to integrate the more superficial nature of artifice into the spirit and meaning of their architecture and furniture. As is so often the case with period styles (Georgian neo-classical furniture, for example), the spirit is conveyed almost entirely through its decoration, relying very little on the basic forms to convey the strong ideas. If we are guilty of anything today, it is that we have forgotten how to express our philosophies through decoration.

Moreover, to the medieval artist, the business of fakery was something that represented the highest goal in his art. Painters tended to decorate whatever was asked of them: panel paintings, altarpieces, statues, rooms and furniture, and their involvement invariably added value and symbolism to the piece that was decorated. The Egyptians had perfected the technique of laying finely beaten gold sheets onto adhesive to simulate solid gold, but this was nothing compared to the lengths that painters were prepared to go in the thirteenth and fourteenth centuries. The Sainte-Chapelle in Paris, built between 1243 and 1248 (a photograph is reproduced on page 11) was a temple to the deceptive art of the painter, as the art historian Paul Binski writes, 'using no more than glass, plaster, putty and tempera paint with gold leaf. The vaults of this lantern-like building were originally a deep, royal blue, spangled with gilt stars.' The walls were 'diapered with colour and gilded. Small medallions...were set with glass placed upon a silver ground to reflect light...Tiny rectangles painted in imitation of enamel patterns were also set into the walls. As in medieval alchemy, the base was converted into the precious.'

Nor was this approach unique to this one building. Many accounts remain of this fascination with mimicry in decoration. Mahaut, Countess of Artois, commissioned Pierre de Bruxelles in 1320 to decorate her residence near Paris. Work involving murals, a wainscot painted in oil paint, gilding, and silvered tinfoil appliqué (a process known as auripetrum, whereby tin shapes were lacquered using varnish tinted with a clear pigment such as

(RIGHT) *The walls of the Schloss Worlitz in Germany demonstrate how truly impressive 'faux' work may depend on mixing a variety of techniques, resulting in almost pure figurative painting. The techniques used here are trompe l'oeil (strictly speaking, coloured versions of grisaille), bronzing, gilding and marbling.*

THOMSON.
MILTON.
ZACHARIAE.
CRONECK.
HAGEDORN.
STOLBERG.
HALLER.

Current fashion for woodgraining is limited to the more sophisticated nineteenth-century effects such as mahogany, rosewood, satinwood, maple and burr walnut. But early eighteenth-century taste extended to more unusual timbers such as cedarwood (the colour of which is reproduced here) and Virginia walnut.

dragon's blood or saffron). The same creative ideas were to be found throughout Europe; in the Holy Cross Chapel at Karlstein Castle in Prague, the walls literally sparkle with gilded texture, the vault is covered with star-shaped mirrors and the dado encrusted with polished stones and glass of various irregular shapes set into gilded plaster.

But what may seem fantastic and whimsical to us was of enormous pride and importance then. Medieval craftsmen believed profoundly in Ovid's tenet *Opus Superabat Materiam*, that the workmanship should surpass the materials. Thus, an elegant advantage was to be had if the jewels, gold and stars of your decoration turned out to be nothing more than of tin and glass. The baser the materials, the greater the satisfaction of the finished result when perfected, and this philosophy is by no means dead. To the modern painter, the greatest satisfaction can come when he marbles and grains with paints that he has made himself, from gums, oils and powdered pigments.

The psychological impact of the great decorated medieval interiors must have been tremendous on the laymen who beheld them. But here, any comparison with modern perceptions must cease. To the monk or farmer of the Middle Ages, these places represented only one thing, they were each a *simulacram* of the glory of God and the world to come. They were true visions. We, on the other hand, perceive our culture, not as celestially determined, self-contained or fixed, but as a hybrid of the many civilizations and cultures that have gone before, and our thinking in this way is typically post-enlightenment. To us these places demonstrate just one more use of materials and effects, an enticing diversion, and yet another interesting historical resonance of gilding or of the use of stained glass.

USING THE HISTORICAL RESONANCES

But let us turn this complex aesthetic view of our lives to our advantage. The fact that almost every building and craft material we perceive does possess several connotations and historical resonances means that in our decoration and architecture we can use them to our advantage and send rich and strong signals to anyone who casts their eye over them. For example, Sir John Soane employed a fake bronze effect on plaster ceiling roundels in his Regency house in London (an effect that has recently been restored) to introduce severely neo-classical resonances to his decorative scheme. Depending on the context in which nowadays such a device could be employed, you might not only suggest the grandeur of Imperial Rome but also Soane's masculine form of English Regency decoration.

In this way, the decorative languages of our past seem more like old, coloured, transparent photographs that can be layered one upon another to build a slightly faded and ghostly image that will inhabit our handiwork every time we employ or simulate a material that has an historic use.

The particular historical uses of bronze each stimulates a resonance within our modern perceptions of the material. Its use in sculpture has left in our minds the ideas of value and importance of the metal, and the notion that when used, or faked, the use of bronze will indicate something of great worth or great antiquity. Equally, the metal has always been used as a grand defensive material to manufacture grand doors and gates, such as those of the church of San Marco in Venice. In this context, the bronze assumes an imperial status and suggests strength and impenetrability. If you exploit these contexts in your work, then it will take on an air of absolute authenticity; by making the correct psychological associations with each material that you use or fake, you will be drawing on all the magic and power that subconsciously we perceive those materials to carry with them.

A key principle to remember is that the fineness of your decorative finishes is entirely dependent on the scale on which you are working. The scale and level of finish of marbling that you might execute on a wall would appear grossly crude when applied to a decorative object such as a table lamp. Equally, walls often require a broad sweep and a fussy hand can produce annoyingly myopic paint effects that have no real weight in a room. Remember that the brushes you use for these different scales of work should be scaled up or down, and mentally adjust your focal length when moving from painting walls to furniture or accessories, and vice versa.

Tortoiseshell

It is baffling how resourceful man is at mining nature for her gems. No one would ever think that the crusty green shell of an extremely ugly reptile would yield a transparent mottled material of such beauty and plasticity that it can be carved or cut into wafers for veneer work.

The technique of tortoiseshell is by no means rigid, and overleaf you will find historical and studio examples executed in different materials. However, for a tortoiseshell of great clarity and general appeal, it is best to use artist's oil-based paints which should be mixed with varnish to aid their flow and permit transparency. The materials employed on this lampshade are varnish, of whatever description (traditional goldsize has good flow properties), burnt umber and Vandyke brown pigments (burnt umber and black would suffice), both useful for their translucency, and raw sienna to lend a golden ochre tint.

When using any wet varnish technique such as this, work as quickly as possible to make maximum use of the flow properties of the varnish. Although varnishes may take many hours to dry, they remain workable for only a few minutes before becoming tacky. A technique such as tortoiseshell is therefore a one-hit technique and you should practise it, getting up to speed and ensuring that all your materials and mixes are ready prepared beforehand.

YOU WILL NEED

Oil or water-based eggshell finish paint
Untinted varnish
Pigments (raw sienna, burnt umber, Vandyke brown)
Artist's paintbrush
Coarse paintbrush
Lily-bristle softener or white bristled jamb duster

A variety of brushes are needed to manipulate the varnish for this effect, most of them rather stiff in order to work the colours and keep the varnish fluid by constantly agitating it. The softest brush (with the blue handle) is the one that is used last.

1 *The object should preferably be primed in cream paint or, as here, manufactured of cream parchment. First coat it with a layer of the untinted varnish, into which all subsequent colours will blend. Immediately, dab on large spots of raw sienna mixed with a little varnish and quickly soften out using the coarse brush.*

2 *Swiftly apply dots of smaller amounts of the burnt umber and Vandyke brown pigments, again mixed with a little varnish. These should be randomly laid, both in terms of the quantity applied and the density of marks over the surface.*

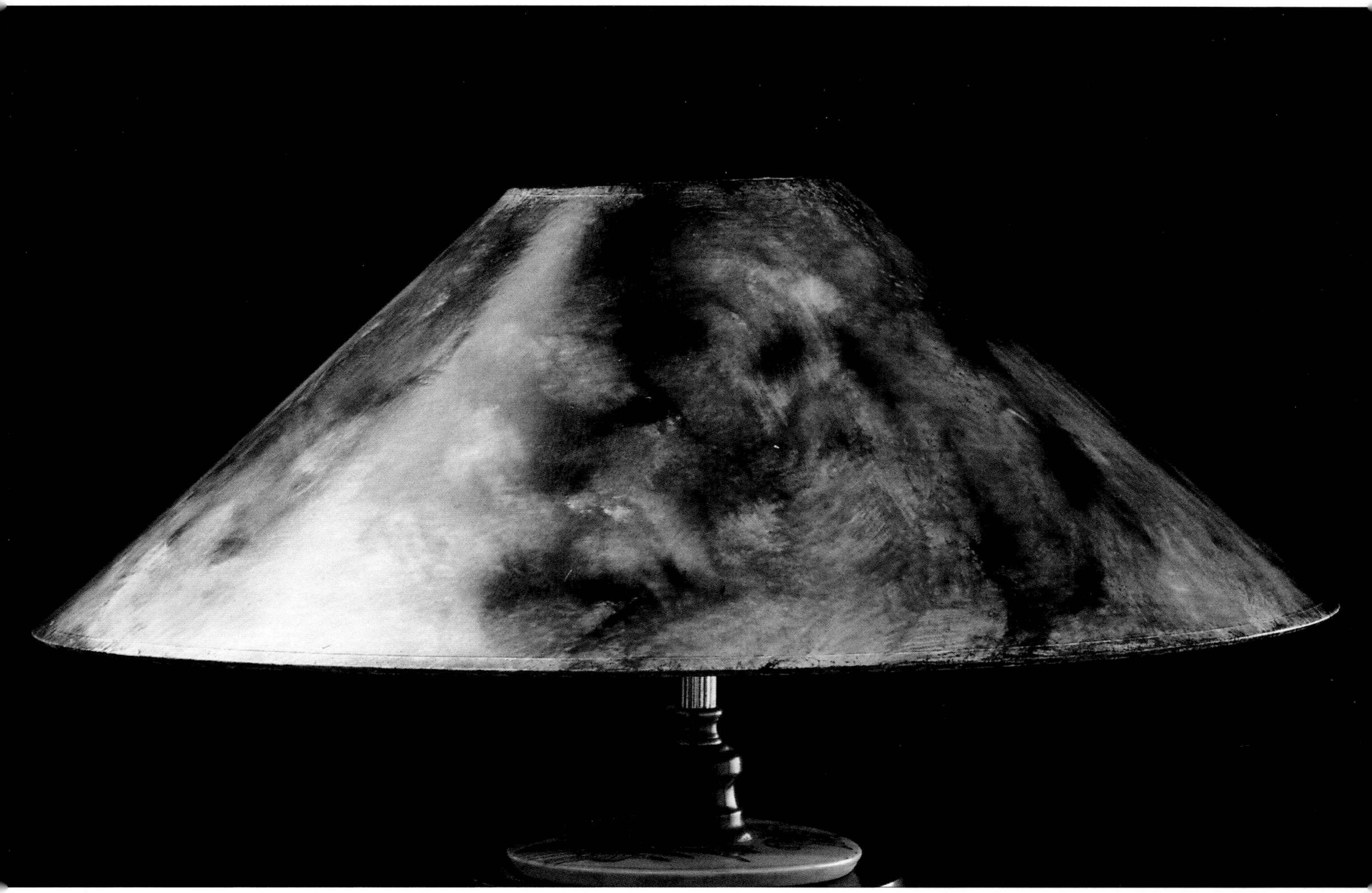

3 *Immediately soften the surface with the coarse brush again. Don't concern yourself with perfection at this stage, you are simply working the colours into the underlying coat of varnish, allowing it to do its job of blending everything together for you.*

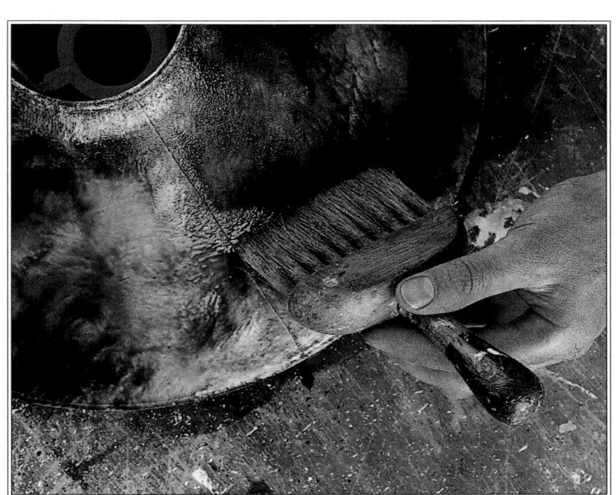

4 *Finally, taking the large soft brush, pass it delicately over the whole surface with the lightest pressure possible to remove as many of the remaining brush marks as possible. Then let the varnish do its job.*

HINTS AND TIPS

* Any object that is to be varnished will benefit from being raised off the table surface with blocks or paint cans; this is to prevent settled dust from coming into contact with the paint film. Equally, any varnished object should be stored in a dust-free environment while it dries; an area where doors or windows will not be opened or shut and where people will not be moving around. For small items, the ideal solution is a plastic 'tent' made by placing a chair or coffee table on the worksurface and draping polythene sheeting over it.

Because of the colouring, the painted effect on this early nineteenth-century French hat box is easier to place than the trunk opposite, despite its forced regularity. It is in direct imitation of earlier painted and inlaid tortoiseshell in the style of Boulle. The red marks are not produced by revealing an underlying layer, but by daubing the colour over a black ground. The surface has also been coated with tinted varnish to soften the crudity of this technique.

THE ESSENTIALS OF TORTOISESHELL

DERIVATION

The use of real tortoiseshell in decoration began in Italy during the Renaissance and grew throughout the seventeenth century. It enjoyed huge popularity as craftsmen such as Boulle in France developed methods for more intricate inlay effects, including the backing of the tortoiseshell with coloured paints, especially red. This trend grew to such an extent that

DERIVATION (CONT)

by the late 1660s painters had begun to imitate the material; a room at Rosenborg Castle in Copenhagen is decorated with this effect. So this technique's pedigree as a faux finish is venerable.

SURFACES

The two requirements for this finish are that the underlying surface is flawless and non-absorbent.

PREPARATION

Smooth cream paint is adequate preparation and cream card that has been sealed with a dilute PVA, acrylic varnish, or shellac is very useful. It can later be cut and used as veneer on picture frames and boxes, for example in imitation of the real material.

FINISHING

Since the technique illustrated involves oil-based varnishes that, if successfully applied, have softened and flowed into each other, the finished

FINISHING (CONT)

surface should be hard, shiny and durable enough. However, specks of dust (nibs) and even bristles may remain! Some 24 hours after varnishing, de-nib the surface with fine wet and dry or sandpaper (440 grade wet and dry or flour grade), and then wax polish, applying the wax with 0000 grade wire wool to ensure its total integration with the varnish coat. When polished, the waxed coat will appear and feel seductively flawless (see pages 138-9).

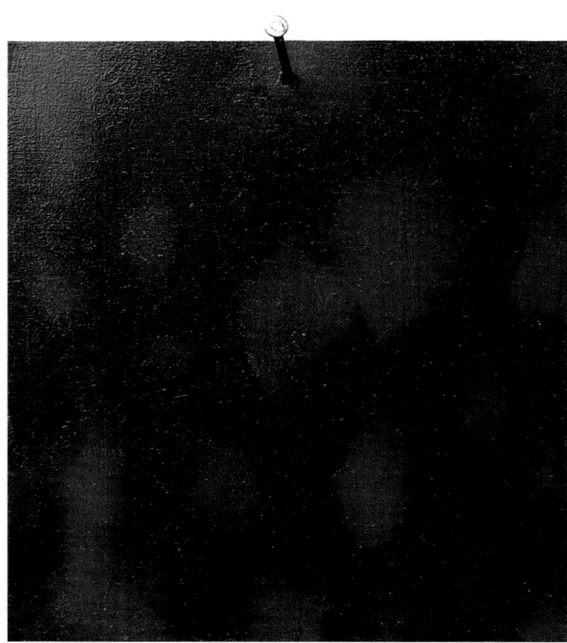

This softly blended and rather subtle effect, in imitation of traditional Boulle red tortoiseshell, is produced very easily. On a perfectly smoothed ground of polished black paint I daubed on varnish that had been heavily pigmented with a mixture of vermilionette and red ochre (the latter affords the mix good opacity). Immediately, this was gently softened in all directions with a lily-bristle softening brush. Care should be taken to use an absolutely dust-free brush and to gently reduce the pressure used throughout softening, to eliminate brush marks.

It is possible to create a highly individual effect with rather strong edges and divisions using water-based media. In this case, a translucent ink was produced by steeping Vandyke crystals (note, not pigment but crystals) in boiling water. Add 1 teaspoon to a pint of water. Different strengths were mixed for different colours, ranging from straw, through amber to brown and black. Traditionally employed for graining, these mixtures can be put to fine effect as tortoiseshell, particularly when dragged out to form very linear patterns. The result was further enhanced by a ground of metal leaf to add brilliance and sparkle; a traditional conceit was to back the tortoiseshell with gold or other fine metal.

The tortoiseshell pattern has been obtained by regularly breaking or scumbling an opaque layer of black paint to reveal a paler ground. The item is a metal nineteenth-century trunk and the pattern so primitive, it is hard to recognize the intentions of the painter.

* If you have ever bought an expensive badger softening brush, never use it for this technique, or for any other in oil for that matter. Badger softeners were designed and introduced for watercolour work only, such as woodgraining; their bristles are too weak to cope with oil and the brush becomes clogged and useless.

* You may try using alternative media for this technique. A passable effect can be obtained by using shellac that has been stained by alcohol (spirit) soluble dyes, or French enamel varnish, as it is known commercially. Water-based media such as acrylic glazes are not suitable for imitating tortoiseshell; they always seem to behave simply as vehicles for paint, developing a muddy opaque quality as they dry. Inks, however, can yield some very interesting results.

Polite marbling

Marbling has gone in and out of fashion as a decorative device, but as early as the seventeenth century the intention was to make it as authentic as possible, and also to be able to imitate the many different kinds of marble. Each marble has characteristic, and highly individual, veining patterns, depending on the geological formation.

Before embarking on this kind of effect, take a good look at real marble so that you can follow the way the veins are formed as closely as possible. For example, no three veins ever meet in a piece of real marble. The actual veins are caused by thinner mineral layers being squeezed between more weighty layers in slightly jagged formations.

To be able to create marbled effects accurately, you need not only an observant eye and a steady hand, but also a paint medium that does not dry too rapidly. To this end, traditionally, boiled linseed oil was mixed with the paint to extend its natural drying time.

YOU WILL NEED

Linseed oil
Gloss emulsion paint (battleship grey)
50mm (2in)-wide flat paintbrush
Wax crayons (black, purple, brown)
Lily-bristle paintbrush
Feather

1 *Mix linseed oil with the gloss emulsion paint in a ratio of 50:50. Mix together thoroughly.*

2 *Using the flat paintbrush, apply the paint as a base coat. You may need two coats, but if so leave the last coat wet.*

3 *Into the wet paint, using the black wax crayon, draw loosely jagged marks. Roll and twist the crayon lightly to create a cracked, broken line, but always in the same diagonal direction.*

4 *Using the purple and brown crayons in turn, add similar marks to the surface in the same way, but making sure that none of the veins meet.*

5 *Go over the marks with the lily-bristle paintbrush, using a fair amount of pressure, to feather out the vein marks, softening across the grain as you go.*

6 *To soften the vein marks still further, go over the surface again with the lily-bristle brush, but this time work with the grain. Do this very gently, just tickling the surface with the brush. For finishing, see The Essentials box, overleaf.*

THE ESSENTIALS OF POLITE MARBLING

DERIVATION

This technique is completely based on panels discovered in the library designed by Sir Christopher Wren at Lincoln Cathedral. It is therefore an entirely mid-seventeenth-century technique, surprisingly sophisticated for its time and unique in its adoption of the crayon as a tool.

SURFACES

Walls, woodwork and plaster ornaments can all be marbled in this way.

PREPARATION

You need to ensure that the base coat is the proper colour – a cold, bluish white or steely pale grey, ideally with a translucent sheen like real marble. This can normally be achieved by ensuring that the paint has a high ratio of linseed oil in it, which imparts the gloss.

FINISHING

To give the marble its final lustrous appearance, it simply requires several coats of varnish, rubbed down between with wet and dry sandpaper (first 220 grit, then 440 grit), and washed with water and allowed to dry before the next coat of varnish is applied. After the last coat has dried, cut it back and sand before waxing with beeswax polish. Walls, or areas of high wear, can be finished with a coat of varnish instead.

(LEFT) *This example of historical marbling is of an eighteenth-century painted shell cupboard belonging to the author. Note how stylized the marbling is and how two types are imitated; sketchy lines on the panelling suggest carrara, while abstract and bold oval marks on the frames are a clear attempt at some kind of brecciated marble. Both are executed by moving a feather, loaded with thick coloured varnish, through a coating of wet clear varnish. The colours used are black and vermilion red; the ground was originally white, although age has turned the coating of varnish a greenish yellow.*

(RIGHT) *All polite marbling is a deliberate attempt to produce a realistic impression of the imitated material. To do this well, the marble must be subdivided to represent real, manageable slabs.*

CHOOSING THE SITUATION

A grey or white ground is the classical colour for seventeenth-century marbling. The exponents of it were highly skilled, and much in demand. One of the best-known travel writers of her time, Celia Fiennes, noted on her journeys in 1697 that the Best Room in Newby Park in Yorkshire was painted just like marble. One of the ways in which marbling was used in the late seventeenth century was to create marbled surrounds to wall panels, which often had mirror glass as the centrepiece – an especially popular conceit in France. By the middle of the eighteenth century, however, this kind of polite, cool marbling was going out of fashion and was confined to decorating wooden or plaster chimney pieces, for example, rather than whole rooms.

When producing this kind of classical marbling, it is clearly important that you pick an appropriate situation for it. It is also important that you create as authentic an effect as you possibly can. If you do not have the time or patience to execute it, you could have a go at the cruder, more theatrical vernacular marbling featured on pages 216-23.

HINTS AND TIPS

* If you use a wax crayon, rather than the artist's brush normally recommended, you will find the crayon slips in the paint, making authentic, and pleasing, veining marks. It does, however, need softening afterwards to diffuse it.

* A feather can also be used for creating the veins in marbling, but instead of working into the wet ground, work on a dry ground and dip the tip of the feather in the appropriate coloured paint (see the picture to the right).

Both of these swatches were executed in variations of the technique described on the previous pages, using materials available to the craftsman prior to the mid-nineteenth century (when oil glazes were introduced).

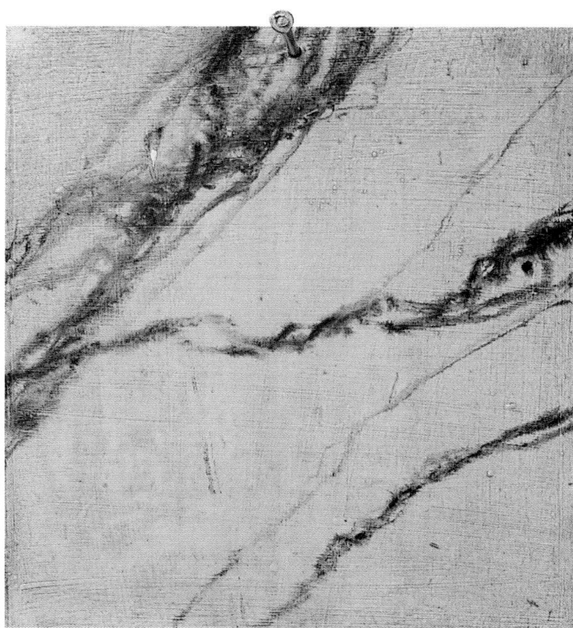

In imitation of the technique used on the painted cupboard on page 212, this sample was executed by dragging a goose feather, loaded with a black-tinted varnish (see photograph above opposite), through a layer of wet clear varnish laid over a white ground. The resulting marks melt and blur into the wet layer. Both varnishes used were oil-based linseed.

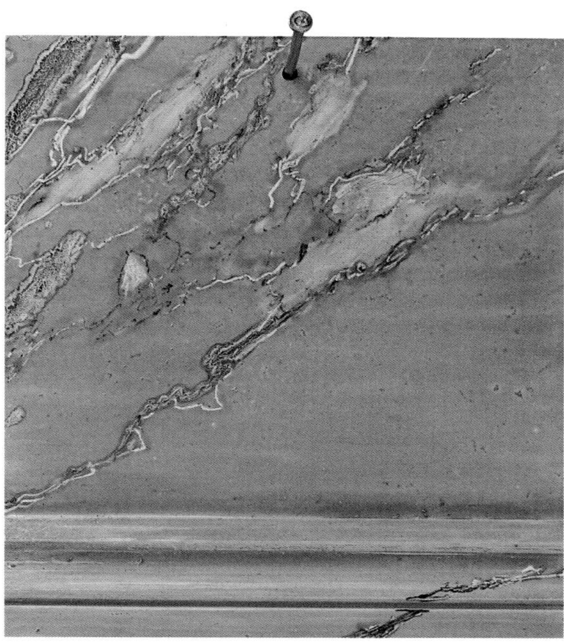

This example is identical to the main technique, save that a yellow coloured varnish was used instead of oil paint, resulting in a more vivid finish. Yellow ochre and a little king's yellow (hansa yellow was used) are the pigments used to colour the varnish. White spirit was dabbed onto the glaze to produce the white marks or 'holes' in the glaze.

* If you use cold-pressed linseed oil (the kind used for oiling cricket bats – linseed comes from the seed of the flax plant), you will find it has a very long drying time, giving you more time for marking in the veins.

(LEFT) *Marbling was extensively used as a finish in Roman decoration and has been popular ever since. Its success has always depended on the way it is applied in blocks, and the choice of different areas, mouldings and panelling, all finished in differing marbles.*

(RIGHT) *Polite marbling may be exaggerated and stylized to more resemble the wilder designs of vernacular marbles, if not executed with the same roughness.*

Vernacular marbling

This exaggerated, almost theatrical looking, marble does not belong specifically to any period. Rather it is an amalgam of different styles and techniques, aiming to produce the widely varying forms of marble, such as the strongly coloured red and grey Breccia marble, so often seen in Venetian churches, or the golden colour of that of Siena. The vernacular marbling technique used here is based on the Italian tradition of marbling in water-based paints that found favour in England possibly as early as the sixteenth century. It is important to note that each of the marbling techniques featured in this book, polite (see pages 210-15) and vernacular, is not rooted in a specific century. Rather, they have run alongside each other, finding favour at different times in different countries.

The veining marks in this technique are more stylistically drawn than in polite marbling, with a more flowing, flamboyant line. They make strong, curving forms rather than the delicate, fragmented broken lines of popular realistic marbling that seek to emulate the real thing more accurately.

This table top had been previously marbled using softened, spattered glazes, in a variation of that same classic standard nineteenth-century method that has enjoyed a revival in the last twenty years. I decided to give it a proper vernacular treatment and so we have shown it opposite both before and after painting.

YOU WILL NEED

Acrylic varnish and pigments (according to your choice of marble) to prepare the paints (see overleaf)
50mm (2in)-wide flat paintbrush
12mm (1/2in)-wide flat paintbrush
Round fitch
Swordliner (designed for lettering but perfect for veining) or other fine brush
Acrylic paint (white)

1 *Daub your first pre-mixed colour (here I used yellow ochre) on the surface in generous quantities, with a standard decorator's brush.*

2 *Using a smaller brush, but one still capable of holding a decent quantity of paint, roll the next colour onto the ground (here a pink formed from the red ochre and titanium white mixes).*

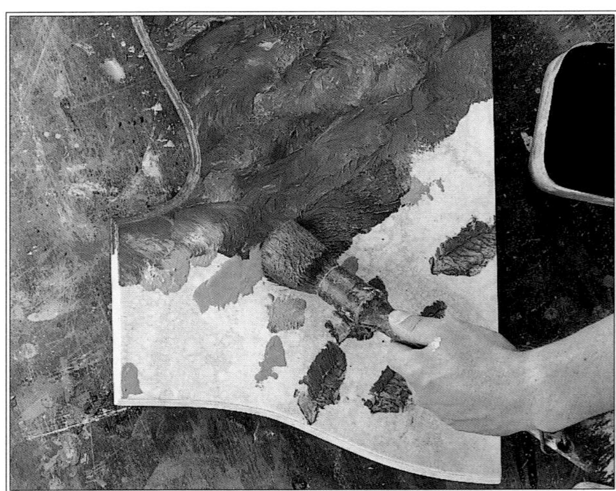

3 *Taking a generously loaded brush, preferably a very large round fitch, apply the main body of colour (red ochre and burnt sienna here) by rolling the brush across the surface in diagonal patterns. This will build texture, obscure the ground and begin to integrate the colours.*

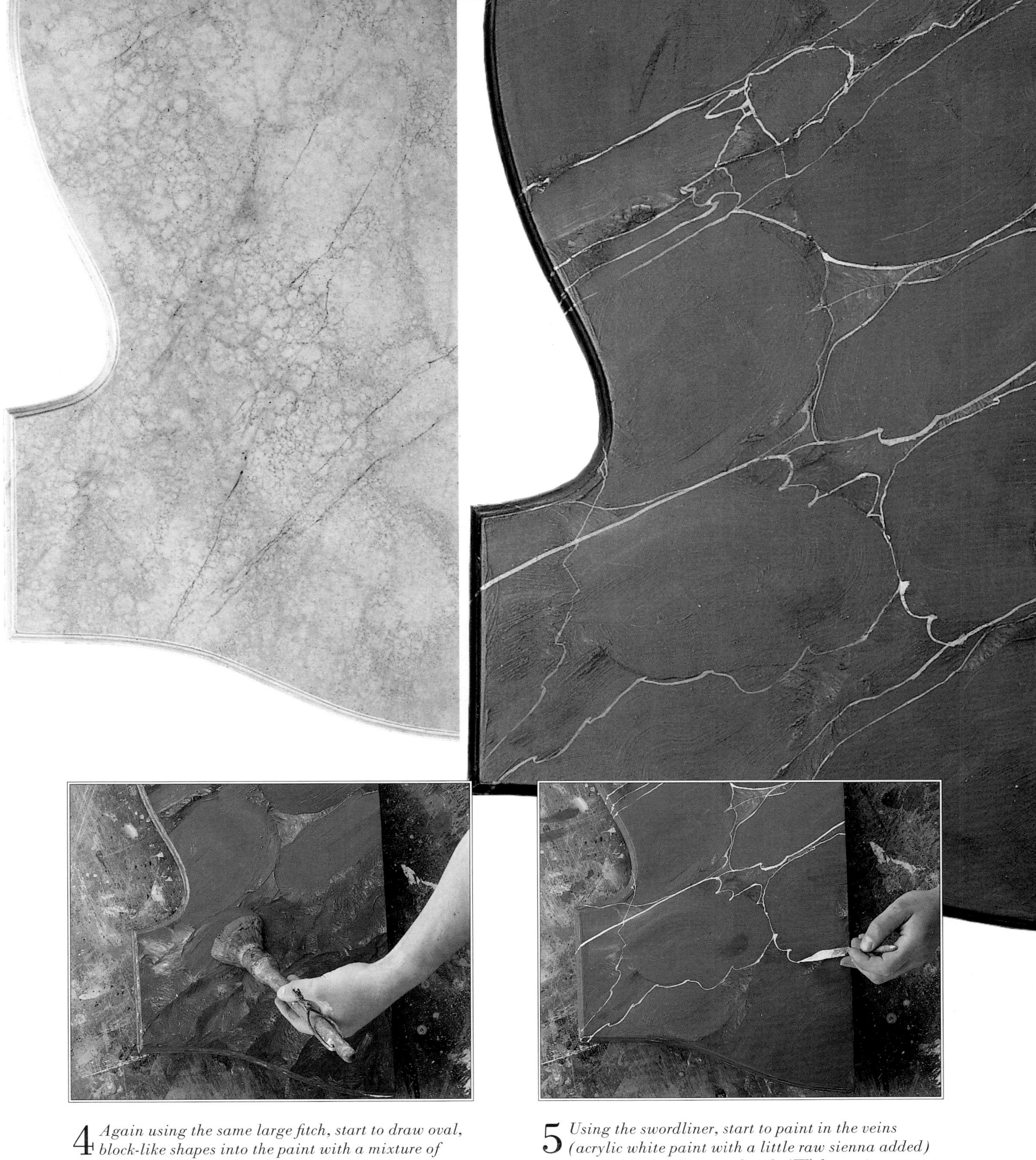

4 *Again using the same large fitch, start to draw oval, block-like shapes into the paint with a mixture of paints on the brush. By this time, the paint on the surface is getting quite thick and you will have to wait some time for it to dry before continuing with step 5.*

5 *Using the swordliner, start to paint in the veins (acrylic white paint with a little raw sienna added) in diagonal broken lines and curly 'W' formations, varying the thickness and the spacing of the lines so that they do not appear too regular. When dry, the surface may be coated with either clear or coloured varnish or wax (I chose a wax coloured with raw umber pigment) (see The Essentials box, overleaf).*

For strength and thickness, the paints I used were made from pigment mixed with acrylic varnish; it is an unorthodox binder but an excellent one.

PAINTS FOR MARBLING

Vernacular marbling is best produced with a paint made from acrylic varnish and pigment mixed together to form a shiny, thick paint that dries to a matt finish. It also makes a very tough paint that emulates the water-based distemper and gesso paints that were often originally used in Italian church interiors.

The pigment colours you will need for this kind of marbling are the earth pigments such as yellow ochre, raw sienna and red ochre, plus titanium white. As far as the surfaces are concerned, this style of marbling tends to look best executed on sturdy items such as table tops, simply designed turned lamps, wooden furniture and boxes, even chunky metal furniture; anything that is butch enough to take it and not too dainty. No one is going to be fooled by this technique as a form of mimicry. It is an entirely painterly marbling technique with a strong character, presence, and a rough-and-ready finish.

Before starting out, you will need to prepare several pots of paint for this technique. I first made a binder by thinning acrylic varnish with water and then to make the four different colours I added the following pigments:

1 Yellow ochre
2 Red ochre
3 Titanium white
4 Burnt sienna.

Firm, round brushes, or fitches, are excellent for producing the thick sworls required for this marbling effect. This is a clear example of how the right tool is sometimes essential for a technique.

USING A ROUND FITCH

For this kind of very textural work you require a stout, round fitch with a long handle. A brush such as this will carry a great deal of paint and you can freely and spontaneously roll it around the surface at arm's length. Ordinary decorator's rectangular brushes will not do; their shape is too formal and their handles too short for you to obtain a suitably random effect from them.

CHOOSING THE MEDIUM

If you have ever tried repeating a paint effect with the wrong materials, you will know how different the

(RIGHT) *The staircase at Parnham House in Dorset has some good contemporary examples of fantasy marbles.*

THE ESSENTIALS OF VERNACULAR MARBLING

DERIVATION

A stylized adaptation of rather crude but lively marbling techniques adopted throughout Europe. Particularly good eighteenth-century examples executed in water paints are to be found in Scandinavia. The Italian tradition is less transparent and often very hastily executed, although to great effect. The designs are graphic adaptations of the more common marbles. Carrara (the great pilasters of the nave of St Peter's in Rome are crudely but effectively painted in fake Carrara), yellow Siena, red

DERIVATION(CONT)

Breccia (the one I chose), travertine and green serpentine are all common, plus a variety of fantasy marbles.

SURFACES

Any can be used, but it must be relatively non-porous to prevent it from sucking the water out of the wet paint and interfering with moving the paint around. Given the eventual thickness of the paint, surface imperfections are not important.

PREPARATION

You will need to paint a smooth, non-porous, neutral-coloured ground on which the marbling can be executed, preferably in a water-based paint. Bare plaster walls should be sealed with a priming coat of diluted PVA. Wooden surfaces should first be sanded and coated with shellac as an isolating coat and to prevent the grain from rising.

FINISHING

The final surface can be varnished or waxed, or varnished and then waxed, as preferred. Areas that are likely to be subjected to hard wear should be given more than one coat. Acrylic varnish is quite acceptable, and indeed an oil-based varnish will sit equally well over acrylic paint. I find that a coloured wax (as employed on the previous pages) sits well into the texture of the dried paint, emphasizing its fluid patterns.

(ABOVE) *Many paint effects develop out of other techniques, and indeed employ other, simpler techniques as part of their more complex structure. This primitive marbling is simply a form of colourwashing and spattering.*

results can be. It is pretty obvious that a classic marble executed in transparent oil glazes will look a mess if exactly the same technique is followed using thinned emulsion paints. But the characteristics of each material should be seen, not as limitations, but as qualities to be exploited. That is exactly what the seventeenth-century decorators responsible for the last technique (see pages 210-15) did. They saw that wax crayons dissolved in oil and turpentine, and so experimented to push the performances of both the crayon and the oil paint a little further than hitherto was possible. It would be pointless to emulate that technique using water-based paints; the result would be uncontrollable and probably a failure.

(ABOVE) *The most exciting and vital vernacular marbles are so obviously painted, it is amazing how the artist got away with it. This is just a succession of brush dabs. The secret lies in the spontaneity of the work.*

(RIGHT) *Scandinavian decoration is unrivalled in its ability to put simple techniques together to create exquisitely sophisticated interiors. This process is theatrical and yet works perfectly well in houses, perhaps because of the delicate colours chosen. Vernacular marbling is here combined with trompe l'oeil work and spattering. None of the techniques is that convincing, but they conspire to produce a charming whole.*

At the Frederic Karlsberg Slott in Copenhagen, the marbling appears to be in the fine nineteenth-century tradition that has been promoted over the last two or three decades. But, in fact, the artist has not used glazes, but impasto oil paint and traditional easel techniques to blend the wet paint; the same technique that I used on these pages, but here they are more painstakingly executed in artist's oil paint.

There are also more subtle distinctions to be made between different types of paint that at first sight appear very similar. I used a tough acrylic varnish as a water-based binder in this instance because I knew that it would dry to a flexible but extremely tough surface – tougher than either ordinary acrylic paint or emulsion.

However, even though an Italian decorator of the nineteenth century would have employed a soft water-based paint to marble, say, a church altar on a table top he would have used thick oil colours. His technique, the one we reproduce here, requires a heavy body of thick opaque paint that for our purposes must dry in a reasonable time. Oil paint is an option, but a slow-drying one and not one with which I would recommend starting out.

Equally, other water-based paints would have been inappropriate here. On a wall I could use soft distemper, casein paint, even pigments bound with gum arabic to make a kind of tempera paint. But on a table top they are all too friable and dusty. They would soon rub off and would darken and smudge under any layer of wax or varnish I might choose to protect them with. Even emulsion would not work; its synthetic pigments would give the finished surface a dead and rather plastic quality. The exception would be a blend of white emulsion coloured with the earth pigments I used; they might introduce some life into the surface, but again, it is doubtful that the dry layer would be as hard as the acrylic formulation I used.

HINTS AND TIPS

* Once you start painting this marbling technique, execute it freely. Take a good look at the example, study it, and then put down the instructions, and simply have a go on some card. If you stop and start, looking as you go, it will lose the fluidity and spontaneity so essential for the final effect.
* Make sure the paint is quite thick, with plenty of texture. If it is too runny, the colours will mix too freely and you will not achieve the necessary varied and textural effect.
* The essence of the stylized veining marks is an italic curling 'W' mark. Practise this first on some card, too.
* If you wish, fine and authentic-looking period effects can be obtained by combining this technique with that of Peeled and chipped paint (see pages 170-3).

This detail from a nineteenth-century French fireplace shows no self-consciousness whatsoever. The paint is applied with a real knowledge of what the artist was trying to emulate, but it is applied very hurriedly, by brush and mainly by sponge.

All these examples were executed in water-based paints.

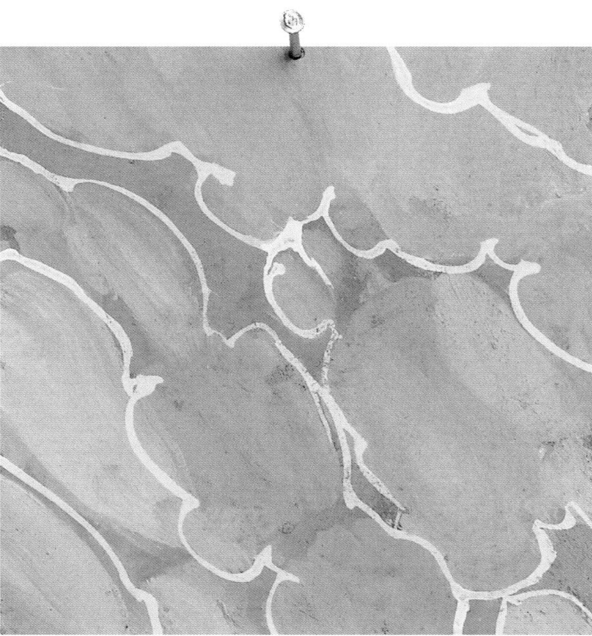

This is exactly the same technique as the one employed on the step-by-step pages. But yellow and raw sienna pigments were employed to produce this imitation of Siena marble .

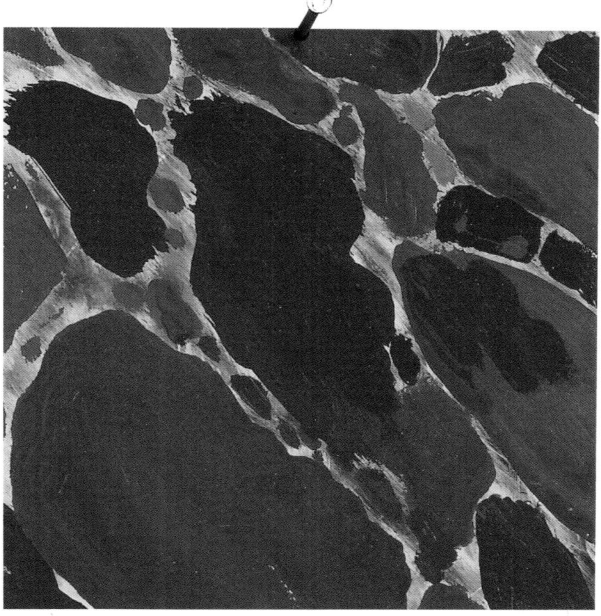

Brecciated marble, can be imitated by a much more careful approach. Here, the ground was laid in a number of greys mixed together on the surface. When dry, several different reds were daubed on thickly and, using a round fitch, manipulated into loose oval shapes that almost touch each other.

This rough form of Carrara was painted using the easiest tradition of all. Each colour had its own brush and the design was worked up by drawing the blocks and veins with thick paint into an already wet paint on the surface.

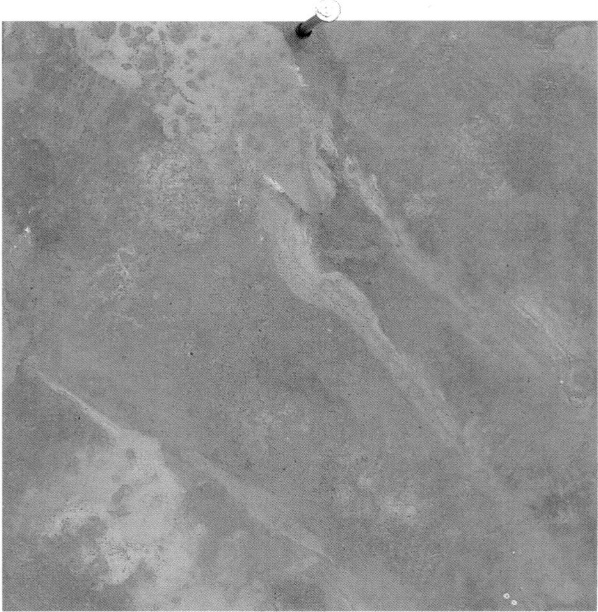

This looser effect is only possible on horizontal surfaces. The surface was wetted and the thick paints applied and worked into each other. More water may be spattered on to assist the colours in blending with each other.

Rustic graining

The simpler fake paint effects are often the ones to be found across all the continents. This straightforward technique, a clear and graphic graining that is more like pattern-making, relies upon a simple medium, be it water- or oil-based, loosely moved and combed in some way. A mixture of gum arabic and pigment dissolved in water is excellent as this will not run or blur. Traditionally, a feather, piece of card or piece of linseed oil putty (see step 4, opposite) was the tool used to either drag or dab the paint. As a result, many of the effects produced were only vaguely suggestive of woodgrain, often merely producing an attractive repeat pattern!

Since the process is virtually a 'one hit' application in every example, the photographs below and opposite are divided into two categories. Pictures 1 and 2 are preparation steps, and then pictures 3 to 6 show four alternative rustic graining effects. More are illustrated on the swatches on page 229.

YOU WILL NEED

Pigments
Water
Gum arabic
Primer
50mm (2in)-wide paintbrush
Shellac
Whiting
Graining medium (see overleaf)
Broken sponge (for step 3); or linseed oil putty (for step 4); or pencil overgrainer (for steps 5 and 6)

1 *Mix your graining paint. The paint I used here was a simple mixture of pigments, water and gum arabic (5 parts water to 1 part gum). The mixture needs to be glossy and oily, and sufficiently thick such that it will not blur or run. Alternatively, use an oil-based glaze (see page 61), but perhaps not one based on varnish; its good flow properties would soften the effects too much.*

2 *Prime the surface and when the paint is dry, apply a coat or two of shellac. Leave to dry once more and then vigorously rub the surface with whiting on your fingertips to absorb any surface grease. Then wipe it clean.*

3 Brush a coat of the graining medium over the ground and immediately drag a piece of broken sponge through it. Experiment to produce different marks by swirling and staggering the sponge. Also experiment with different pressures.

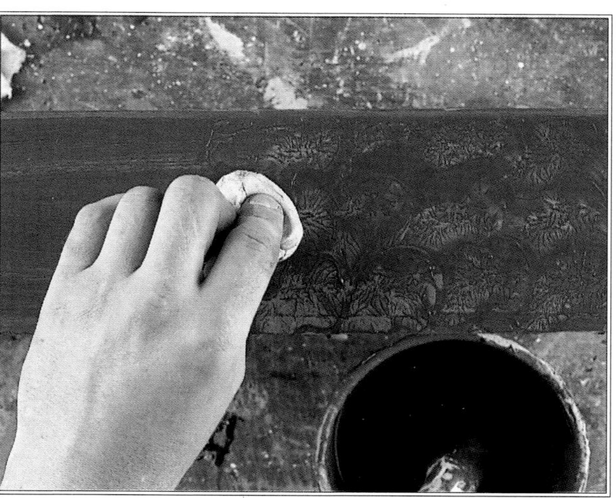

4 Take a lump of linseed oil putty (preferably from an older pot in which the putty has had a chance to go stiff) and dab repeatedly through a wet surface of graining medium. The pattern should be regular and the dabs overlapping. Note the tiny reticulated patterns made by pulling the putty away from the paint. This is a popular effect on folk-art furniture.

5 A special tool, the pencil overgrainer, can be employed to make a wide variety of strong marks through a layer of graining medium. Even a decorating brush will suffice to produce this grain. Drag the surface one way and then make definitive, stylized curving marks through the paint.

6 This technique differs in that for once the paint or graining medium is put on *by the brush. Take a pencil overgrainer, load it with paint and experiment with a variety of stylized grains such as whorls and curves.*

(ABOVE) *The French decorator who painted this tray in the nineteenth century probably just used a piece of card to do it. With one edge ripped into a jagged blade he could drag it through a coloured glaze, forming the whorls of this simple mahogany design, and stop the card every now and then to make the radial lines. It is worth experimenting to see what a piece of card is really capable of.*

GRAINING MEDIUM

For this type of clear and graphic graining, which is more like pattern-making, a medium is required that will not run or blur and for this a mixture of gum arabic and pigment is excellent. The gum is sufficiently glutinous for any pattern made to stay in place. Early recipes from the seventeenth to the nineteenth centuries call for graining media bound with simpler, more readily available liquids such as vinegar or stale beer. Stale beer is interesting because as it deteriorates (over the course of a week or so, on open exposure to the air), it gets thicker; when ready for use, it is as glutinous as gum arabic. Skimmed milk is also a traditional binder for washes, understandable since it contains casein, a long-recognized powerful binder for paints.

To experiment, you may wish to begin with artist's gouache – pigment paints bound with gum arabic – although for permanent work these are unsuitable since their high chalk content will render the colours darker and more transparent if and when varnished. Another alternative is Vandyke crystals, prepared as for the graining recipe on page 232, but, of course, these provide a more limited colour range than pigments. When thinned they are also transparent, a quality not normally associated with this rustic type of graining.

(RIGHT) *Historic Scandinavian interiors often demonstrate the clever integration of both rustic graining and marbling. This is primarily achieved by a process of abstraction; the effects are executed in colours that are derived from the colour scheme of the room, and not necessarily from real marbles or woods.*

COLOURS

Almost inevitably, the best graining colours are those provided by earth colours; particularly raw sienna, raw umber and burnt umber. If white is to be added, choose a pigment that will not be rendered transparent under subsequent oil or shellac varnishes; titanium white is best.

(BELOW) *This is an exuberant, restored, example of American eighteenth-century graining in water paints, from Captain William Perley's house built in 1763 in Boxford, Massachussetts. The wood imitated is cedar, popular for the period and executed in an interesting deep ochre/pink on a delicate pale beige-pink ground.*

Mitt hem är vårsol
i vintertid
Mitt hem är vila
i arbetstid

A set of graining rollers for introducing the heart graining for oak, made at the turn of the twentieth century. Each wooden roller is covered with a 5mm (1/4 in)-thick strip of sewn leather which has been hand gouged, like a lino printing block, with the pattern. When dampened, the roller would have lifted wet paint or glaze from a surface. Note the different sizes required for the varying timber widths on panelling and doors.

EXPERIMENTING WITH RUSTIC GRAINING

The joy of this particular technique is that by using a very simple paint you can produce extremely effective results just by letting your imagination run wild. In early historical examples, the graining medium used for the job was much cruder than the clearer, more transparent glazes developed for the job in the late eighteenth/early nineteenth centuries. But it is interesting to note that even the more sophisticated and realistic wood graining techniques, such as that represented on pages 230-5, have always relied on a combination of water and oil media.

HINTS AND TIPS

* Practise these techniques on flat card and aim for speedy execution and total confidence. The charm of these graining patterns depends on your ability to abstract the pattern in your mind's eye, to produce a simple graphic version of it, and to work as spontaneously as possible. In short, you must work and place yourself in the same frame of mind as the decorators who originally did this

THE ESSENTIALS OF RUSTIC GRAINING

DERIVATION

Much seventeenth-century panelling was painted and, if made from cheaper softwood, grained in imitation of the timbers used in grander schemes; oak, walnut and chestnut. Until recently it has been assumed that early graining was applied only to timber surfaces, relying on the mouldings and relief of the panelling to add interest. However, the paint historian Helen Hughes has discovered that the remains of some late seventeenth-century graining at Cogges Manor in Oxfordshire are much more sophisticated. Not only did the artist grain both the timber dado and the plaster wall above, he created trompe l'oeil panelling both on the flat wall and the real timber panelling. This was heightened by applying the paint thickly in places to produce a type of impasto graining, adding texture for extra realism.

But simpler graining techniques were also well in

DERIVATION (CONT)

evidence throughout the seventeenth and eighteenth centuries. Captain William Perley's house built in 1763 in Boxford, Massachusetts (see page 226) contained cedar-graining; a popular faux woodgrain of the time, as was Virginia walnut, on both sides of the Atlantic.

However, we must not get bogged down by dates. Rustic graining, by definition, is lowly and has been healthily produced by folk artists and decorators for centuries, regardless of the technological advances or fashionable styles of advancing history. Many of the examples I have seen have been French or American dating from the nineteenth century, a period that decorative historians associate with more polite and sophisticated forms of oil-glaze graining. The work at Cogges Manor is so sophisticated (for any period) that, ironically, it almost falls outside the definition of rustic graining.

SURFACES

Clearly wooden objects and simple country furniture are the most appropriate objects to paint, but the nineteenth century has bequeathed tin trunks, lanterns and metal trays that have all received a dash of graining. Sophisticated furniture or fine panelling dating from the eighteenth century onwards, if it is to be grained, should generally be painted with a little more respect, employing a polite graining technique (see pages 230-5).

PREPARATION

Surfaces should be prepared as well as possible, sanded, filled and polished smooth before the ground colour is applied. This is usually an oil-based undercoat and eggshell finish topcoat, although acrylics, if smoothed out under the brush, can be used. In the examples on pages 224-5, I used shellac that had been coloured with raw sienna pigment to make a

PREPARATION (CONT)

lacquer-type paint. This is more brittle than oil paint but quicker drying and quite suitable for objects that will receive little wear.

FINISHING

Since the media used for this type of graining are soft, ie they will dissolve in water even when dry, the finished graining should be varnished to waterproof and stabilize it. A coat of shellac is possible, but great care must be taken in applying it so that the alcohol in the shellac does not lift or smudge the water-based graining medium – something it can do all too easily, especially if overbrushed. An oil-based varnish is therefore best.

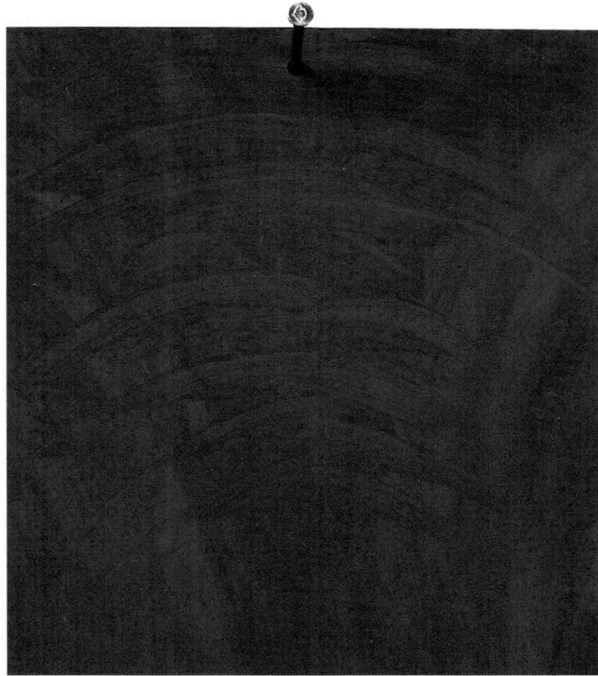

(TOP LEFT) *When painted by vernacular decorators, rosewood may appear wildly different to the real wood, as here. A strongly coloured oil-based varnish, thickened and darkened with a mixture of burnt umber and black pigments, was applied over an orange-beige ground and dragged through with a comb.*

(TOP RIGHT) *This example of mahogany was produced by using a brush to roughly grain a water-based wash into a fan shape. I then quickly passed my thumb through the wet paint to produce the rays of the heart graining. It is precisely this crude form of water graining that was used in many vernacular applications. The ground was painted a beige-pink and the graining was executed in burnt sienna pigment bound with gum arabic in water.*

(LEFT) *This sample of oak was executed in raw sienna pigment bound with gum arabic in water. The mix was lightly brushed over the surface, quickly grained (dragged) with the side of the brush and then flogged with the side of the brush. The figure of the heart grain was then added by taking a cloth and pulling it tightly over a thumbnail. By moving the nail through the paint layer, the trailing, comma-like marks so distinctive of oak were created. It only then remained to re-flog the surface.*

kind of work. All these processes are only possible with rigorous practice that will, in the end, give way to total confidence.

* The easiest media are the most traditional ones. A glaze medium made with gum arabic or stale beer will remain water-soluble, even when dry. These media are therefore ideal for experimenting and practising with; you can rework them time and again until you find that you are happy with the result.

* The finest examples of this type of graining are to be found on European and American furniture and accessories, dating mainly from the eighteenth and nineteenth centuries. Museums, collections of folk art and books on the subject all provide excellent references.

Polite graining

This form of graining, popular in the nineteenth century, is a refined form of rustic graining (see pages 224-9). In it, several layers of translucent glaze are built up, using a mixture of water and oil colours. Water colours are used initially, and then an oil glaze applied as the finishing coat.

For the water glazes, you need either pigment in a beer solution (to make it sufficiently sticky) and Indian inks (which dry waterproof) or Vandyke crystals (from a polish supplier), which are dissolved in water. These last are very dark, and the darkness of the final finish will be determined by the strength of the Vandyke solution (see recipe overleaf). A weaker one will produce an almost yellow colour, a strong one an almost black colour.

It is the translucency of these crystals that makes the finish so naturally appealing, coupled with the fact that it is built up layer by layer. Start with a general light grain, flogged, dragged or cross-grained over the surface to give a broken effect, then add some pores, followed by figure graining, if needed, and finally give it a general glaze as a last coat, which you can mottle if you wish, depending on the wood finish you are imitating. In rosewood, this mottling is clearly part of the overall pattern; in mahogany and satinwood it produces a shimmering pearlescence on the surface. The technique described below creates a good walnut grain.

YOU WILL NEED

Paintbrushes (50mm [2in] flat, flogging or 60mm [2 1/4in] flat, 25mm [1in] fitch, small badger softener, sable liner, sable fantail, soft bristled)
Whiting
Vandyke crystal solution (see recipe overleaf)
Indian inks (sepia, black)
Sponge
Oil-based varnish
Pigments (raw sienna, burnt umber)

1 *Prime your surface with acrylic or oil-based base coat tinted with white, yellow ochre and raw umber, and leave it to dry. You may find it necessary to dust the surface with whiting to absorb any surface grease or oil before applying the solution so that it adheres better (see preparation in The Essentials, overleaf). Wipe the surface clean and brush on a weak solution of Vandyke crystals.*

2 *Flog the solution while it is still wet using a long flogging brush (for a large surface) and an ordinary decorating brush for a smaller one. Push and tap the brush against the glaze, rather than pulling it through it.*

3 *Start the spattering to create the pores, using the fitch paintbrush and a mixture of the sepia and black Indian inks. To spatter, flick the brush against your finger. Then use the small badger softener to elongate the ink marks. When dry, give the surface a coat of oil-based varnish and allow it to dry. Rub whiting into the surface to remove any grease and wipe clean.*

4 *Paint on a coat of thicker Vandyke mixture and then with small pieces of sponge, figure the wood by dragging the sponge lightly through the mixture to produce bands of darker colour.*

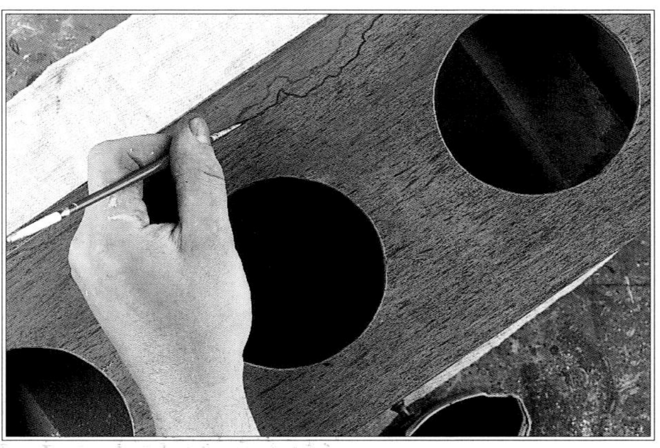

5 *Using the sable liner and the thickest Vandyke mixture of all, create watery and near-parallel lines, softening them out with the badger softener in the direction of the grain.*

6 *At this stage, darken the wood by applying a coat of oil varnish to which raw sienna and burnt umber pigments have been added in equal quantities*

7 *Using the tip of the sable fantail, mottle the oil varnish. This removes some of the varnish to create some very subtle cross-banding.*

8 *Finally, soften across the grain once again with the soft-bristled brush. Finish as described in The Essentials box, overleaf.*

VANDYKE CRYSTAL RECIPE

Put the crystals in a container and pour on boiling water, while stirring. For a thick mixture, add a teaspoon of crystals to a half a cup of boiling water. This produces a blackish-brown mixture particularly useful for rosewood graining. A thinner recipe produces a transparent, mid-brown wash, as used in varying strengths, for the technique demonstrated here. A paler version again can be achieved by further diluting the solution. Test your mixes on a piece of card.

CHOOSING THE MEDIUM

The aim of this kind of graining is to achieve an authentic simulation of fine veneer at a tiniest fraction of the price you would have to pay for the real thing. A huge variety of graining patterns can be copied using this technique, but rosewood, mahogany and satinwood are among the most popular.

Polite graining is time consuming to do well, and requires patient attention to detail. What is absolutely necessary is a real love of wood for its own sake. Only through careful study of a timber's physical characteristics will you be able to reproduce them in your final effect.

(ABOVE) *Tools for woodgraining, from left to right: 50mm (2in)-wide flat paintbrush, sable liner, small badger softener, sable fantail, overgrainer (optional and only necessary for large areas), Indian ink, Vandyke crystals.*

(RIGHT) *This rosewood sample was executed on a pale orange ground. The colour is clearly visible where the paint has chipped away.*

THE ESSENTIALS OF POLITE GRAINING

DERIVATION

Principally a mid-nineteenth-century invention, polite graining is a development of the water-based or (occasionally) oil-based techniques of the eighteenth century. By mixing the two disciplines, a near-perfect imitation of the real wood is possible. Earlier traditions produced very stylized and painterly imitations of wood of whatever grain. However,

DERIVATION (CONT)

given its complexity, polite graining tends to be used to fake the more expensive hardwoods such as mahogany, teak, walnut or rosewood.

SURFACES

Must be coloured as the lightest tint of the wood, and be perfectly smooth and flat – any bump or hole will catch the washes and glazes and show up.

PREPARATION

Ideally use a non-porous ground, such as oil-based eggshell, lightly sanded with flour-grade sandpaper. Dust down with talc, whiting or fuller's earth to remove any grease.

FINISHING

Traditionally, two coats of oil-based gloss varnish and then wax. Varnish to be cut down with flour-grade sandpaper between coats.

(ABOVE LEFT) *The grain of rosewood is particularly varied and unusual; the finely detailed bands of grain laid next to each other seem to run in opposite directions and are separated by dark lines. The cross-banding varies in colour from walnut to reddish hazelnut. It is a grainer's delight to imitate, although, when broken down, it has the same steps as those described on the previous pages. The graining has been worked over a pink-beige ground and the coat of tinted varnish was in two colours, one redder than the other. It was brushed over the top and selectively wiped or mottled out over some of the graining, always following the darker lines beneath.*

(ABOVE RIGHT) *Clairebois is the generic name given to any pale inlaid wood, and specifically satinwood or maple. This effect demands an especially subtle approach. A thin coat of Vandyke crystal mixture was applied which was lightly flogged and dragged to give the slightest indication of pore graining with a little figure. This was then followed by at least two layers of glaze or varnish to build up the body colour of the wood. The varnish layers were mottled out to procure the effect of cross-banding; in this case, wide horizontal pale marks across the pore graining.*

(RIGHT) *Simple pine graining can be easily produced with two brushes; one a small fitch and the other a flat-sided decorator's brush. Using a water-based paint, the grain was drawn in and then dragged out using the side of the decorator's brush, always in one direction. The ground was a dark, rich cream paint and the graining was executed in raw sienna pigment bound with gum arabic in water.*

(BELOW) *Do not underestimate the degree to which you can exaggerate and stylize your graining once you have mastered the figure of a particular wood. Moreover, you can apply your technique to more than the obvious surfaces, remembering that for a realistic impression it is best to subdivide large area with divisions such as dados. Achieve this either for real by using, for example, timber panelling, or fake it with painted panelling or inlay designs.*

HINTS AND TIPS

* To analyse what is required, look at different woods in photographs, painted effects and furniture. Do not, however, copy slavishly from life. The finished effect will look curiously flat and dead if you do. The success of the technique relies upon both a conscious and unconscious

absorption of the character and detail of the original woodgrain pattern.
* Do not get confused by the name Vandyke; Vandyke brown is an earth-type pigment and relatively opaque in water, whereas Vandyke crystals are a derivative that is totally transparent in water. Vandyke crystals require no binder, since they are naturally sticky.
* Just as each timber has its own colouring, so each fake graining technique requires the colour of both graining media and the painted ground to change. The ground for the walnut technique on pages 230-1 was made by tinting a white oil-based paint with yellow ochre and a little raw umber pigment. Oak and pine will require lighter grounds, while rosewood and mahogany are best served by a light orange ground.

(ABOVE) *The balcony room at Dyrham Park, south-west England, showing some splendid examples of woodgrained panels.*

Bronzing

It is arguable that this is not a fake finish as the method, in fact, calls for bronze powders as the main material. However, this technique does emulate antique bronze.

Enough books have been written about gilding as a technique that I felt it unnecessary and repetitious to cover the same material again in this book. It is sufficient to say that water gilding is virtually unteachable in print, and oil gilding requires huge practice, particularly over large areas. However, acrylic size gilding (with a latex-acrylic product) is easy, new and yields reasonable results for all but the restorer. The size is brushed on and brushed out quickly to avoid coarse brush marks, and when touch dry and lightly tacky, covered by pressing either loose or transfer Dutch metal (brass) leaf into place. From our experiments, a harder and much brighter finish is obtained if the acrylic size is left overnight, not a problem since it seems to remain ready for leafing for about two to three days.

Bronze finishes offer much greater scope for experimentation and variation. They may be red, orange, green or brown, and can reveal some of the underlying metal, which ordinarily has a warm orange cast to it that is more pleasing than brass (an alloy of copper and zinc, while bronze is an alloy of copper and tin). When weathered, bronze may assume a smattering of verdigris, or turn bright green over its entirety; on pages 240-1 you will find some variations.

1 *Start by making a general-purpose gold paint by mixing bronze powder (really powdered brass) of a good gold colour with ordinary brown shellac (button polish and so-called French polish are variants) and a little methylated spirit. Stipple this onto your surface generously, and when half dry, re-stipple to produce some texture in the coating.*

YOU WILL NEED

Bronze power
Brown shellac
Methylated spirit
Paintbrushes (35mm [1½in], 100mm [4in]
Beeswax polish
Turpentine
Pigments (red ochre, burnt umber)
Round paintbrush
Clean soft cloth
Abrasive paper (fine)

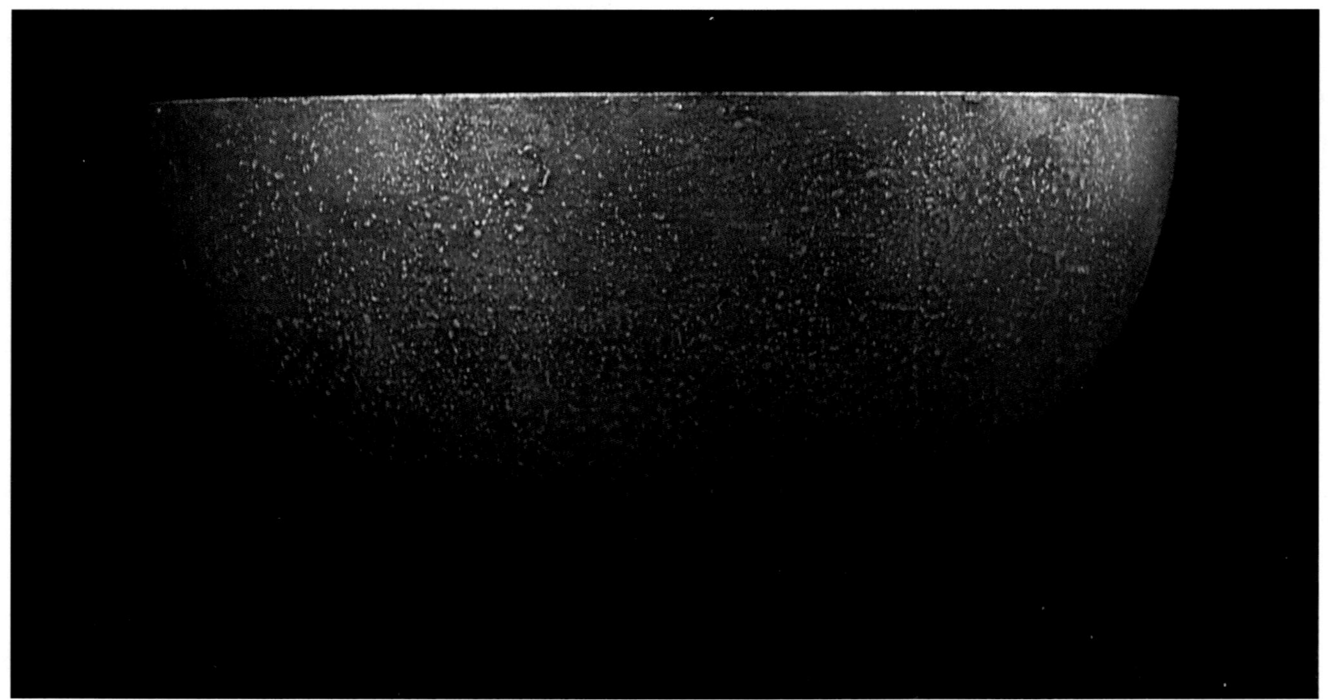

2 Leave for at least 2 hours to dry and then brush beeswax polish thinned with a little turpentine and coloured with pigment liberally onto the surface. Here, I chose red ochre, but virtually any earth colours and most greens are acceptable. Give the solvent a few minutes to evaporate, then rub off the majority of the wax to reveal the ground.

3 You must wait for this coat to give off all its solvent and harden before applying a second coat of wax (I discovered that placing the object in the freezer was a useful quick method). Then apply a second coat of thinned beeswax (here, tinted with burnt umber pigment). Put it on quickly so that the solvents in the wax do not awaken the previous layer.

4 Brush out the wax coat a little and lightly stipple it with a clean dry brush. This action should do several things; soften any crude brush marks left during application, blend the two wax colours together here and there, and reveal some of the underlying metallic colour.

5 Leave the object in a warm dry place for at least 24 hours to allow the solvents to evaporate and the coatings to harden. To obtain a sharp textural contrast, lightly rub the surface with extremely fine abrasive paper to cut back to the metallic powder beneath on all the ridges and high points.

HINTS AND TIPS

* The most important point to remember about bronze powders concerns the health risk they pose. Copper, zinc and tin, all freely available in bronze powders, may produce allergic skin reactions and induce a condition known as metal fever or the zinc shakes when their fumes are inhaled in moderate quantities. However, brass, even in

The particular historical uses of bronze each stimulates a resonance within our modern perceptions of the material. Its use in sculpture has left in our minds the ideas of value and importance of the metal, and the notion that when used, or faked, bronze will indicate something of great worth or antiquity. Equally, the metal has always been used as a defensive material to manufacture grand doors and gates, such as these of the church of San Marco in Venice. In this context, the bronze assumes an imperial status and suggests strength and impenetrability.

THE ESSENTIALS OF BRONZING

DERIVATION

It is difficult to tell when first bronze was faked, but even the great bronze doors to the Pantheon in Rome are not of solid metal, but of sheet material fastened over wooden panels and frames. The material has always been associated with its early widespread use throughout Greece and Rome, and was popularly employed as a decorative finish during the Greco-Roman revival of the early nineteenth century. At the John Soane museum in London, ceiling roundels, previously thought of as being painted in simple colours, were recently discovered to have been bronzed, apparently by dusting a coat of bronze-coloured or green paint with

DERIVATION (CONT)

dull metal powders. This can be easily emulated by mixing bronze powder with a transparent brown pigment such as Vandyke brown.

SURFACES

Historically, the use of this effect was limited to accessories, lamps and architectural details that in all probability were to be found in ancient Rome in the real material. This is a good lesson to learn, since it is interesting how a fake finish can be entirely convincing when in context but entirely obvious when applied to inappropriate surfaces or objects such as a panelled wooden door, or a telephone.

PREPARATION

Shellac is a material widely employed as a surface sealant, primer, or isolating coat. It prevents layers of material from interacting with each other; it used to be widely used to seal damp marks on walls and ceilings. Consequently, in this technique, the first shellac-based coat finds no problem in adhering to most surfaces, including the steel dish shown, which had simply been washed and cut back with wet and dry paper to key it. More porous surfaces such as plaster and timber would benefit from a coat of diluted shellac to give them an appetite for the thicker coat to follow.

FINISHING

In the technique illustrated, no further finishing is necessary or practicable on top of the waxes already used. However, in place of the abrasive rub, you may wish to add other colours or traces of verdigris in the form of paint smudges (paint will create its own effect by unhappily sitting over the wax and will instead cling to the texture of the surface). If an alternative medium to that of wax is used for a metallic finish (see Hints and tips), a final coating of varnish and/or wax may be desirable.

powder form, may also contain small amounts of lead or arsenic which are highly poisonous.
* A face mask should always be worn when working with metal powders and full eye protection afforded to avoid nuisance reactions. A controlled environment is also desirable, with no movement of air other than from an extractor.
* Bronze powders are usually available in a wide variety of colours; experiment with these and by intermixing them either with pigments or ready-prepared paints, choosing colours that are known for their transparency to maximize the effect of the metallics. Auripetrum, or false gold, was known to decorators of the Renaissance as a technique whereby polished tin was coated with a transparent varnish containing a highly transparent pigment; Jehan le Begue proscribed 'Spanish Saffron distempered with very clear glue or liquid varnish'.

(ABOVE LEFT) *This is an ingenious nineteenth-century variation of Renaissance auripetrum, where, instead of polished tin, a pressed tray has been galvanized in zinc. The resulting crystalline formations that emerge on the surface catch the light well, but only begin to appear attractive when the object is lacquered, as shown on the underside of the tray to the left (the object may have been oil-varnished with a colorant or shellacked). However, when printed with a black pattern that masks most of the surface, the metal gleams brilliantly, resembling mother-of-pearl inlay* (ABOVE RIGHT).

(LEFT) *This tray has been bronzed by gently dusting bronze powder onto tacky goldsize (oil goldsize is by far superior for this) that has been painted onto a black ground. The pattern, however, was not established by painstaking application of the size, but by drawing with black paints over the bronze powders afterwards when the surface was thoroughly dry. This way, much finer effects are obtainable.*

* If you are concerned about using bronze powders, execute the first stage of this technique with a ready-prepared gold paint.
* As an alternative to coloured waxes, the tinting layers can be built up with coloured acrylic scumble glaze or transparent oil glaze. Coloured varnishes, heavily pigmented, can also be employed for a very durable finish, and for a rock-hard coating, the first metallic coat can also be produced by mixing the bronze powder into a brown-tinted varnish, either oil or water based.

(ABOVE LEFT) *A huge variety of patinated finishes are procurable on metals by the action of chemical solutions or fumes. Most patinas are produced by exposure of the metal to alkalines or acids, and very often in alternate succession. Consequently, many recipes call for ammonia compounds and acids, such as acetic acid, and sometimes compounds that will introduce gases to the surface to assist the reaction, such as hydrogen peroxide. This finish resulted from an application of a ready-prepared acid solution made by Liberon, together with water and a little common salt. Such experiments must be conducted in a controlled environment because of the health risks.*

(ABOVE RIGHT) *This green bronze sample was executed in exactly the same way as the sample technique in the step-by-step sequence, but the coloured waxes were burnt umber followed by a green wax coloured with cerulean blue and yellow ochre.*

(LEFT) *Like the aluminium examples opposite, brass leaf was employed here to fake its superior. It is commonly known as schlag or Dutch metal and is only rarely applied via the technique of water gilding over a gesso ground properly prepared with coloured bole. For such effort in preparation, the additional cost of true gold would be merited. Instead, schlag is today most often applied using acrylic size. This example was not severely rubbed back and shows all the marks resulting from the action of laying on the schlag; even these have some kind of decorative charm. Note that schlag will tarnish very quickly when exposed to the air and must be sealed. Many varnishes dull the reflections of the metal because they are quite alkaline. They can also turn the metal greenish. The best coating is either shellac or cellulose lacquer. Note the brownish marks left on the surface; these are areas of patination due to the slightly acid skin oil left by fingerprints. Prevent these by using gloves when leafing, and seal the surface as soon as possible.*

(ABOVE LEFT) *A stunning polished pewter effect can be obtained with a little effort. An ordinary gesso was made up (see page 90) and when hot and ready it was poured, a little at a time onto a small pile of graphite powder (a dessertspoon of powder to a cupful of gesso). The mixture must be constantly stirred while the gesso is being added, and for a little time afterwards to thoroughly integrate the graphite. The gesso was then applied and polished as normal to produce a metallic finish of great depth.*

(ABOVE RIGHT) *Silver leaf can be bought, or palladium for a non-tarnishing surface. However, for everyday use, aluminium leaf will suffice. Here it was laid onto a tacky, water-based acrylic size that had been applied over a dark blue ground. The ground had been textured slightly for two reasons; to assist in later rubbing back to reveal the blue, and to present many different facets of the leaf to the light to produce a shimmering effect. The squares of leaf were deliberately butted in a regular way to reveal the joints; a technique that is useful for introducing some structure to the surface over a large area such as a wall. The surface was then rubbed to reveal the ground in places and to exploit the texture, before being given a thin coat of shellac to seal it and prevent the aluminium from oxidizing. Finally, the leaf was toned with a spatter and wash of a pale brown acrylic paint.*

(RIGHT) *Lead is an easy metal to imitate. Here, the surface was painted with a very dark grey acrylic paint to which a little aluminium powder has been added for sparkle. On top of this, a coat of mid-grey paint was applied, again with the addition of a little aluminium, and it was then rubbed through here and there with methylated spirits. Finally the 'patina' was added by washing over the surface with a pale grey paint, thinned to a watery consistency, that was moved about with a damp sponge as in Veiling on page 85. For a simpler effect, the first coat may be eliminated.*

Verdigris

It is difficult to explain why, as a decorative finish, verdigris has become so popular in the last ten or so years. I suspect that the reason is a very prosaic one; that manufacturers have realized that a coat of paint of a carefully chosen green, that is then ragged or wiped onto a sprayed coat of dark primer, will add a thousand years to a lamp base or candle stick, and double its retail value.

This formula for adding value to an object actually works, and ironically so, since verdigris is perhaps the easiest faux technique to do well. On these pages, a basic paint process for producing lookalike verdigris is given that can be reproduced using conventional acrylic, casein or even emulsion paints. In addition, overleaf there is a recipe for producing the real thing, copper acetate, on a ground of bronze powder (actually brass powder) using a proprietary chemical.

YOU WILL NEED

Acrylic, casein or emulsion paints (dark bronze, mint green, pale blue, yellow ochre)
Paintbrushes (large and small round artist's)
Lint-free cloths or tissues

1 *Onto a dark ground (I start with a brownish bronze basecoat) roughly apply a coat of paint thinned to single cream consistency of a pale mint-green colour using the round artist's paintbrush. Then add a small quantity of pale blue and randomly stipple and push the mixture over the surface with the brush.*

2 *Rag the surface with a lint-free cloth or tissue. In order to prevent the surface from appearing too contrived, re-rag it as the paint dries, refining the marks.*

3 *An option is then to apply a little yellow ochre paint. This should be of the same consistency as the green and it is either spotted or dribbled onto the object. Take care not to overdo this.*

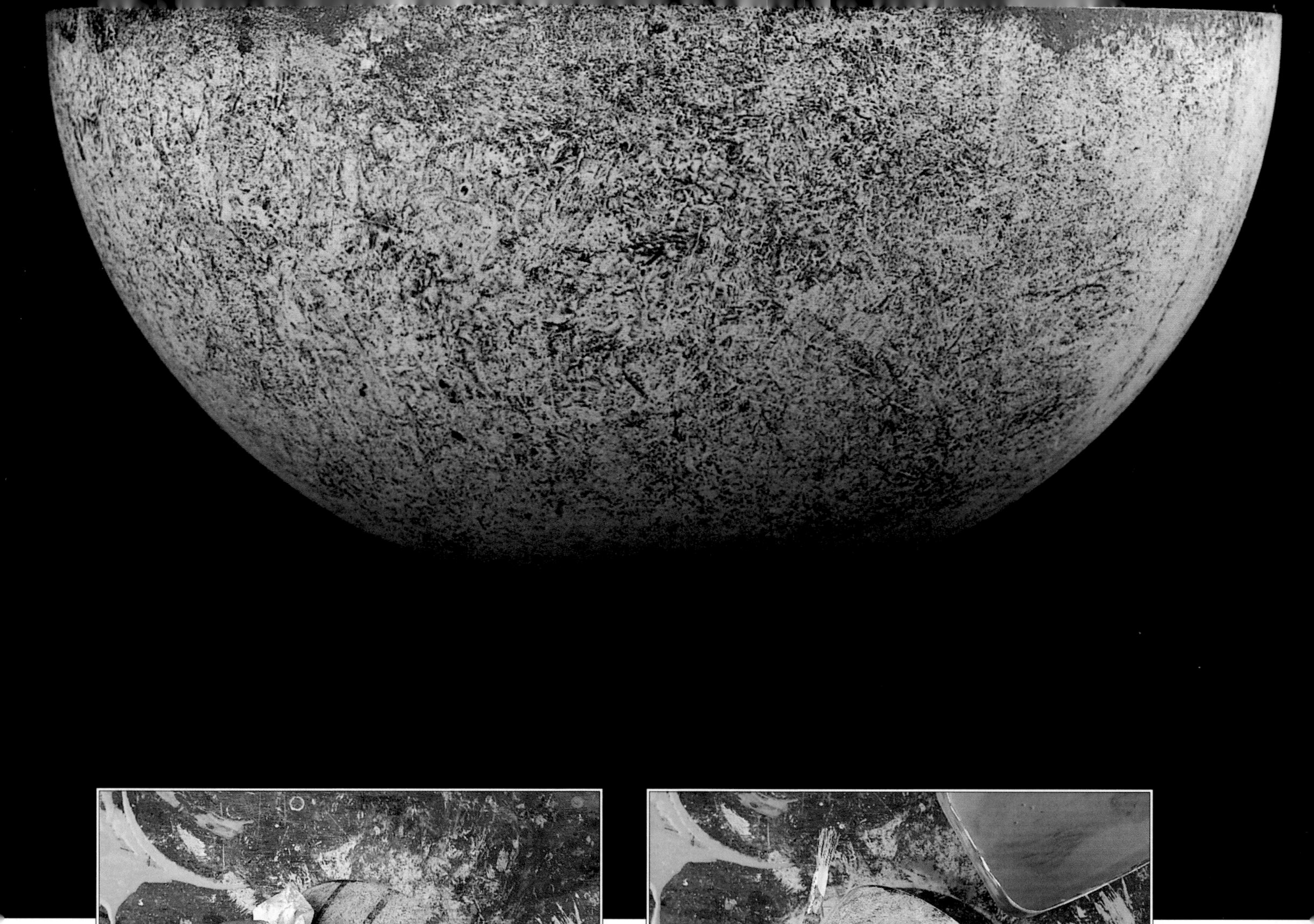

4 *These marks and dribbles will also require blending into the surface and even blotting out with the rag again. Work quickly at all times, since some of the more interesting marks come when wet paint is applied to half-dry or damp paint.*

5 *Take the small artist's brush loaded with your original green paint, and a rag. Repeat steps 1 and 2 of the technique but on a smaller scale, filling in objectionable holes in the paint layer, covering thumb marks and crude brush marks.*

PRODUCING VERDIGRIS WITH A PROPRIETARY CHEMICAL

In general I am not in favour of do-it-yourself chemical patination; it is often unpredictable and the chemicals used (and gases produced) can be highly dangerous. But in this case, the manufacturer (see Suppliers) has made it very easy. That, of course, doesn't mean you shouldn't read the label on the bottle.

YOU WILL NEED

Primer
Paintbrushes (50mm [2in]-wide flat, round fitch)
Goldsize
Bronze or copper powder
Verdigris solution

Note: the finished effect is entirely real and therefore poisonous. This technique should not be used on food vessels, and the final verdigris should be sealed with varnish to prevent it dusting off.

1 *After priming your object, coat it with some form of goldsize, be it a modern acrylic water-based type or the traditional oil-based type. When tacky to the touch (a stage past sticky), gently dust on bronze or copper powder. You will require much less on the brush than you think, and surplus may be dusted off the surface with the same brush.*

2 *What you have just done is a form of gilding but with powders. The effect is much superior to that of gold paint, but the powders would tarnish quickly unless sealed (preferably shellacked to conserve the brightness). In this case, however, we need to leave the coating of powder exposed to react with the chemical cocktail that is to be applied. Take care with the verdigris solution; it contains acids and other active compounds. After about 2 hours, a verdigris coat should have formed. The solution may then need to be stippled on again to build the layer of verdigris.*

The Paris Opera. The roofs of great public and institutional buildings around the world are covered with copper that has assumed the noble patina of verdigris. Its public connotations are hence of value, authority and decorum.

HEALTH AND SAFETY

Some room is given over to the toxicity of phthalo blue and green pigments (on pages 34 and 35). They are suspected of carcinogenic effects. However, when used in liquid form to colour other paints they can be considered as relatively safe. *Do not* handle them in powder form and take care when using them in concentrated liquid form.

The chemical preparations that are available for patinating metals, including the liquid I used for verdigris, are corrosive and toxic. They *must* be used in a well-ventilated area and you should wear goggles, a mask and rubber gloves. They should not be stored or even used near children or pets. Above all, read the label and strictly adhere to the manufacturer's instructions and health warnings.

HINTS AND TIPS

* The base coats that appear through verdigris are not as important as you might think. Any dark brown, green or even black paint will suffice; as long as it is relatively matt. My preferred choice is for a paint comprising bronze (brass) powders, Vandyke pigment (a good transparent brown) and acrylic varnish. The combination provides a realistic brown bronze. However, I have worked using opaque green paints over black grounds to equally good effect. An alternative ground would be the recipe given for bronze paint on pages 236-41.
* The texture of the underlying surface is critical, especially over large surfaces. On cast or worked detail, a verdigris-coloured paint will sit in the crevices and appear natural all by itself. But on flat areas, some texture is essential to hold the film of paint and provide surface interest. If none is present, introduce it by stippling the basecoat. Again, the recipe for bronze on pages 236-7 is useful for providing this.
* Virtually any type of modern synthetic paint is suitable for this technique, even oil-based eggshells. The importance is that it is opaque; ie when brushed out to a film they do not appear glaze-like but instead create a translucent, chalky film of pale colour.
* You may find it an improvement to add whiting (powdered chalk) to water-based paints to add to the chalking effect. However, this will be reduced if later varnished, especially with oil-based varnish, in which chalk turns transparent.
* A wide variety of greens is found in naturally occurring verdigris; it is important to study them carefully. From the palette, you should start with white coloured with a copper-type green (see page 35) such

Because so much (now) patinated bronze work has been recovered from classical civilizations, when verdigris is formed on, or applied to, objects, sculptures and domestic metalwork, it invests those things with the connotations of historical worth, antiquity, and even aesthetic value, whether or not this is actually present in the object. Hence it is possible to commercially increase the value of a poor piece of metalwork by simply painting it verdigris, a fact that manufacturers of furniture and accessories understand.

as phthalocyanine green. The green stainers widely available to colour your own paints rely on this pigment. To this, yellow ochre and raw umber should be added to tone the colour to a respectably subdued shade. Terra verde also offers a range of interesting, more earthy verdigris colours when mixed with white. Both phthalo and terra verde pigments have a bluish cast, essential for the minty quality of most verdigris.

* The technique for painting verdigris that I give is by no means definitive; it is simply a relatively easy way. Of all the techniques covered in this book, verdigris is perhaps the most flexible. Simply by using verdigris-coloured paint combined with other techniques you can produce many pleasing results. Other techniques to combine with verdigris colours are Veiling (pages 82-5), Sponging off (pages 104-7), Cracked paint (pages 166-9), Peeled and chipped (pages 170-3), Rubbed paint (pages 174-9) and Bronzing (pages 236-41).

THE ESSENTIALS OF VERDIGRIS

DERIVATION

Verdigris is a naturally occurring compound of copper acetate. Since man began refining copper and bronze for use in jewellery, sculpture, architecture and the machinery of war, verdigris has always formed on the surface of these metals. Its connotations are therefore ancient, stretching back to Rome, Greece and the Celtic world.

SURFACES

The patina of verdigris is a suitable finish for any metalwork, be it for outside or inside use. Table lamps, furniture and lighting are all commercial applications, and even planters, statuary and pots for the garden. However, verdigris should not be applied to those surfaces that have the obvious textures of the underlying material, such as terracotta, stone or carved wood. Objects in these materials often look absurd dressed in verdigris. Bear in mind the historical and archaeological resonances of the finish and ask

SURFACES (CONT)

yourself whether this finish is appropriate for the context of the piece, and not just another pretty paint finish.

PREPARATION

Surfaces should be clean and dry, but not necessarily smooth. Thinned opaque paint leaves a film when thinly brushed or rubbed over a surface, and a texture, however fine, will assist in articulating that film and giving it some surface interest. The ground should be dark.

FINISHING

Chemical verdigris requires varnishing both to preserve the finish and to prevent it coming into contact with the skin – if ingested it can have poisonous effects. Painted verdigris, however, is much safer, and merely requires a sealing coat of varnish (preferably matt) to protect those areas of high wear.

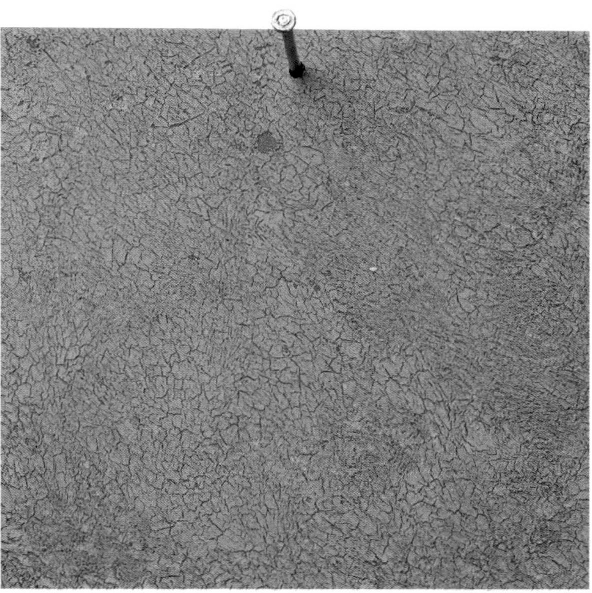

A very good verdigris effect can be produced by combining cracked paint and antiquing techniques. A layer of gum arabic was brushed over a bronze-coloured ground and allowed to dry. Next, a flat-surfaced car sponge was generously coated with a mint-green emulsion paint. Then, with great speed (so as not to blend the dried gum and wet paint into a coagulated mess), the sponge was dabbed over the surface. As the paint dried, so it cracked. When hard, it was antiqued with a thinned brown oil paint and waxed a few days later.

An entirely different technique was used here to equally good effect. I thickly stippled a coat of pale mint-green emulsion onto the sample and let it thoroughly harden. When dry, I then washed it with a thinned coat of pale green-blue emulsion, which was also allowed to dry. Finally I sanded the surface, softening the stipple texture and revealing the green undercoat.

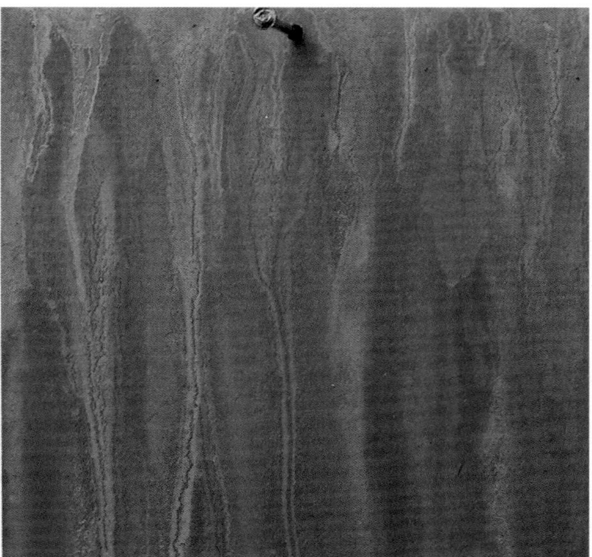

This dribbled effect is extremely effective if pigments are used as well as acrylic paints or emulsions because the coarser-sized pigments collect in a granular pattern as the paint runs down the surface. Surfaces to be dribbled should be held vertically, the paint thin, and the surface (here ready-painted a dull, dark bronze colour) washed with water to allow the dribbles to disperse. Finish with varnish or wax so the surface does not rub off or darken.

I have seen this technique used to great effect on statuary in London. The surface is painted a pale green, anything from mint to apple green, and then given one or more coats of varnish tinted with pigment, in this case raw umber. The result is a general, all-over effect of patina.

Part Three

REFERENCE

Paint colour and light theories

This appendix is a brief summary of several theories and principles about the way in which colour, and paint colour in particular, behaves. In addition, I have inserted several elaborations and criticisms of these theories that I have developed. You may not find these ideas relevant or necessary to your work, but you may find them interesting.

THE NEED FOR TRADITIONAL MATERIALS

In the traditional paints and techniques section, I have already said plenty about the importance of traditional colours and paints on old buildings. Their use is demanded principally by the need for old buildings to breathe, that is, allow moisture in their walls to pass through the walls both inside and outside the house, into the atmosphere. They are also historically accurate coatings that are sympathetic to older building materials such as lime and stone.

I have also mentioned how traditional paints are relatively environmentally friendly, and also how important their aesthetic appeal is, not just on older buildings but also on new ones. This last point is the one that I want to elaborate on.

The pigments available from the natural world dominated colour theory for millennia. At Roussillon, native coloured earths have always been mined in enormous quantities for paint-making.

A soft or oil-bound distemper is pigmented primarily with fine powdered chalk or whiting. Chemically, it is calcium carbonate, formed from the skeletons of billions of minute marine creatures that have been compressed in the earth. As such, it has a microscopically crystalline quality. Chalk is also the principal colorant of casein wall paints. And in another form, calcium carbonate is the single constituent of limewash, once it has dried back as a film on a surface.

In all these paints, to a greater or lesser degree, the common quality of the calcium carbonate layers is that under a microscope they all appear somewhat crystalline. The surface of the paints does not simply reflect light like a layer of plastic does, it refracts light as well, passing the light through the top crystal surface layer, and bouncing it back into our eyes together with the ordinary reflected light. This process accounts for the alluring chalky, sparkling and luminous qualities that most people can immediately spot on being presented with a limewashed or distempered surface. Because of the non-crystalline molecular structure of synthetic paints, such as acrylics or emulsions (including exterior masonry paints), these products appear lifeless and dull when placed next to their traditional equivalents.

This idea may, therefore, be summed up as follows. Traditional water-borne paints have a primitive crystalline-like structure when dry which imparts attractive surface qualities to the dried coating. Modern, synthetic plastic paints are formulated to much more demanding specifications, using high-opacity pigments such as titanium oxide white. Their ability to form semi-opaque refractive layers is poor.

Moreover, there is another aesthetic plus on the side of traditional paints; pigments. Traditional paints have been coloured by ground minerals and metals for thousands of years. Most are dug out of the earth and refined; colours such as the earth iron oxides like red ochre. Many have been chemically synthesized for centuries, but all are added to paints as some form of fine granular powder. If added to artist's oils, they are closely blended by grinding in small quantities. However, in house paints, they are ground with the paint in mills to a coarser quality.

The result is that when traditional house paints are brushed out, they offer a surface that is composed of a medium of, say, chalk and glue, interspersed by small particles of randomly dispersed pigment. Microscopically, these particles may appear very large indeed, and may even be visible to the naked eye as tiny dots of colour.

This effect is obvious in the oil paint film shown on page 87. Moreover, as that picture shows, if two or more pigments are intermixed and added to a paint, then it is possible that they may 'settle out' and be just visible as separate dots of colour.

This phenomenon occurs even in paint layers which have been ground at length; and the resultant visual effect is quite charming, rather like that of a pointillist painting. It is another example of how traditional paints, including oil paint this time, take on individual identities and subtle surface qualities when dry that modern synthetic paints cannot. The latter are pigmented with many dye-based pigments and superfine particles that render the microscopic surface of the paint film bland and uninteresting.

To sum up, traditional water-borne and oil paints have larger, more randomly dispersed pigment particles that add aesthetic qualities to the dry paint film. Modern synthetic paints do not and therefore appear bland and uniform. The aesthetic effect may be further emphasized by not fully mixing the paint/pigment blend, so that there will remain in the can pockets of paint which are perhaps a shade lighter or darker. When brushed out these will produce a barely discernible movement of colour across the wall. This is a feature of paints that were traditionally mixed on site using hand tools. Modern mixing methods are designed specifically to achieve an evenness of tint to ensure customer satisfaction with a guaranteed product; manufacturers want the customer to be able to retouch painted areas unobtrusively and to obtain a reliable colour. As a result, our expectations as consumers are high: a hundred years ago, such a wide variety of synthesized colours as we have today was not possible. If paint colours varied a degree or two when dry, this was acceptable; today, such variations are considered as different colours.

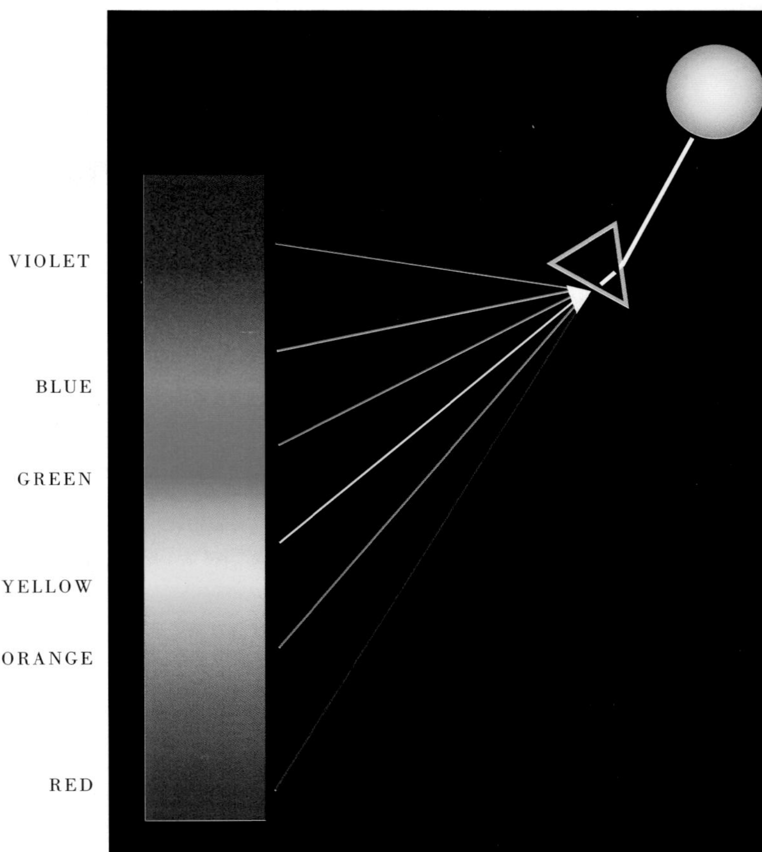

When visible light hits a prism, it is split into its component colours, those of the rainbow. Infrared ('below red') light is below the visible spectrum, and ultraviolet ('beyond violet') is above the visible spectrum.

LIGHT AND COLOUR

When we look at a red rose we think of its colour as being a property of the flower itself, it 'is' red. Equally, when we handle a red paint, we think of it as being the colour red itself, somehow mystically embodied as paint. But both these ideas are complete fallacies. Under a green light, both paint and rose will appear black; at night, they will seem an indeterminate brown-black. This is because neither is, in fact, red. They have actually no colour within them, they simply respond to the light that is hitting them.

Sunlight contains many separate frequencies of light, including infrared and ultraviolet, but the frequencies that we are able to see are those contained in the rainbow; red through to violet, via orange, green, etc. When pure white sunlight hits a prism, it splits into these seven separately visible colours, establishing that together they make up white light. A red rose, if lit in full spectrum sunlight, will absorb every frequency of light that hits it, except red. Red is the colour it does not want and so it throws it back, reflecting it into our eyes.

Red pigment behaves similarly; it reflects red light, absorbing every other frequency. It is not surprising that, when under a green light, the pigment can find no red light to reflect – it is being bombarded with light of a colour that it will readily absorb. No red light is reflected and so we perceive it as black.

Conversely, under a red light bulb, the rose and pigment will appear to glow or pulsate with colour, because they are such efficient reflectors of red light. Some pigments, those that are prized, like vermilion, are very efficient reflectors, producing an intensely bright effect of redness. Others, like red ochre, appear dull because they reflect much less red light, absorbing some of it, while reflecting one or two other frequencies of light as well. The effect is a rather dull, muddied colour. White pigments, on the other hand, are extremely effective at reflecting every single frequency of light which together make white light. Black pigments, of course, reflect little or no light of any frequency.

So, colours are not intrinsic to objects or pigments, but are a function of their light-reflective properties. The brightness or intensity of an object's or pigment's colour will be determined by how efficient it is at reflecting certain frequencies. We must therefore think of pigments not as embodiments of colours but as minerals with a particular talent for reflecting certain frequencies of light.

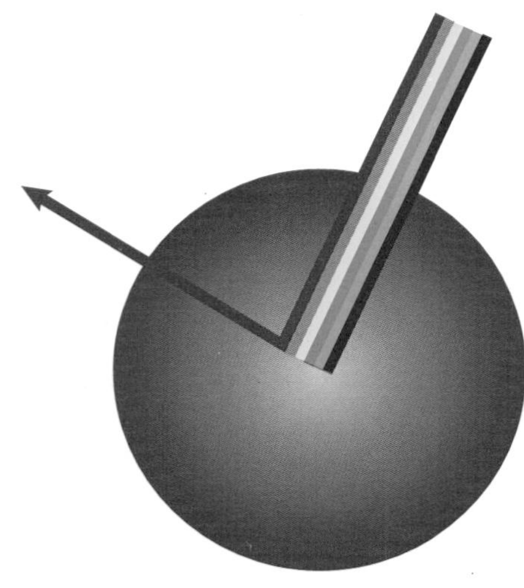

When full spectrum light hits a so-called 'red' object or pigment, the surface absorbs every frequency, or colour, of light that is hitting it, except red, which it reflects away. So what we perceive as being an object's colour is, in fact, the one colour it has rejected!

In reality, most surfaces reflect more than one frequency, but in differing strengths. This red pigment is actually reflecting a lot of red and orange light, giving it a red-orange tinge. But it is also reflecting a considerable quantity of violet light, some yellow and blue and even a little green. This phenomenon gives rise to visually satisfying effects, 'rich' and 'complex' colours, dark colours and muddy colours.

It is possible to find pigments that reflect more than one frequency of light; vermilion, for example, reflects red and also orange light, giving it a characteristically orangey quality. Its efficiency at this is proved by its brightness. Red ochre reflects a little purple light but is an inefficient reflector all round; it is consequently dark.

A step behind red ochre are those indeterminate colours that we see all around us in nature: browns and muddy greens, neutrals and deep complex colours that result from surfaces reflecting small amounts of a mixture of frequencies. A dark green leaf may be reflecting green, yellow, red and blue frequencies, a wide selection of colours from across the spectrum. But it will also be reflecting each of them inefficiently, resulting in the darkness of its surface.

What is so interesting here is the wide variety of frequencies that one surface can reflect. Paint colours will always seem more interesting if a complementary colour is added in minute quantities or if it is mixed with brown or another colour. It is as though the surface when dry will offer more interest as a result of more frequencies being reflected.

There are certain areas of colour in the decorator's palette that respond extremely well to this treatment. For example, paints made with greenish-blues and bluish-greens vary enormously in character as the day passes. In full sunlight, they will appear as true as possible; on a cloudy day, they will turn bluer in response to the enormous amount of blue light in the atmosphere (clouds filter light, allowing through blue frequencies), and in the evening, they may turn very green under electric lighting, since tungsten and tungsten/halogen light sources produce much more warm yellow-green light than blue. Red ochre paints may behave in the same way, appearing much more orange at night, and bluer by day. Because these colours seem so reactive to changes in normal lighting, I have termed them cusp colours.

Not all paints behave like this. Primary colours are generally of such intense hues and presence that such changes are hard to detect in them; their intensity waxes and wanes, but they do not change colour so markedly. Indeed, even secondary colours of a pure nature, orange, green and purple, seem to respond little. The colours that do respond, however, are the weaker mixes, where a proportion of neutral grey or brown is already present in the colour, and where the subtle changing of a type of light source, from one with a greater degree of blue light in it, to one with more yellow light, can effectively shut down one set of receptors in the paint film and start up another. The neutrality of the colour seems to be important as a background against which these changes become visible. The other important factor is that the separate identities of the changes in the colours must be recognizable; perhaps it is because green, uniquely, appears to be such a different colour to blue (although they are next to each other on the colour wheel), that the divide between them has room for a cusp colour.

Whatever the susceptibility of standard colours to providing cusp colours, it is clear that the blue-green cusp colour will be the most common, simply because it is in this area that natural and artificial sources of lighting fluctuate most.

To conclude, many surfaces in this world reflect light inefficiently and so appear dark, brown, or indeterminate. Very few surfaces reflect just one colour of light, many reflect at least two. Most pigments are extremely efficient reflectors, some of just a few frequencies. Mixes of pigments in a neutral base that will respond to changes in the light colour that hits them, will react correspondingly and appear to change colour. These may be called cusp colours.

COLOUR BIAS AND HOW TO BECOME COLOUR MIXER OF THE YEAR

Of all the colours of the rainbow that are present in light and in the world, why is it that we have three primary colours, red, yellow and blue? And why is this 'full-colour' book you are reading, printed not in those three colours but in a cool yellow, a greenish blue (cyan), and a purplish red (magenta)?

The answer is that, in both cases, the colours have been settled on more out of convenience than anything else. Historically, scientists and print technologists have been very keen to apply theorems and simple structures to colour mixing. You can see them both represented on the colour wheels shown on the following pages.

The standard 'process' colours that were used to print this book (other than black). From left to right, yellow, cyan blue and magenta. Between them they can produce most strong colours, but they have their limitations: some art books are printed using several more ink colours.

As children, we were brought up to believe that these were the true primary colours, somehow God-given. In fact, they were identified in the eighteenth century with relative arbitrariness.

When process yellow and magenta are mixed, they form muddy oranges; no amount of fiddling will enable the colour printer to produce an exciting orange in his work unless he uses a special mix – poor oranges are the one great failing of modern printing methods.

The three swatches below illustrate how important it is to choose the right primary colours if you want to make a really good secondary colour.

A) Yellow ochre (which is dull) is mixed with Prussian blue (tending towards the green). The result is a dark and muddy disaster, because the yellow is not up to the job.

B) The right blue, Prussian blue, which tends to the green, is mixed with a good mid-yellow with a slight green tendency. The result is a range of vivid greens.

C) When ultramarine replaces Prussian blue, predictably darker and muddier greens follow, despite the fact that the yellow is bright and greenish. This is because the ultramarine tends away from green, to purple.

The important point is that neither system works very well. To give you an example, if a printer tries to print orange using cyan and yellow, the resultant colour is dull. Equally, on the painter's palette a mid-red and a mid-blue, such as cadmium red and cobalt blue, will yield a very dull and unimpressive purple. Why is this? The answer lies with an Australian artist Michael Wilcox and his book *Blue and Yellow Don't Make Green* in which he expounds his own theory of 'subtractive mixing'.

I have already noted at the beginning of this appendix how any surface is only the colour it is because of the particular frequencies of light that it reflects. If pigments were absolutely pure and you mixed together a yellow and a red, you would not achieve orange. Instead, the red element of the mixture would absorb all the yellow light hitting it, and the yellow would absorb all the red. The resultant perceived colour would therefore be not orange, but black!

Of course, in reality, when red and yellow pigment molecules are mixed, they never blend to physically become one and the same molecule, instead they sit side by side in the paint film. Moreover, because no pigment is totally pure, each of the original colours is not wholly dedicated to reflecting only one pure frequency of light. Nearly all pigments reflect other

Don't ever think of good colour mixes resulting just from bright red, mid-blue and mid-yellow. We really need nine primary colours in our palettes, three reds, three yellows and three blues, each group comprising a true mid-hue, a cooler version and a warmer version. For example, if we want to mix good, vibrant oranges and purples, we will not only need a proper post-box red, but also a warm vermilion-type red for the orange mix, plus a cool, crimson-type red to make a good purple. The best secondary colours come from a mixture of those colours on either side of them; so the richest purples will be formed from a crimson-type red and an ultramarine (ie purplish) blue.

frequencies than the one they principally represent. And so, even if I were to take the finest and most intense primary-coloured pigments and mix them together (cobalt blue, cadmium yellow and cadmium red, for example), I would still not produce a black paint, but a muddy brown one. All the constituent pigments would still be reflecting other colours as well, and in the case of some colours this is very obvious; ultramarine blue, for example, is clearly a very 'reddish' blue, it almost looks purple in some lights.

Taking this argument one useful step forward, imagine that you have a tube of warm orangish-yellow in one hand and ultramarine blue in the other. If you mix them together you will produce a muddy dead green – because each of the constituent colours is reflecting other frequencies of light that are actually taking these colours further around the colour wheel, away from each other. Result: failure.

Now imagine you are mixing a greeny yellow with, say, Prussian blue, which also has a greenish cast. Each primary colour, although still yellow and blue, is reflecting quite a lot of green light already, even before mixing. The result is that when mixed they will produce a vivid, vibrant green because a significant number of molecules in both pigments is reflecting green light. In this case, both primary colours are moving around the colour wheel towards each other. Result: success.

It is exactly this fact that explains why the orange print in a book is so dull. The yellow used is rather cold and slightly green, and the red used is not at all orange and warm, but blue and cold.

So you can see that we should perceive our colour palettes as being not just simply composed of three primary colours, but of three primaries with a total of six intermediate colours, positioned either side of the primaries, producing three vivid secondary colours. If you want good green colours, don't use ultramarine blue pigment, but Prussian blue. If you want a good purple, use ultramarine blue, not Prussian. If you want a good mid, sky-coloured blue, choose cobalt blue!

To conclude, our understanding of primary and secondary colours is over-simplified; the conventional red-blue-yellow theory can be supplanted with the magenta-yellow-cyan theory, but neither yields good bright secondary colours. All pigments for any practical use are impure and reflect other frequencies of light. By taking advantage of that and establishing that there should be six intermediate colours for good colour mixing, we can achieve bright and intense secondary colours.

DON'T FORGET OUR BROWNS, MR PAINT-MAKER

Just as physicists have been content with a three-colour primary palette (even though this proves useless for the painter and artist), so paint manufacturers and paint theorists work to another colour model which is totally useless to us. Nearly all colour models ever imagined are variations of the double cone, or globe model, rather like our own planet. Imagine that the

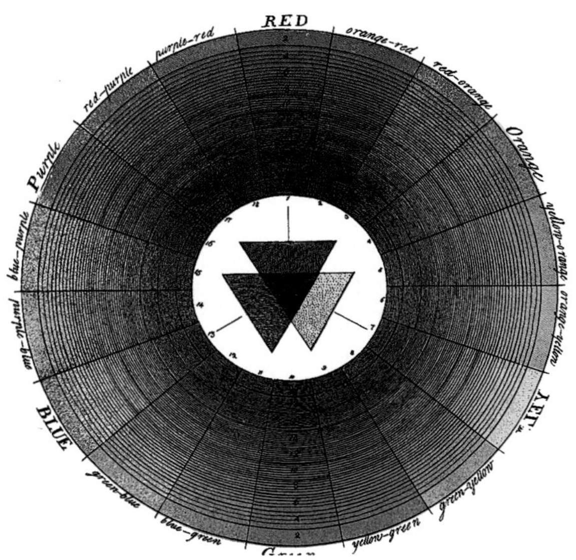

Moses Harris's eighteenth-century colour wheel, an early attempt at colour theory. Harris's system really created the myth that all colours could be reproduced from three primaries: red, yellow and blue.

north pole is white and the south pole black. Imagine, too, that the equator has passing around it in succession all the intense hues of the colour circle, each one occupying a segment. If you were to cut through the Earth you would find a central axis running in a straight line from the north to the south poles with varying strengths of grey on it, changing from total white at the north to total black at the south. On the equator would be the purest hue of one of the colours on the colour wheel, blue for example, and everything in between would be a mixture of that blue with varying amounts of white, grey or black. Every colour on that slice could be defined by exactly

A three-dimensional version of the modern Munsell colour-model. Because of the inability of paint manufacturers to synthesize deep and powerful colours, many of the commercial colour models have often been constructed to be 'incomplete', as here. However, modern technologies are rapidly remedying this problem.

how much black, white or pure hue it contained.

This is the paint industry's beautiful model theorem, and is how the manufacturers want us to think paint is made; with intense hue, black and white, as though colour mixing is scientific. In fact, the opposite is true. Bright hues in some colours (notably blues) are notoriously difficult to achieve using modern synthetic pigments, so that, for a start, our globe's equator is somewhat wobbly, and not a perfect circle at all!

Moreover there is something extremely sinister about these black-white-colour models. They are fundamentally flawed for one reason. If you take two complementary colours (which always occupy opposite positions on the colour circle) and mix them, they will always produce a sort of murky brown. Decorators know this because to tone a colour and add interest to it, they will often add a dot of its complementary.

If we do this on the colour model, we are mixing two colours on the equator but which are on the opposite sides of the globe. Where they meet, they make brown, but where they meet on the colour model is bang in the centre of the Earth at a midway point between the north and south poles where the colour on these models is always grey, not brown.

The fact that these colour models have no place for brown is their biggest failing. In fact, it makes a nonsense of them. Brown colours, the most common on the planet, are often the most useful to the decorator and represent the true phenomenon of what happens when different colours are mixed together – even the colours that the manufacturers make. We know this because in the repertory of pigments available to the manufacturer, browns and ochres figure quite substantially; do not believe that the bought paint colour you see is simply a mixture of a particular hue that has been manipulated with black and white pigments. Black is seldom used as a paint colorant, browns are. Black will not darken yellow when mixed with it, instead it will turn it green. To darken it, you need yellow ochre, raw sienna, burnt umber, or a little purple, its complementary.

Remember how important brown is when you next buy paint, or mix it for yourself, and remember how the manufacturers are trying to get you to forget about brown, because it is 'unscientific'. It is they who are unscientific.

Glossary

Words in bold represent entries in the glossary.

ACETATE
A petroleum-based plastic material, used in clear sheets by some decorators for cutting stencils as an alternative to stencil card.

ACETONE
A **solvent** of relatively simple chemical structure with relatively low toxicity. Can be used to clean dried oil paints and as a protein hardener, ie to waterproof soft protein **binders** such as **casein** and **gelatine.**

ACRYLIC
A plastic **polymer** that has found much use in paints. Acrylic polymers can be made to emulsify in water, providing water-borne acrylic paint vehicles and varnishes. Stronger than the common vinyl polymer **binders** found in ordinary **emulsion** paint.

ACRYLIC SCUMBLE GLAZE
See **scumble glaze**.

ACRYLIC SIZE
An adhesive for applying metal or gold leaf or bronze powders to a surface. Water borne, it dries to a tacky state that takes several days to dry. Replaces oil **goldsize**, which should still be used outdoors.

ALKYD RESIN
A synthetic resin that has supplanted traditional vegetable oil resins as a **binder** or vehicle for most commercial 'oil-based' paints and varnishes. It is often combined with vegetable oils such as soya oil to improve its performance, when it is known as 'oil-modified alkyd resin'. The name is a supposed improvement on its earlier identity, 'alcid' stemming from the fact that it is a product from an alkaline-acid reaction.

ALUM
A salt which has the effect of hardening protein. It is therefore added to protein **binders** such as **gelatine** hide glues and casein to render them water resistant when dry.

AMMONIUM CARBONATE
An alkaline compound. When mixed with oils or fats, alkalis will form a soap of them. Ammonium carbonate is sometimes mixed with **linseed oil** or beeswax to render them easier to emulsify in water.

ANIMAL GELATINES
The protein content of animal hides and bones which can be rendered up by boiling them. Available in many grades and separated by those grades into glue, size and paint **binders**. One of the oldest paint binders known to man.

ANTIQUING SOLUTION
Any thinned paint glaze or varnish that is coloured or stained, and applied to allow the underpainting to appear through it, usually with the effect of ageing the surface.

AQUEOUS
Watery. An aqueous paint medium is one that will dissolve in water.

AZO DYES
Oil-soluble dyes based on coal-tar, slightly dullish and not, as a whole, considered permanent. Hansa yellow is one of the brighter and more permanent exceptions. In use from the nineteenth century and still used in the making of cheap paints and inks.

BAIN MARIE
See **Double boiler**.

BEESWAX POLISH
A ready-made dilution of beeswax with a **solvent** such as **turpentine substitute**. The resultant paste is easy to apply.

BINDER
Literally a substance, usually a liquid formed with a **solvent** that will hold pigment particles and form a durable film when dry. Proteins do this very well, which accounts for the large number of animal and vegetable proteins that are used for the job: **linseed oil, casein, gum arabic, gelatines,** etc. Without the binder, paint would powder away. When a binder is mixed with a pigment without any solvent, it is sometimes known as a vehicle.

BOLE
An extremely fine coloured clay, effectively an earth pigment, that is usually applied over **gesso** as an underlying coating beneath gold leaf. After application, the dry surface of the leaf may be burnished with a hard tool which, in fact, brings the bole beneath to a high gloss as part of the process. Common colours for bole are yellow, red and black.

BONE GLUE
A crude, dark form of **gelatine** glue made by boiling up animal bones.

BRECCIATED MARBLE
Consisting of angular fragments of material interspersed with veining and fissures.

BRONZING
The process whereby a surface is painted or coated to imitate bronze, whether of a bright metal or patinated, weathered colour.

BROWN GUM
Common water-based liquid glue used for sticking paper, usually **dextrine** based.

BURNISHING
The process of polishing using manual pressure behind a hard tool, such as a polished piece of agate, to procure a mirror-like reflective shine on gold or metal leaf. It is only possible to do on **water gilding**.

CALCINATION
The process of heating a pigment to irreversibly change its colour. The usual colours are earth colours, which by this process lose water molecules and change from ferrous to ferric compounds. An example is yellow ochre, which when heated changes to red ochre.

CARBORUNDUM
Silicon carbide, an extremely effective abrasive, formed into blocks, cutting tools and applied to paper.

CARNAUBA WAX
A vegetable wax which is collected in small quantities from palm fronds. Very hard and brittle, it is often added to **beeswax** to render it tougher and able to take a high polish.

CASEIN
The protein content of milk (consisting additionally of lactose and fats), ie curds. Used for millennia as a paint **binder** both by artists and decorators, and as an adhesive. Skimmed milk consists mainly of casein. Since it is a long, complete protein, it is able to form tough **polymers** in a dry film, and having done so (well after water has evaporated), becomes remarkably water resistant.

CELLULOSE LACQUERS/ PAINTS
Developed in the twentieth century, cellulose **binders** are semi-synthetic products derived from wood, pulp and cotton cellulose. They are extremely quick drying and therefore generally unsuitable for use under the brush. Cellulose media will, however, intermix with **shellacs** and alcohols.

CHALK
Calcium carbonate. A natural mineral deposit consisting of crushed exoskeletons of minute prehistoric life. Used as a filler in modern paints and as a principal white pigment in traditional water-based house paints (see also **Whiting**).

CISSING
The reticulating action of wet paint that will not adhere to a surface.

CLAIREBOIS
Literally 'palewood'. A generic name for pale wood veneers, such as satinwood, and paint effects used to imitate them.

CLAIRECOLLE
A dilute, pale, literally 'clear glue', usually a **gelatine**-type glue traditionally used for sizing absorbent surfaces such as wood and plaster, prior to painting or wallpapering.

COLOURWASH
Nowadays a decorative paint technique, the term historically was used to describe coloured whitewash or **limewash**.

COPPER ACETATE
The chemical definition of verdigris.

CRACKLE VARNISH/ CRAQUELURE
A two-part varnish process, available as a two-pack commercial product. The French word, craquelure, is sometimes used to describe the effect.

CROCODILING OR ALLIGATORING
The effect produced in an old oil paint film that has broken down and shrunk, resembling a miniature crocodile skin pattern.

CUTTING BACK
Abrading, or sanding down.

DEXTRINE
Carbohydrate produced from starch. Used traditionally as a water-based **size**. May also substitute the second **gum arabic** coating in **crackle varnish**.

DISTEMPER
Commonly a simple interior house paint comprising simple **binders** such as **gelatine size** or **casein**, with basic pigments. A cheap traditional paint that allows walls to transpire moisture.

DOUBLE BOILER
Also a bain-marie. An arrangement of one pot over another for heating on a stove. The lower pot is filled with water, the boiling of which prevents the contents of the top pot from ever reaching boiling point. Essential for heating **gelatine** glues, which will spoil if boiled.

DRYER
An additive or agent, usually metallic, to speed the drying of a coating. An example is cobalt stannate, another is raw umber pigment, containing manganese. These agents catalyse the paint by introducing oxygen to the paint film at a greater rate.

EGGSHELL PAINT
A common name for paint of a mid-sheen, or semi-matt finish.

EMULSIFIER
An agent that will assist in the formation of an **emulsion**. **Toluene**, **xylene** and **methyl alcohol** will all form emulsions of plastics in water.

EMULSION
A suspension of an oil in water, and therefore thinnable with water, or (less commonly) the opposite: of water particles in an oily medium that must be thinned with a **solvent**. Plastic water-borne paints are considered emulsions, as is milk. Butter, however, is a water-in-oil emulsion. More commonly, emulsion is used in a restricted sense as a description in Britain of a vinyl water-borne paint used for interior walls.

ETHYL ALCOHOL
Common drinkable alcohol, not available to the public in concentrated form. Manufacturers use it in the formation of **shellac** solutions, etc. (see also **Methylated spirits**).

EVA
EthylVinylAcetate, a more durable and waterproof vinyl **polymer** than **PVA**.

FORMALDEHYDE
Also known as formalin. A powerful preservative and poymerizer. As such it can be carefully added to, or applied over dry coats of, protein-type paints such as those based on **gelatine** or **casein**, ensuring that they **polymerize** completely and provide a more water-resistant coating.

FRENCH ENAMEL VARNISH
A manufacturer's name for **shellacs**, which are sold in a variety of ready-dyed colours.

FRIABLE
Liable to crumble or disintegrate.

FULLER'S EARTH
A fine dark clay powder traditionally used for fulling (de-greasing) sheep fleeces. Its ability to absorb makes it useful as a preparatory dry rubbing agent for removing grease and oil from surfaces prior to painting.

GELATINE
Or gelatin. The protein content of animal tissues such as skin as well as bone, hooves

and horn, which are boiled to procure it. It is a weak, incomplete protein that will not perfectly **polymerize** on drying. It is thus water-soluble when dry. Used for millennia as a **size**, glue and **binder** in paints.

GESSO
An extremely tough but brittle coating traditionally used in the painting and **gilding** of the finest furniture, etc. Made from **gelatine** and powdered **chalk** (or **gypsum**), it is built in many layers and can be finely polished. In use for several thousand years.

GOLDSIZE
Traditionally an oil-based varnish with excellent flow properties used for adhering gold or metal leaf in work of secondary or inferior quality, but used uniquely outdoors on railings, gates, etc. where other gilding methods cannot weather. The leaf is normally applied after several hours when the surface reaches a gentle 'tack'. There is now a sticky water-based acrylic formulation to replace it that is easy to use and remains 'tacky' for several days. It yields inferior results.

GOUACHE
A tube/paste paint used by artists. Usually comprises pigment, **gum arabic** and **chalk** as an agent to render the paint characteristically opaque, and different to water colours, which are otherwise identical.

GRISAILLE
The technique of painting trompe l'oeil representational subjects such as landscapes, architectural details, etc., in purely grey or monotone.

GUM ARABIC
A water-soluble tree resin from a type of acacia. Used as a **binder**/vehicle in water colours, **gouache** paint and in certain techniques such as **craquelure**.

GYPSUM
Calcium sulphate, a naturally occurring mineral which when burned becomes plaster of Paris.

IMPASTO
The technique or effect of paint that has been obviously thickly applied to create visible texture.

ISOLATOR
In painting terms, a coating, usually of a clear nature, which is interposed between, and serves to prevent a physical or chemical reaction between, two layers of paint or varnish. **Shellac** is often used as a quick-drying (30 minutes) isolator in techniques such as marbling where many layers need to be built up. It may be applied over a half-dry coat of oil paint or glaze, permitting another coat of oil paint to be applied soon after without dissolving or destroying the underlying layer.

JAPANNING
So-called after a technique in imitation of lacquerwork, the application of a clear varnish that traditionally had no **linseed oil** content. The resultant finish is smooth and highly glossy. Nowadays used indiscriminately.

LACQUER
Like **japanning**, a term that has now been devalued. Originally applied to a painstaking Chinese process of building dozens of layers of thin varnish obtained from indigenous trees. Nowadays, a lacquer may be a single-coat product based on **polyurethane**, **cellulose** or even water-soluble **acrylics**.

LEVIGATION
The process of water filtration whereby pigments can be refined.

LIME
A generic name for a number of chemical compounds based on calcium. Commonly used to describe building lime, a putty of calcium hydroxide.

LIME SLAKING
The process whereby dry **lime** (calcium oxide) is steeped in water for months or even years to produce building lime or **quicklime** (calcium hydroxide).

LIMEWASH
An extremely dilute form of **quicklime** made by adding water to building lime putty. Applied to walls, most often externally, as a traditional protective and decorative coating.

LIMING WAX
A mixture of furniture wax polish and a white pigment (usually titanium white) used as a decorative finish on open-pored woods such as oak. It imitates the traditional finish achieved on oak by the early technique of scrubbing and disinfecting the wood with dilute **quicklime**.

LINOXYN
The hard, oxidized crust that forms on old oil paints.

LINSEED OIL
Refined pressed oil from the seeds of the flax plant, used as a vehicle for oil paint.

MARBLING
The art of faking marbled patterns with paint.

METHYLATED SPIRITS
A form of methyl alcohol (see also **Ethyl alcohol**), denatured and coloured to render it undrinkable. Methyl alcohol is poisonous.

MILK PAINT
An American term to describe **casein**-based paint.

MORDANT
A glue or **size** used for adhering powder or metal leaf to a surface. Literally, a 'biter'.

MULLER
A hand-grinding tool, usually of glass, employed to grind pigments.

MUNSELL SYSTEM
An American system of colour recognition and analysis used by many paint manufacturers.

OIL GILDING
The traditional method for gilding a surface where expensive **water gilding** cannot be applied (see also **Goldsize**).

OIL GLAZE
See **Scumble glaze**.

OIL OF TURPENTINE
A clear, colourless, oily distillation from pine resin used traditionally as a thinner

and matting agent for household and artist's oil paints. Now supplanted by the inferior **turpentine substitute** (turps subs) and **white spirit**.

OLEAGINOUS
Oily, or of a viscous, oily nature.

OVERGRAINER
A specialist brush, often with short bristles, employed in **woodgraining** to manipulate or remove an already grained wet glaze. When pointed, it is known as a pencil overgrainer.

PALLADIUM
A form of platinum that is non-tarnishing and with a dark silver colour. Available in metal leaf for decorative work.

PATINA
The coating, transparent or opaque, that slowly builds on a surface with the passage of time. An example is verdigris.

POLITE ARCHITECTURE
Refined genteel architecture of whatever period, usually architect designed to include informed references and built for the aristocracy and gentry (see also **Vernacular architecture**).

POLYMERS/POLYMERIZATION
Long, repeating molecules that are able to join to each other (polymerize) to form long chains. When present in a paint vehicle they form these chains as the coating dries, thus producing a hard, impenetrable film. The process can be further improved by the addition of catalysts, which encourage the molecules to form as many connections as possible, called cross-linking. These additives are called cross-linkers.

POLYURETHANE
A synthetic plastic product (hence petroleum/chemically based) used as a varnish resin and as a vehicle in some industrial and specialist paints.

PVA
PolyVinylAcetate. A vinyl **polymer** that will happily form an **emulsion** in water. A simple **binder** with many uses, such as in concrete, plaster, paint, and as a wood glue (see also **EVA**).

QUICKLIME
Calcium hydroxide, or building lime (see also **Lime**).

RABBITSKIN GLUE
A **gelatine**-type glue used as the adhesive content of **gesso**. A very fine grade, obtained by boiling rabbit skins.

REFRACTIVE INDEX
The degree by which a material will refract, distort or bend light that passes through it.

REGISTRATION
The process by which a stencil or printing block can be correctly repeated in the right place. Marks or holes (registration marks) that do not necessarily form part of the design, are used to ascertain the correct position.

RETARDANT
A paint additive used to slow down the drying time of a paint and keep it open and workable for longer. An example in water paint is glycerine.

ROTTENSTONE
A finely powdering stone dust used under linen cloths as a loose abrasive on paint and varnish films to provide a substrate with sufficient key for the next coat. Unlike paper abrasives, rottenstone will not heavily scratch the surface.

RUBBER
An arrangement of cotton sheet over a small bundle of cotton wadding that is held in the hand and used to apply **shellac** in the processes of French polishing and **lacquering**.

SCUMBLE GLAZE
A medium that is used in decoration to facilitate decorative effects by providing a paint or colour with a longer drying time. A nineteenth-century invention, until recently oil scumble glaze was the only product available, formed by mixing **chalk** and **linseed oil**. Since the verb to 'scumble' means to break through an opaque layer of paint, and this product invariably provides a transparent medium, the name is a misnomer; indeed, many manufacturers prefer to call it transparent until recently oil glaze. It is really a simple extending medium for artist's oil paints which allows them to be thinned without becoming too liquid and unworkable on a wall, for example. It may also be mixed with oil stainers and household oil-based paints to improve their workability.

Latterly, manufacturers have formulated water-borne acrylic scumble glaze, a gelatinous and translucent medium that will do the same job for **acrylic** paints and acrylic-bound stainers. Its drying time can be extended even further by the addition of so-called 'tropical drying extenders'. Acrylic scumble will supplant oil scumble in most applications, but has more limited flexibility and can produce muddier and cruder effects.

SHELLAC
A sticky exudation from insects that swarm on trees in South East Asia. It is collected, dried and shipped, then dissolved in alcohol to produce a quick-drying varnish that can be brushed or applied with a **rubber** as in French polishing. Used for several centuries as a fine indoor finish for wood and a useful varnish and **isolator** for the decorator.

SIKKENS FOUNDATION
A Dutch institute concerned with the development and promotion of the use of regional colour in Europe.

SILICATE PAINTS
A process developed by Keim in the nineteenth century of applying potassium silicate paints to exterior porous walls such as those of lime render or concrete, with an aesthetic quality similar to that of **limewash**. The paint, however, is not strictly a coating since it penetrates the top layer of the substrate and locks itself to it.

SIRAPITE PLASTER
Internal plaster used for walls.

SIZE
Strictly speaking, a coating used to reduce the porosity of a substrate, ie a sealant used prior to painting or papering; it is often the same glue or **binder** used for papering or painting, but diluted. Used on canvas, linen, wood,

plaster and paper. Is also used as an abbreviation of **goldsize** to mean an adhesive or **mordant** for gilding.

SLAKING
See **Lime slaking**.

SOLVENT
A liquid used to dilute a paint or varnish that has the effect of thinning the **binder**. Thus water is a solvent for **gum arabic** and **turpentine** a solvent for **linseed oil**.

STAND OIL
Raw **linseed oil** which has been heated to above 525°C (977°F) and then allowed to clarify, producing a pale and thick oil.

STIPPLER
A large brush, usually with a large surface area of hundreds of bristles, that can be presented to a wet paint or glaze film to produce a mottled, stippled pattern.

STUCCO/STUCCO LUSTRO
Stucco is the Italian word for plaster but in English has come to mean plasterwork modelled or cast with **lime** plaster (slow setting) in the traditional manner, as opposed to the nineteenth-century technique of casting in fibrous **gypsum** (fast setting) plaster. Stucco lustro, or Stucco Veneziano, is a technique whereby pigments, marble dust and glue are added to the plaster, allowing it to be finely polished under the trowel and then laboriously polished to a gloss when dry.

TEMPERA
A painting technique popular with easel artists in the Middle Ages, employing an **emulsion binder** such as egg yolk. Because the works are usually waterproof when dry and do not discolour because there is no vegetable oil present in the paint, tempera colours remain remarkably vivid and undamaged with the passing of time.

TOLUENE/TOLUOL
An aromatic hydrocarbon **solvent**, and as such to be treated with extreme suspicion as a probable carcinogen.

TROMPE L'OEIL
Literally to 'trick the eye'. A technique of realistic figurative painting on walls, introducing landscapes, architecture, etc.

TURPENTINE
See **Oil of turpentine**.

TURPENTINE SUBSTITUTE/ TURPS SUBS
Cheap petroleum distillate product to replace **oil of turpentine**. Thin and foul smelling.

UNIVERSAL STAINER
A pigment-in-oil mixture, usually castor oil, which has the benefit of being miscible with alcohols, oils and water. Thus the 'stainer' can be used to colour any type of paint or varnish.

VANDYKE CRYSTALS
Dark brown dye crystals formulated for staining wood, but useful in **woodgraining**, since they require no **binder**. Made from bituminous earth.

VEHICLE
See **Binder**.

VERNACULAR ARCHITECTURE
Ordinary historical everyday architecture, such as cottages, farmhouses and industrial buildings, expressive of regional architectural styles and local building materials.

WATER GILDING
A delicate process whereby 7.5cm (3in) squares of gold (usually, but other metals such as **palladium** or silver are used), a few microns thick, are laid with a brush onto a film of dilute, fine wet glue (usually the finest **gelatine** glue, such as parchment glue or **rabbitskin glue**). By way of preparation, the surface is usually built up with many layers of **gesso** which have been scraped and polished when dry, and then one or two layers of **bole**. The dried film of leaf can be subsequently polished or **burnished**. This is the finest quality gilding work and the most expensive. (See also **Goldsize** and **Size**.)

WHITE SPIRIT
A cheap petroleum distillate thinner used for oil paints.

WHITING
Finely powdered **chalk**.

WOODGRAINING
The art of faking woodgrains with paint.

XYLENE/XYLOL
An aromatic hydrocarbon **solvent**, and as such to be treated with extreme suspicion as a probable carcinogen.

Suppliers

TOOLS AND MATERIALS

JW Bollom / JT Keeps
15 Theobald's Road
London WC1 8SN
Tel: 0171 242 0313
Fax: 0171 831 2457

Other branches:

314-316 Old Brompton Road
London SW5 9JH
Tel: 0171 370 3252
Fax: 0171 370 3253

L A Cook & Co Ltd
130-132 Coporation Street
Belfast BT1 3DH
Tel: 01232 230947
Fax: 01232 246910

1-3 Callaghans Lane
Georges Place
Dun Laoghaire
Co. Dublin
Tel: 01280 8263
Fax: 01280 7461

General painting supplies, manufacturers of Pervalac crackle glaze, range of palette colour emulsions and specialist paint brushes. (MAIL ORDER)

C Brewer & Sons Ltd
327 Putney Bridge Road
London SW15 2PG
Tel: 0181 788 9335
Fax: 0181 788 8285

General painting supplies and specialist paint brushes; branches throughout south-east England — call 01323 411080 for details. (MAIL ORDER)

Brodie and Middleton Ltd
68 Drury Lane
London WC2B 5SP

Decorating brushes, French enamel varnish, glues, metallic powders, paints, pigments and powder colours. (MAIL ORDER)

Byron & Byron Ltd
4 Hanover Yard
Islington
London N1 8BE
Tel: 0171 704 9290
Fax: 0171 226 7351

Verdigris materials. (MAIL ORDER)

HJ Chard & Sons
Albert Road
Bristol BS2 0XS
Tel: 0117 977 7681
Fax: 0117 971 9802

Other branches:

Springway Lane
The Old Airfield
Western Zayland
Bridgwater
Somerset TA7 0JS
Tel: 01278 691193

Limewash and traditional building limes. (MAIL ORDER)

L. Cornelissen and Son Ltd
105 Great Russell Street
London WC1B 3RY
Tel: 0171 636 1045
Fax: 0171 636 3655

Bone glue, brushes, casein powder, gilding materials, gum arabic, pigments, rabbitskin glue. (MAIL ORDER)

Craig & Rose plc
172 Leith Walk
Edinburgh EH6 5EB
Tel: 0131 554 1131
Fax: 0131 553 3250

Other branches:

4 Westgate House
Spital Street
Dartford
Kent DA1 2AH
Tel: 01322 222481

Dixon Blazes Industrial Estate
30 Lawmoor Road
Glasgow G5 0UX
Tel: 0141 429 4347

Unit 5A
Lissua Road Industrial Estate
Moira Road
Lisburn
Northern Ireland BT28 2RF
Tel: 01846 622273

Casein paint, extra pale dead-flat varnish, gold leaf, goldsize, scumble glazes, specialist brushes and transparent oil glaze.

Cy Pres (Brigstock) Ltd
14 Bells Close
Brigstock
Kettering
Northants NN14 3JG
Tel and fax: 01536 373431

Limewash and traditional building limes. (MAIL ORDER)

Daler-Rowney Ltd
12 Percy Street
London W1A 2BP
Tel: 0171 636 8241
Fax: 0171 580 7534

Other branches:

Daler Gallery
4 Westover Road
Bournemouth BH1 2BY
Tel: 01202 297682

Artist's materials including tri-acetate, acrylic gesso, artist's acrylics, artist's oil paints, gouache, powder colours and paper. (MAIL ORDER)

Farrow & Ball Ltd
33 Uddens Trading Estate
Wimborne
Dorset BH21 7NL
Tel: 01202 876141

Limewash and traditional building limes, National Trust paints, specialist paints, wallpapers. (MAIL ORDER)

Foxell & James Ltd
57 Farringdon Road
London EC1M 3JB
Tel: 0171 405 0152
Fax: 0171 405 3631

Gilding materials, glues, metallic powders and paints, pigments, scumble glazes, specialist brushes, varnishes, wood finishes. (MAIL ORDER)

Green & Stone
259 King's Road
London SW3 5ER
Tel: 0171 352 0837
Fax: 0171 351 1098

Artist's materials including acrylic varnish, crackle varnish, gesso, gum arabic, linseed oil, powder colours, scumble glaze, shellac, specialist brushes, stencilling materials. (MAIL ORDER)

W Habberley Meadows Ltd
5 Saxon Way
Chelmsley Wood
Birmingham B37 5AY
Tel: 0121 770 0103
Fax: 0121 770 6512

Artist's brushes, gilding materials and paints. (MAIL ORDER)

AS Handover Ltd
Unit 37H
Mildmay Grove
London N1 4RH
Tel: 0171 359 4696
Fax: 0171 354 3658

Manufacturers and suppliers of specialist brushes. (MAIL ORDER)

FA Heffer & Co Ltd
24 The Pavement
London SW4 0JA
Tel: 0171 622 6871
Fax: 0171 498 3990

Specialist brushes. (MAIL ORDER)

Hirst Conservation Materials Ltd
Laughton
Sleaford
Lincs NG34 0HE
Tel: 01529 497517
Fax: 01529 497518

Limewash and traditional building limes. (MAIL ORDER)

Bruce & Liz Induni
11 Park Road
Swanage
Dorset BH19 2AA
Tel: 01929 423776

Limewash and traditional building limes. (MAIL ORDER)

The Lime Centre
Long Barn
Morestead
Winchester
Hants SO21 1LZ
Tel: 01962 713 636

Limewash and traditional building limes.

E Milner Oxford Ltd
Glanville Road
Cowley
Oxford OX4 2DB
Tel: 01865 718171
Fax: 01865 770942

General painting supplies including crackle varnish, specialist brushes, transparent oil glaze and universal stainers. (MAIL ORDER)

John Myland Ltd
80 Norwood High Street
London SE27 9NW
Tel: 0181 670 9161
Fax: 0181 761 5700

Artist's brushes, bone glue, French enamel varnish, liming wax, oil-based varnish, palette-colour emulsions (including earth colours), pigments, powder colours, rabbitskin glue, rottenstone, shellac, transparent oil glaze and universal stainers. (MAIL ORDER)

Omnihome Ltd
77 Golborne Road
London W10 5NP
Tel: 0181 964 2100
Fax: 0181 964 2080

Specialist brushes, glazes, varnishes, Harmony water-based paints, paint mixing service. (MAIL ORDER)

Paint Service Co Ltd
19 Eccleston Street
London SW1W 9LX
Tel: 0171 730 6408
Fax: 0171 730 7458

Specialist brushes, transparent oil glaze and varnishes. (MAIL ORDER)

Paper and Paints
4 Park Walk
London SW10 0AD
Tel: 0171 352 8626
Fax: 0171 352 1017

Suppliers of many specialist paints and decorating materials, casein paints and 'historic' colours. (MAIL ORDER)

E Ploton (Sundries) Ltd
273 Archway Road
London N6 5AA
Tel: 0181 348 0315/2838
Fax: 0181 348 3414

Artist's materials including acetate, acrylic gesso, acrylic varnish, artist's acrylics, artist's oil paints, crackle varnish, gouache, gum arabic, metallic powders, specialist brushes and transfer gold leaf. (MAIL ORDER)

Potmolen Paint
27 Woodcock Industrial Estate
Warminster
Wiltshire BA12 9DX
Tel: 01985 213960
Fax: 01985 213931

Specialist paint suppliers including casein, distempers, gilding materials and traditional materials. (MAIL ORDER)

JH Ratcliffe & Co (Paints) Ltd
135a Linaker Street
Southport PR8 5DF
Tel: 01704 537999
Fax: 01704 544138

Brushes and tools for graining. (MAIL ORDER)

C Robertson and Co
1A Hercules Street
London N7 6AT
Tel: 0171 272 0568
Fax: 0171 263 0212

Acrylic-based scumbles, gilding materials, pigments, Plaka (casein emulsion) and varnishes. (MAIL ORDER)

Jane Schofield
Lewdon Farm
Black Dog
Crediton
Devon EX17 4QQ
Tel: 01884 861181

Limewash and traditional building limes.

Scottish Lime Centre Trust
PO Box 251
Edinburgh EH6 4DW
Tel: 0131 553 4999
Fax: 0131 553 7158

Limewash and traditional building limes. (MAIL ORDER)

The Shaker Shop
322 King's Road
London SW3 5UH
Tel: 0171 352 3918
Fax: 0171 724 6640

Other branches:

The Shaker Shop
25 Harcourt Street
London W1H 1DT
Tel: 0171 724 7672
Fax: 0171 724 6640

Furniture and woodwork paints.

Simpsons Paints Ltd
122-4 Broadley Street
London NW8 8BB
Tel: 0171 723 6657
Fax: 0171 706 4662

Gold leaf, specialist brushes, traditional paints and finishes, transparent oil glaze. (MAIL ORDER)

Stuart R Stevenson
68 Clerkenwell Road
London EC1M 5QA
Tel: 0171 253 1693
Fax: 0171 490 0451

Artist's and gilding materials. (MAIL ORDER)

J Varco
Tabbs Barn
Nanscawen
Par
Cornwall PL24 2SR
Tel and fax: 01726 812389

Stocks Lyn Le Grice's stencil books, kits and materials. (MAIL ORDER)

Lewis Ward & Co
128 Fortune Green Road
London NW6 1DN
Tel: 0171 794 3130
Fax: 0171 435 2346

Distributors of Omega brushes and manufacturers of Whistler brushes for faux finishing. (MAIL ORDER)

Wood Finishes
30 The Vineyard
Richmond
Surrey TW10 6AN
Tel: 0181 332 1772
Fax: 0181 332 1773

Acrylic varnishes, gilding materials, lacquer paint, powder pigments and spirit dyes. (MAIL ORDER)

USEFUL ADDRESSES

CADW - Welsh Historic Monuments
Brunel House
2 Fitzalan Road
Cardiff CF2 1UY
Tel: 01222 500200

English Heritage
Fortress House
23 Savile Row
London W1X 1AB
Tel: 0171 973 3000

The Georgian Group
6 Fitzroy Square
London W1P 6DX
Tel: 0171 387 1720

Historic Buildings & Monuments for Scotland
20 Brandon Street
Edinburgh EH3 5RA
Tel: 0131 556 8400

Society for the Protection of Ancient Buildings (SPAB)
37 Spital Square
London E1 6DY
Tel: 0171 377 1644

Bibliography

BASIC GOOD HOUSEPAINTING

F Hamilton Jackson, *Mural Painting* (Sands and Co, 1904)
An important work covering the history of wall painting and various historical practices, including techniques that form the basis of much experimental work today, such as Keim's mineral fresco process, Gambier Parry's spirit fresco technique, plus encaustic painting.

Arthur Seymour Jennings, *House Painting and Decoration, a Popular Guide* (1912)
Arthur Seymour Jennings, *The Modern Painter and Decorator*, 3 vols (Caxton, editions from 1921 to 1950s)
Arthur Seymour Jennings, *Paint and Colour Mixing* (1926)
Arthur Seymour Jennings, *Wallpapers and Wallcoverings* (1910)
These are a few of the books on the subject written by Arthur Seymour Jennings at the beginning of the twentieth century. Jennings was Editor of *The Decorator* and an examiner for the City and Guilds Institute, and although his knowledge of chemistry and of history of art must be treated suspiciously, he was highly knowledgeable about decorating practice of his period. Much of what he writes represents basic good practice that is often lacking in the work of modern decorators. The three-volume set of *The Modern Painter and Decorator* should be considered his major work on the subject.

CHEMISTRY AND PAINT COMPOSITION

Thomas Lambert, *Glue, Gelatine and their Allied Products* (Charles Griffin and Co, 1905)

Robert Massey, *Formulas for Painters* (1967), ISBN 0 8230 1877 6
A paperback with 134 recipes for paints, varnishes, glazes, etc., using both traditional and modern materials.

Ralph Mayer, *The Artist's Handbook of Materials and Techniques* (editions from 1940, but still in print), ISBN 0 571 18033 7 and 571 11693 0
The most authoritative and thorough analysis of artists' and decorators' materials from ancient times to modern synthetic products. Plenty of science and thorough research from Mayer, an American and this century's most gifted paint technologist. An absolute essential for anyone interested in paint.

Michael McCann, *Artist Beware* (1979), ISBN 0 8230 0295 0
An exhaustive survey of painting materials including solvents and pigments with a full description of their toxicology. A terrifying read but absolutely necessary for those who wish to experiment with unknown materials.

Paul I Smith, *Glue and Gelatine* (Chapman and Hall Ltd and the Chemical Publishing Co Inc, 1943)

HISTORICAL SOURCES

A great number of historical treatises deal with the materials and techniques of the artist's studio. Some deal also with the decoration of buildings. This is a short list, and since most are widely available in several translations and editions, I have only listed specific editions for particular reasons.

Leon Battista Alberti, *On Painting (De Pittura)* (fifteenth-century work)

Cennino Cennini, *The Book of the Art (Il Libro dell'Arte)* (fifteenth century)
Influential treatis on the studio methods for Renaissance panel painting, tempera and gilding.

Mary P Merrifield, *Original Treatises from the Twelfth to the Eighteenth Centuries on the Arts of Painting, etc.* (1849, reprinted by Dover under the title *Materials and Methods of Painting*, 1967)
A comprehensive volume translated into English.

Pliny the Elder, *Natural History* (middle of first century)
The books on mineral subjects (books 33-37) are particularly useful.

Rudolph Erich Raspe, *A Critical Essay on Oil Painting* (1781)
The one reliable and properly researched study of painting made in the eighteenth century. It contains translations of many ancient manuscripts.

Theophilus, *The Various Arts* (probably twelfth century)
A guide to the practice of several disciplines in northern Europe.

Theophrastus, *History of Stones* (fourth century BC)
Mentions pigments and materials.

Vasari, *Lives of the Artists* (1550-1586)
Most contemporary versions exclude the technical chapters to be found at the end of the Lives. LS Maclehose translated these with notes under the title *Vasari on Technique* in 1907. It was reprinted by Dover in 1960.

Vitruvius, *On Architecture (De Architettura)* (first century BC)
Contains detailed descriptions of Roman fresco technique.

HISTORY OF DECORATION

Owen Jones, *The Grammar of Ornament* (1856), reprinted as ISBN 1 85007 072 5

Peter Thornton, *Authentic Decor* (1984), ISBN 0 297 78504 4
A large and excellent sourcebook of decorative schemes from 1620 to 1920, relying on hundreds of reprinted engravings and paintings of interiors.

See also works listed under History of paint, below.

HISTORY OF PAINT

Patrick Baty, 'My True Colours', *The Architect's Journal* (15 June 1994)
Patrick Baty, 'Palette of Historic Paints', *Country Life* (20 February 1992)
Patrick Baty, 'Palette of the Past', *Country Life* (3 September 1992)
Patrick Baty, ed., *Traditional Paint News*
For those with a true fascination for historical paint, this magazine is published annually and is available from Simpson and Brown Architects, 179 Canongate, Edinburgh EH8 8BN. It includes articles by all the leading authorities such as Patrick Baty, Ian Bristow, Peter Hood, Helen Hughes and the American, Frank S Walsh.

Dr Geoffrey Beard, *Craftsmen and Interior Decoration in England 1660-1820* (1981), ISBN 0 906223 49 0

Paul Binski, *Painters* from a series called *Medieval Craftsmen* (1991), ISBN 0 7141 2052 9
An art historian's view of paint, colour and decoration in the Middle Ages.

Dr Ian Bristow, 'Cost Constraints on Historical Colour', *The Architect* (March 1977)
Dr Ian Bristow, 'Historic Town-houses: The Use of Paint and Colour', *The Saving of Spitalfields*, ed. Mark Girouard (Spitalfields Historic Buildings Trust, 1989)
These two essays represent a fraction of the work of this most eminent paint historian.

A and A Gore, *The History of English Interiors* (1991), ISBN 0 7148 2611 1

Roger W Moss, ed., *Paint in America – The Colours of Historic Buildings* (1994), ISBN 0 89133 255 3 and 089133 263 4
A thorough survey of American paints and colours that dispels several myths and forms a corner stone of the study of traditional paints around the world. Indispensable to the serious student.

Dr Steven Parissien, *Paint Colour* (Georgian Group Guides No. 4, 1994). This is an excellent introductory guide to paint colour in the eighteenth century. You can contact The Georgian Group at 6 Fitzroy Square, London W1P 6DX (telephone: 0171 387 1720)

Dr Steven Parissien, *Palladian Style* (1994), ISBN 0 7148 2921 8
A sumptuous look at decorative and architectural styles of the early and mid-eighteenth century, including a chapter on paint and coverings.

REGIONAL COLOUR

Alec Clifton-Taylor, *The Pattern of English Building* (1962), ISBN 0 571 14890 5 and 0 571 13988 4
A solid look at the traditional building materials of England including some mentions of paint.

Richard Fortey, *The Hidden Landscape* (1993), ISBN 0 7126 6040 2
A vibrant and exciting book that will awaken an interest in geology in anyone. Beautifully written.

Michael Lancaster, *Britain in View – Colour and the Landscape* (1984), ISBN 0 907621 29 5
A comprehensive and unique study of colour around the world and how light and landscape affect our views on the colours of landscape and buildings.

JP and D Lenclos, *Les Couleurs de la France* (Moniteur, 1982)
The seminal work on the subject of integrating building colours into landscape and the environment.

T Porter, *Colour Outside* (The Architectural Press, 1982)

E Taverne and C Wagenaar, eds, *The Colour of the City* (1992), ISBN 90 74265 03 0
An extensive collection of studies of building colour programmes from around the world.

SPECIALIST PAINT TECHNIQUES

Yannick Guegan, *Imitation des Marbres* (1989), ISBN 2 249 27791 5
Yannick Guegan, *Imitation des Bois* (1989), ISBN 2 249 27835 0
These books represent the highest standard of decorative graining and marbling that you can aspire to, especially the book on graining.

IB, A and R Marx, *Professional Painted Finishes* (1991), ISBN 0 8230 4418 1
A demanding and excellent book based on the teaching practices of the Marx family in New York.

Isobel O'Neill, *The Art of the Painted Finish*
The late Isobel O'Neill ran a decorative painting school in New York and was a stickler for correct method. This book is an unsurpassable textbook.

John P Parry, *Graining and Marbling* (1949, revised 1985), ISBN 0 00 383 131 0
A stalwart introduction to professional standard work.

TRADITIONAL PAINT TECHNIQUES

Viola & Rosamund Borradaille, *Practical Tempera Painting* (1949, Dolphin Press)
Not one illustration, yet this is simply the most accurately written manual for the tempera painter, with extremely useful chapters on preparation, gesso and gilding. Also available in a 1941 edition under the title *A Student's Cennini.*

Jane Schofield, *Lime in Building, A Practical Guide* (1995), ISBN 0 952 4341 0 5
A small volume but the best on the subject of using lime in building, including limewash.

Daniel V Thompson Junior, *The Practice of Tempera Painting* (Yale University Press, 1936).
Another excellent reference work based on Cennino Cennini's teachings.

The Society for the Protection of Ancient Buildings (SPAB) publish a number of leaflets on the use of traditional building materials, of which the following are useful to the painter. They can be obtained from SPAB, 37 Spital Square, London E1 6DY (telephone: 0171 377 1644):
Philip Hughes, *The Need for Old Buildings to Breathe* (SPAB Information sheet No. 4)
Jane Schofield, *Basic Limewash* (SPAB Information sheet No. 1)
Michael Wingate, *An Introduction to Building Limes* (SPAB Information sheet No. 9)
Bruce & Liz Induni, *Using Lime*
A useful booklet also sold by the SPAB.

Acknowledgments

The publisher thanks the following photographers and organisations for their kind permission to reproduce photographs in this book:

1 Robert O'Dea; 4-5 Agence Top /Pascal Chevalier /Designer Giorgio Silvagni; 7 Lars Hallen; 8-9 Paul Ryan/International Interiors/Architects Hariri & Hariri; 10-11 Bridgeman Art Library /National Gallery, London; 11 Matthew Weinreb; 14 Simon McBride; 14-15 Hutchison Library /John Wright; 16 Hutchison Library /P W Rippon; 17 Vincent Motte; 18 below Kevin McCloud; 19 Edifice /Darley; 20 below Reproduction by permission of the American Museum in Britain; 21 Simon McBride; 23 left Explorer /Christophe Boisvieux; 23 right Simon McBride; 24 Explorer /Ameller; 27 Hutchison Library /Tim Beddow; 29 Bridgeman Art Library /Pushkin Museum, Moscow; 31 above Agence Top /Olivier Garros; 31 below The Interior Archive /Fritz von der Schulenburg; 32 Collections /Paul White; 33 above right ET Archive /Asciano Museum, Italy; 33 below left Hutchison Library /Jackum Brown; 34 right Arcaid /Richard Bryant/ Homewood House Museum of Johns Hopkins University, Baltimore; 35 above Collections /David Bowie; 36 right Bridgeman Art Library /Richardson and Kailas Icons, London; 37 right Arcaid /Richard Bryant/ Claydon House Bucks; 38 Paul Ryan /International Interiors /Designer John Saladino; 42-43 Tim Street-Porter /Designer Annie Kelly; 64-65 Stock Image Production /Cote Sud/Eric Morin; 66-67 Paul Ryan/International Interiors /Architects Hariri & Hariri; 68 Elizabeth Whiting & Associates /Nadia Mackenzie; 69 Ianthe Ruthven; 74-75 Dominique Vorillon /Architect Tom Wuelpern; 75 above Elizabeth Whiting & Associates /Huntley Hedworth; 75 below Robert Harding Syndication /Woman's Journal /James Merrell; 78 Jerome Darblay; 81 Lars Hallen; 84 Reproduction by permission of the American Museum in Britain; 98 Jerome Darblay; 99 Christian Sarramon /Architect Claudio Silvestrin; 100-101 Elizabeth Whiting & Associates /Andreas von Einsiedel; 102 Jean-Pierre Godeaut/Designer Roberto Bergero; 102-103 Abode /Spike Powell; 106 Tim Street-Porter; 107 Paul Ryan/International Interiors; 110 Jan Baldwin; 116 Arcaid /Lucinda Lambton; 128-129 Studio Verne /Designer Rodolpho Dordony; 130 Kevin McCloud; 131 Elizabeth Whiting & Associates /Michael Crockett; 140-141 Paul Ryan/International Interiors /Laura Bohn; 142 above The Interior Archive /James Mortimer (Gabhan O'Keefe); 142 below Christian Sarramon /Designer Roberto Bergero; 143 Dominique Vorillon /Architect Michael Lehrer /Designer Joanne Belsen; 150 Philadelphia Museum of Art (W P Wilstach Collection) - Portrait of Antonie Renniers and Family by Cornelius de Vos; 154 Elizabeth Whiting & Associates /Tom Leighton; 154-155 The Interior Archive /James Mortimer (Christophe Gollut); 156-157 The Interior Archive /Simon Brown; 158 Robert Harding Syndication /Homes & Gardens /Trevor Richards; 159 The Interior Archive /Fritz von der Schulenburg; 160 Arcaid /Belle/Rodney Weidland /Designer Terry Brooks; 161 Arcaid /Richard Bryant /Designer James Broadbent; 168 Ianthe Ruthven; 172 Dominique Vorillon /Designer Michael Anderson; 177 Ianthe Ruthven; 178 below Agence Top /Pascal Chevallier /Designer Giorgio Silvagni; 184-185 The Interior Archive /Fritz von der Schulenburg; 186 right Jean-Pierre Godeaut /Designer R Bergero; 187 above Jean-Pierre Godeaut /Designer Roberto Bergero;187 below Edifice /Drury; 190-191 The Interior Archive /Fritz von der Schulenburg; 192 above Reproduced by permission of the American Museum in Britain; 194 The Interior Archive /Fritz von der Schulenburg (Tullgarn, Sweden); 195 Arcaid /Lucinda Lambton; 196-197 Elizabeth Whiting & Associates /David Giles; 199 above The Interior Archive /Ari Ashley; 199 below David George; 203 Arcaid /Nic Barlow; 204 Arcaid /Robert O'Dea; 205 Paul Ryan/International Interiors /Designer S Blount; 213 Agence Top /Ronald Beaufre/Designer Giorgio Silvagni (Provence House, Irene and Giorgio Silvagni); 214 below Paul Ryan/ International Interiors; 215 below The Interior Archive /Simon Brown; 219 Collections /Michael Allen; 220 above Camera Press /Appel; 220 below Lars Hallen; 220-221 David George; 222 above Elizabeth Whiting & Associates; 226 below Reproduction by permission of the American Museum in Britain; 226-227 Lars Hallen; 234 Elizabeth Whiting & Associates /SIP/I Snitt/Cote Sud; 234-235 National Trust Photographic Library /Angelo Hornak; 238 Edifice /Weideger; 245-246 Robert O'Dea; 248-249 David George; 250 Vincent Motte.

Special photography by Michael Crockett on the following pages: 12-13, 18 above, 20 above, 22, 26, 28, 30 left, 33 above left, 34 left, 35 below, 36 left, 37 left, 39-41, 45-63, 71-3, 76-7, 79-80, 82-83, 85-97, 104-5, 108-9, 111-5, 117-127, 132-9, 144-9, 151-3, 162-7, 169-171, 173-6, 178 above, 179-183, 188-9, 192 below, 193, 198, 200-2, 206-212, 214 above, 215 above, 216-218, 222 below, 223-5, 226 above, 228-233, 236-7, 239-244, 247.

Every effort has been made to trace copyright holders. We apologize in advance for any unintentional omission and would be pleased to insert acknowledgment in any subsequent edition of this publication.

Index

Page numbers in *italics* represent illustrations
Entries in **bold** represent techniques